It's the Disney Version!

It's the Disney Version!

Popular Cinema and Literary Classics

Edited by
Douglas Brode and Shea T. Brode

ROWMAN & LITTLEFIELD
Lanham • Boulder • New York • London

Published by Rowman & Littlefield
A wholly owned subsidiary of The Rowman & Littlefield Publishing Group, Inc.
4501 Forbes Boulevard, Suite 200, Lanham, Maryland 20706
www.rowman.com

Unit A, Whitacre Mews, 26-34 Stannary Street, London SE11 4AB

British Library Cataloguing in Publication Information Available

Library of Congress Cataloging-in-Publication Data

Names: Brode, Douglas, 1943–, editor. | Brode, Shea T., 1984–, editor.
Title: It's the Disney version! : popular cinema and literary classics / edited by Douglas Brode and Shea T. Brode.
Description: Lanham : Rowman & Littlefield, 2016. | Includes bibliographical references and index.
Identifiers: LCCN 2015043566 | ISBN 9781442266063 (hardcover : alk. paper)
Subjects: LCSH: Walt Disney Company—History. | Film adaptations—History and criticism. | Literature and motion pictures.
Classification: LCC PN1999.W27 I88 2016 | DDC 384/.80979494—dc23 LC record available at http://lccn.loc.gov/2015043566

Printed in the United States of America

For Sue Anne Johnson Brode: wife, mother, and our very own
Disney princess come to life

Contents

Acknowledgments   ix

Introduction: Once Upon a Time at the Movies   xi
   Douglas Brode

1   "And They Lived Happily Ever After???!" : Disney's Animated
    Adaptation of *Snow White and the Seven Dwarfs* (1937) and
    Fleischers' *Gulliver's Travels* (1939)   1
    David McGowan

2   The Perils of a Masculine Upbringing: Pinocchio, from Carlo
    Collodi to Walt Disney   13
    Jean-Marie Apostolidès

3   Here Be Gay Dragons: Queer Allegory and Disney's *The
    Reluctant Dragon* (1941)   23
    Tison Pugh

4   Zip-a-Dee-Doo-Dah: The Re-enslavement of Uncle Remus   33
    Peggy A. Russo

5   "Glory in the Flower": Disneyfying *Bambi*   45
    David Payne

6   Through the Cinematic Looking Glass: Walt Disney's 1951
    Animated Version and Tim Burton's 2010 Film   51
    Sarah Boslaugh

7   Walt Disney and Robert Louis Stevenson: Haskin's *Treasure
    Island* or Stevenson's *Kidnapped*?   61
    Scott Allen Nollen

8 Of Medieval Ballads and Movie Musicals: Walt Disney and the Robin Hood Legend 71
Shea T. Brode with Douglas Brode

9 "Do You Believe in Fairies?": *Peter Pan*, Walt Disney, and Me 79
Elizabeth Bell

10 "In God's Good Time": *20,000 Leagues Under the Sea* and Cold War Culture 93
Cynthia J. Miller and A. Bowdoin Van Riper

11 Perchance to Dream: A Narrative Analysis of Disney's *Sleeping Beauty* 105
Alexis Finnerty with Douglas Brode

12 "It's a Jungle Book out There, Kid!": Walt Disney and the American 1960s 117
Greg Metcalf

13 "Higitus! Figitus!": Of Merlin and Disney Magic 129
Susan Aronstein

14 "This Is Not the Mary Poppins I Know!": P. L. Travers Goes to Hollywood 141
David S. Silverman and Olga Silverman

15 The Wonderful Worlds of Dickens and Disney: Animated Adaptations of *Oliver Twist* and *A Christmas Carol* 151
Shari Hodges Holt

16 The Tao at Pooh Corner: Disney's Portrayal of a Very Philosophical Bear 165
Anne Collins Smith and Owen M. Smith

17 From Icon to Disneyfication: A Mermaid's Aesthetic Journey 177
Finn Hauberg Mortensen

18 Disney's *Pocahontas*: History, Legend, and Movie Mythology 189
Gary Edgerton and Kathy Merlock Jackson

19 "Driven to Sin": Victor Hugo's Complex Vision of Humanity in Disney's *The Hunchback of Notre Dame* 201
Michael Smith

20 The Integrity of an Ape-Man: Comparing Disney's *Tarzan* with Burroughs's *Tarzan of the Apes* 211
Stanley A. Galloway

Index 225

About the Editors 229

About the Contributors 231

Acknowledgments

Many thanks to Shane J. Brode for his endless contributions of time, effort, skill, and talent as a computer expert in creating the technical means to organize this book and properly convey the package to our publisher. Also, to the remarkable array of gifted writers who not only contributed fascinating essays but were willing to also rewrite, again and again in some cases, in order to hopefully achieve something as close to perfection as possible. Our thanks to the journals that granted permission to reprint the following articles:

"'And They Lived Happily Ever After???': Disney's Animated Adaptation of *Snow White and the Seven Dwarfs* (1937) and Fleischers' *Gulliver's Travels* (1939)" by David McGowan was originally published in *Peer English*, issue 5 (2010).

"'Do You Believe in Fairies?': *Peter Pan,* Walt Disney, and Me" by Elizabeth Bell was original published in *Women's Studies in Communication*, volume 19, issue 2 (Summer, 1996), pp. 103–126.

"'It's a Jungle Book Out There, Kid!': Walt Disney and the American 1960s" by Greg Metcalf was originally published as "It's a Jungle Out There, Kid: The Sixties in Walt Disney's *Jungle Book*" in *Studies in Popular Culture*, volume XIV, number I (1991), pp. 85–97.

"From Icon to Disneyfication: A Mermaid's Aesthetic Journey" by Finn Hauberg Mortensen was originally published as "'The Little Mermaid': Icon and Disneyfication" in *Scandinavian Studies*, volume 80, issue 4 (Winter 2008), © Society for the Advancement of Scandinavian Study. Reprinted by permission of the University of Illinois Press.

"Disney's *Pocahontas*: History, Legend, and Movie Mythology" by Kathy Merlock Jackson and Gary Edgerton was original published as "Redesigning Pocahontas: Disney, the 'White Man's Indian,' and the Marketing of Dreams" in *Journal of Popular Film and Television*, volume 24, issue 2 (1996), pp. 90–98. Reprinted by permission of Taylor & Francis, LLC.

Introduction

Once Upon a Time at the Movies

Douglas Brode

"It's *only* a movie."—Alfred Hitchcock, 1954

Born in 1901, at the cusp of what *Time*'s publisher Henry Luce would acknowledge as the American Century, Walt Disney emerged as a full equivalent in the realm of Hollywood entertainment of Henry Ford in Detroit's new
automobile industry, Horatio Alger in popular culture, and Jay Gatsby in the
"serious" novel *The Great Gatsby*: an embodiment of the American Dream, a
concept unique to our nation, founded on the notion that democracy and
capitalism can exist in a yin/yang relationship.

Disney's was a rags-to-riches story like many others, in which some
young male, born with no assets other than his own pluck (and, as an outside
force, blind luck), becomes part of a specifically *American* aristocracy: un-
concerned with bloodlines, open to anyone who achieves great status by
"making it" (financially, though in other ways as well), in a rat race that
destroys the majority of his competitors. To achieve this, the most essential
element has proven to be a full, rich sense of self: a refusal to fail, no matter
how many times failure appears imminent, a notion that success is to a
degree preordained and that one's life mission is to prove this true through
accomplishments in one's own chosen field.

When Disney and his friend Ubbe Iwerks began turning out short advertising cartoons, known as Laugh-O-Grams, circa 1920 in Kansas City, few
Midwestern theatergoers perceived them as anything but a passing fancy. As
Shakespeare's Hamlet said of wandering medieval players who puckishly
satirized the styles, politics, and conventions of their own moment in the
limelight, they were but the brief and abstract chronicles of our times. When

idea man Walt, artistic genius Ubbe, and Disney's older brother Roy (the brain for business) settled in Los Angeles three years later, their crude cartoon entertainments, initially with Oswald the Rabbit and then Mickey (his name would have been Mortimer if Mrs. Lillian Disney hadn't put her foot down), were applauded as raucous fun, easily ranked among the best of such stuff then being turned out.

Still, no one paid any close attention to such giddy fluff. Movies had only recently been accepted as an entertainment form worthy of attendance by respectable middle-class people, who only a few years earlier ignored such boardwalk attractions as they would a déclassé freak show. Still, a small coterie of theorists in academia and Europe's avant-garde intellectual circles had already invoked the heady term "art."

Everything changed when Walt and company began turning out Silly Symphonies, a series of ambitious short-subject pieces that furthered the possibilities of film in general and animated movies in particular. Most notable was *The Old Mill* (1937), which introduced three-dimensionality thanks to technical whiz Iwerks's invention of the multiplane camera. As some of these cartoons employed fairy tales and other old fables for their subject matter, the issue arose of whether Disney's work might in fact relate to the long tradition of children's literature (finally taken seriously at about this time in our country's cultural history). Disney's feature-length *Snow White and the Seven Dwarfs* (1937), a dazzling full-color screen musical drawn from a tale that long preceded its best-known Grimm origins, changed the pop culture landscape. No one could argue that this was, taken as a movie, anything other than a masterpiece, aesthetically flawless as well as emotionally satisfying from its first moment to its last.

No longer, though, could champions of the now respectable genre of children's literature, along with the act of reading rather than watching, remain silent. There was a second and, as time would reveal, one of an all but infinite number of ways the swiftly amassing celluloid library of Walt and his chief competitors (most notably, Max and Dave Fleischer) could be considered, often a less positive view of what the public had immediately fallen in love with.

In "The 'Disney Touch' and the Wonderful World of Children's Literature," Dewey W. Chambers, an eminent library commentator who apparently perceived his career as endangered by then-new media, insisted that he found no problem with the "harmless, delightful fun for the entire family" provided by the Oswalds and Mickeys. Indeed, Chambers was willing to admit that these were worthy of being considered not only fine examples of entertainment but also "art." Still, by moving on to Grimm, Perrault, and others, "Disney and his studio have gone far beyond their depth," causing not only librarians but also educators of young children to "wince."

Disney versions of any such classic, at least for Chambers, represented a "catastrophic revision." Mostly, Chambers castigated Uncle Walt for altering plots, drastically changing the nature of specific characters while retaining their names, adding "cute" animals not present in the originals, and disregarding the intended themes of earlier storytellers to include Walt's own theme, while reimagining old texts by taking into consideration the temporal tastes of Americans (and, later, global customers) of his own time. Notably, Chambers failed to mention that, when Charles Perrault in late seventeenth-century France and Jacob and his brother Wilhelm Grimm in early nineteenth-century Germany set down what were already sturdy old classics in print, often for the first time, neither felt any compulsion to remain true to any earlier version (indeed, in most cases, multiple predecessors existed). As true auteurs rather than simple scribes, they brought to the process (as do all noteworthy artists in any medium) their individual visions. And they certainly reflected the tenor of their times.

Any adults or children, living and consuming in their countries of origin, who might receive these remodeled fairy-tale texts were taken into consideration in those separate time periods, precisely as Walt would eventually do. This would seemingly legitimize Disney doing the same with his evolving worldview and acute awareness of what a typical U.S. family would, and would not, accept. Significantly, Walt's feature-length animated work appeared precisely as the Great Depression finally receded and World War II exploded, followed by a postwar period of suburban conformity. However quiet the Eisenhower era may have seemed on its surface, the beginning of an atomic age, the Red Scare, and the birth of rock 'n' roll strongly suggested that this was a brave new world with which Americans must learn to cope. As always, the modern media helped create many of the changes while commenting on them, through art and entertainment, even as they occurred. There is no reason why this ought to have been any less true of Disney's work than those of other contemporary filmmakers and writers, artists, and musicians, who absorbed the zeitgeist and shared their view of it in their diverse mediums of expression.

Children's, or more correctly, family-oriented, literature (or, in the twentieth century and beyond, cinema) is not, and never has been, sacrosanct, though small groups of people with their own clearly defined agendas may wish that were the case. It has lately become fashionable to complain that the corporation that today carries Disney's brand (WDC) subjects classic stories to what is trendily dismissed among an intellectual elite as consumer-oriented marketing, or the "culture industry." While that can't be denied, it's also essentially what Perrault and the Grimms did during periods in which mass marketing had not reached the advanced stage of today, or, more likely than not, they would have taken advantage of every opportunity, even as Disney did. If Walt and his studio were happy to announce themselves as capitalists, so were the writers he has adapted, most notably Charles Dickens.

Yet another librarian, Jill P. May, appears more sensitive to Disney's unique situation if also aware of and concerned about some of Walt's changes. She wrote, "Since all of these feature-length films were designed to be first shown in movie theatres and were not planned around educational or literary objectives, they represented a *calculated* look at children's stories" (emphasis added). Here an early understanding of media and mediums, as well as a work's admittedly capitalist identity, emerges. As to the latter, truth be told, many librarians chose to "Disneyfy" their children's literature sections, largely because this proved an easy way to attract large hordes of kids. If anyone, it is they, not Disney, who should be blamed for the decision to include in an educational context products that were openly and honestly offered up as commercial materials.

Likewise, literature is literature, and cinema is cinema. While books, plays, and short stories provided raw material for movies since the very birth of narrative cinema, circa 1900, anyone who grasped the distinction between the two storytelling forms simply assumed it was not preferable, or even possible, to film any book page by page. This was proven at once by France's Georges Méliès with his groundbreaking fantasy film *Le Voyage dans le Lune* (1902), based in part on a space travel novel by Jules Verne. However, Méliès also included elements of another early science fiction story by H. G. Wells, without crediting that work, while totally reimagining the piece as an expression of his own genius-level fantastic imagination (the "cute" if somewhat menacing moon creatures we see are Méliès's invention) as well as taking his audience into account. Scantily clad beauties dancing about did not appear in either Verne or Wells, though they absolutely did provide cinematic cheesecake moments, much to the delight of Paris's fin-de-siècle boulevard strollers searching for some new divertissement.

And, of course, those lengthy novels were not only combined but stripped down to manageable plots. In truth, then, Disney, some thirty-five years later, did not initiate this method of book-to-film adaptation but followed in the path of an earlier master. (American Winsor McCay was yet another.) This explains why May, while raising issues similar to Chambers, appears to understand that Walt's situation was, essentially, the only route open for doing what he set his mind to do, for better or worse

> Disney sought the memorable drama, the action, and the villainy long remembered by the reader after finishing the original version. He planned his versions around satisfying emotional experiences that would remain with the viewer. . . . Seldom did he reflect the book's theme or original characters with accuracy. While his settings depended upon the (particular) author, the scene rarely maintained its original cultural and geographic heritage.

Still, May admits, "It was this manipulation of children's stories that has continuously raised the ire of professionals in the field of children's literature." It's all well and good that people protest, just so long as it's acknowledged that they constitute a special interest group—a voice crying out in the print-medium wilderness against the sudden populist acceptance of celluloid texts as, at the very least, a necessarily evil.

Things change. They always have, always will. We can, like nineteenth-century makers of wagon wheels for stagecoaches, bemoan the fact that Detroit perfected the automobile. A kinder, gentler time may indeed have passed. Or that may only be the way we choose to nostalgically recall the old days. Either way, the car, like the animated film for children, was clearly here to stay.

In truth, though, Disney—like the original avatars of the fairy-tale form—never had an audience of children in mind, at least not exclusively. As Chambers noted, even as Perrault and Grimm intended their earliest stories for adults, Walt made films targeting the *entire* family. This necessitated performing an odd if amazing juggling act, tossing all sorts of wondrous stuff up in the air simultaneously, each appealing to adults, teenagers, and children. Even those who dismiss Disney on various critical grounds cannot deny that he and his company performed that virtual magic act better than anyone else. We might well conclude, then, that at least according to this one possible route into the oeuvre, most Disney films are successful owing to the degree to which they provide precisely what they promise—and, in truth, what the mass audience wants, even demands, from popular entertainment.

This is, of course, how the public at large, as well as reviewers (like the late Roger Ebert), whose coverage of films constitutes a *Consumer's Guide* to current film offerings, views movies. People return to films bearing the Disney label simply because, so often in the past, they left the theater satisfied, having received their money's worth, ticket-wise, when the product carried the Disney brand. A precious few can bemoan that we live in a consumer-oriented world; most people simply accept that as the status quo, the way things work in the cosmos that we find ourselves living in. All the same, while Ebert and others embody the primary view of film for the majority of moviegoers, not only in the United States but worldwide, such an approach represents but the beginning for those who make academic or intellectual inroads into cinema, considering this medium on serious levels of study, as of course well they should.

One such angle of perception constitutes what Val Perkins has referred to as "film as film"; earlier, Hans Richter referred to film as an original art form—"original" meaning unique, specific, containing qualities that cause it to appear distinct from any earlier preexisting art form. True, movies share "narrative" with novels, and drama or comedy with plays. Yet movies approach both elements in ways entirely different from the manner that those two preexisting art forms did and still do. Most essentially, films (to be properly understood) must be seen as a visual medium. Any attempt to film a book "as is" would only provide something on the order of a cinematic Monarch Notes, an appendage to rather than distinct version of the work. The great moviemakers, Disney included, grasped at once that their approach should not be to transfer words to the screen with accompanying images, but rather to translate a work originally presented in a verbal medium into images that vividly convey the ideas. In movies, words ought not to be employed as narration but in limited form, as basic to the telling of the tale as music.

The Soviet genius Sergei Eisenstein, a huge fan of Disney, argued that in the sound era, the story and soundtrack should be inseparable, fused together; the influential British critic Penelope Houston coined the phrase "sight and sound" to suggest the very same thing. Few movies so well illustrate that concept of the film as Disney's animated musicals.

Movies, then, are not literature—at least, not *literary* literature. They instead constitute something new (original) and at the time of their inception groundbreaking: *cinematic* literature, which must be understood and accepted as every bit as worthy as the earlier form, different yet equal, at least when approached via those examples most effective at employing the medium's own special "vocabulary": montage, camera movement, the chosen angle for filming, and so on. Once this is acknowledged, it must also be grasped that these twentieth-century and beyond storytellers have as much of a right to adapt earlier texts as did Perrault, Grimm, and anyone else who rethought oral tradition for the printed page, endowing the work with their own original visions, adjusting these materials for an audience that at that moment did not actually exist yet had to be taken into account if the work would have any resonance.

Whether by Disney or someone else, whether the project was designed for adults, children, or both, a film, at least according to this approach (often referred to as Pure Cinema), ought to be based on the degree to which it proves effective at achieving precisely this. Though diehards, dedicated to certain books by specific writers, can hold to the belief that the quality of a book-to-film adaptation is determined by the degree to which the latter conveys the former, few movies drawn from truly great novels have abandoned as much of the original text as the 1975 film version of Ken Kesey's 1962 *One Flew Over the Cuckoo's Nest*. Yet the film has been hailed, and rightly so, as perhaps the greatest single case of turning a major novel into an equally classic film. Not surprisingly, Kesey despised it for betraying his style and his substance. He was precisely right in doing so, though that hardly negates the film's greatness.

Simply, there are many ways to evaluate a film in general, a film adapted from an earlier tale in particular. Such a line of reasoning was what provided the jumping-off point for this anthology. The title term, "the Disney Version(s)," has become so much a part of our informal public discourse that Richard Schickel chose it in 1969 for his critical (in the negative sense of that term) biography of Walt Disney, who had passed three years earlier. Yet, at least until now, no book has directly addressed the *issue* of the Disney Version in all its complexities. The approach here was to take a wide variety of Disney feature-length films, each derived from some acclaimed preexisting work, and assign them to scholars uniquely suited to the particular subject. The through line necessarily had to be an intense interest in Disney, though whether any individual essayist happened to be pro-, anti-, or neutral/balanced on Walt, his films, and his company was left completely up to each.

The second was that the contributor also had to possess expertise on the particular literary piece in question.

Their essays provide a wonderfully open spectrum of ways we might consider books in relationship to films as well as the overriding focal issue of Disney as storyteller to the world. Some of the most fascinating essays are those that in a poststructuralist manner refuse to simplify, seeing any one film as neither a success nor a failure but a compendium of artistic decisions, some of which "work," while others do not.

Taken together, these essays provide an extensive intellectual feast for anyone interested not only in Disney but in the possibilities of cinematic narrative for uniquely expressing ideologies that, in verbal contexts, can be communicated by books.

WORKS CITED

Chambers, Dewey W. "The 'Disney Touch' and the World of Children's Literature." *Elementary English* 43, no. 1 (January 1966): 50–52.

May, Jill P. "Walt Disney's Interpretation of Children's Literature." *Language Arts* 58, no. 4 (April 1981): 463–72.

Chapter One

"And They Lived Happily Ever After???!"

Disney's Animated Adaptation of Snow White and the Seven Dwarfs *(1937) and Fleischers'* Gulliver's Travels *(1939)*

David McGowan

Walt Disney's *Snow White and the Seven Dwarfs* (1937) was the first American feature-length animation.[1] This adaptation of the Grimms' fairy tale played an important part in justifying a production more than eight times the length of the usual seven-minute cartoon.[2] Several commentators questioned whether animated drawings could sustain an audience's interest over this extended running time, and some even dubbed the film "Disney's Folly" ahead of its release.[3] The film ultimately became one of the highest-grossing of the year, proving that animators could break away from their sole reliance on the limited revenue stream of short films. Reviews were largely positive, and Disney was presented with an honorary prize at the Academy Awards: a full-size statuette and seven miniatures. The Fleischer brothers, Max and Dave, responded by producing *Gulliver's Travels* (1939), based on Jonathan Swift's novel.[4] These films set the pace for all animated features adapted from preexisting texts.

SNOW WHITE AND ADAPTATION

The credits for Disney's *Snow White* announce that the film is "adapted from Grimms' Fairy Tales," without referencing any other source. The opening sequence underscores the literary heritage by showing a lavish hardback book, which provides a text-based prologue before the animation begins. Despite the "old-fashioned" design of the volume's typeface, it does not quote directly from any extant version of the story, instead offering an adaptation created specifically for the film.[5] Numerous academics have faulted Disney for the various omissions and changes to the tale, arguing that the movie's iconic status—and its implicit claims of authenticity to the Grimms' version—obscures the meaning of the original text.[6] This process is often termed "Disneyfication," described by Richard Schickel as "that shameless process by which everything the studio . . . touched, no matter how unique the vision of the original . . . was reduced to the limited terms Disney and his people could understand."[7] It is certainly true that the film emphasizes the romantic within its narrative, including having Snow White and the prince meet much earlier. A common criticism is that the Disney film softens the sense of the grotesque found in the Grimms' tales. The prince's kiss revives Snow White in Disney's adaptation, rather than the poisoned apple being dislodged (and, in some interpretations, literally vomited) from her throat after the prince's servants stumble with the coffin.

M. Thomas Inge lists eighteen significant differences between the Disney film and the Grimms' text, but also attempts to justify the decision-making process from page to screen. He notes that many changes were simply "common sense," such as toning down the scenes of violence, and increasing Snow White's age from seven in the Grimms' text to a teenager in the film to make the romance more palatable for contemporary audiences. Furthermore, Inge highlights that the Grimms' "Snow White" was not the origin of the tale, but itself a version of an existing work:

> The basic plot structure of the story of "Snow White" can be found in hundreds of variants collected by folklorists in Europe, Asia, Africa, and North and South America, many of which pre-date the Grimm version. . . . If we place the Disney version in this tradition, we see that he has made only one major change in the structure: that of deleting the first element, the birth of Snow White and the death of her mother. . . . There were plenty of technical and dramatic justifications for this deletion, but the remainder of the traditional structure was maintained. Thus, Disney's version is a legitimate variant in the "Snow White" cycle of tales.[8]

Such assertions have not always led to a significant reappraisal of Disney's work. While acknowledging that the Grimms were at times also "creative 'contaminators'" of existing fables, fairy-tale scholar Jack Zipes distinguishes between their "finishing touches" and "the prudish changes made by that twentieth-century sanitation man, Walt Disney."[9] Although his analysis of the films is often revealing, Zipes arguably overemphasizes his own neo-Marxist reading, isolating Disney's adaptive process in an attempt to argue that the studio has "obfuscated the names of Charles Perrault, the Brothers

Grimm, Hans Christian Andersen, and Collodi."[10] His (somewhat pejorative) assertion that Disney "Americanized" *Snow White* by turning it into an "entertainment [commodity]" downplays the existence of many other versions of the story already available for mainstream consumption in the United States ahead of Disney's film.[11]

The Grimms' text was clearly the best-known prose version in 1930s America, which may explain why the film's credits posit it as the sole source of adaptation. However, production material highlights that Disney's team consulted a variety of other incarnations of "Snow White," such as Joseph Jacobs's "retelling" in the collection *Europa's Fairy Book*.[12] Publicity for the film also included Disney's recollection of seeing, as an adolescent, a silent feature-film version (1916), adapted from a 1912 Broadway production written by Winthrop Ames under the pseudonym Jessie Braham White.[13] Ames had purchased the rights of an earlier play, *Snowwhite and the Seven Dwarfs* [*sic*] by Marguerite Merington, an English adaptation of a nineteenth-century German play by Karl August Goerner. Disney reportedly received a waiver from the publishers of the Braham White play in 1936 and bought out Paramount's rights to the play (but not the film) in 1937. Karen Merritt has argued that these works offer precedents for the alterations and omissions from the Grimms' story that are found in Disney.[14] The 1916 film, for instance, also brings the initial meeting between Snow White and the Prince to the beginning of the narrative, and somewhat anthropomorphizes a number of animal characters, albeit more awkwardly in live-action than Disney would later achieve in animation. Each of the theatrical versions introduce musical sequences, a precedent for the integration of (original) songs in Disney's film. As such, many accounts that criticize Disney in comparison to the Grimms' narrative fail to consider how the process of adaptation was already worked-through in these intermediary texts.

It should not be suggested, however, that Disney's version was entirely derivative of these works. Merritt argues:

> By choosing a children's play that was a proven property, both as a children's theater staple and as a silent film, Disney was creating an element of security for his risky venture. . . . As the feature developed over time, the scaffolding provided by the plethora of sources fell away, as the animators created original solutions to the dramatic problems posed by expanding the slight fairy tale to a feature-length narrative.[15]

Many of the scenes, as realized in the finished film, were specifically designed to showcase the sophistication of the Disney Studio's animation techniques. This was a unique trait in terms of previous versions of *Snow White* and, due to the film's pioneering feature-length, was also a significant modification of the approach to adaptation within the American cartoon industry as a whole.

THE EARLY HISTORY OF ANIMATED ADAPTATION

Fairy tales and other "classic" (read: out of copyright) literary texts provided a recurring source for one-reel American animated films from the silent era onward, but often only as a loose structure for unrelated gags. Disney's short-lived animated series the *Laugh-O-Grams* nominally presented "modernized" fairy stories, though the surviving cartoons display extended scenes with only a tenuous link to the original narratives. The pilot film, *Little Red Riding Hood* (1922), begins with the mother preparing doughnuts for Grandma while the family cat creates the holes with a shotgun. It ends with a title card stating "And they lived happily ever after???!", highlighting the processes of parody and burlesque which permeate the entire narrative. This cartoon displays none of the sincerity in its happy ending that Disney would later bring to *Snow White* and many of his subsequent feature-length adaptations.

Donald Crafton has outlined the consolidation of the "character continuity series" during the 1920s, in which cartoons were constructed and promoted around a central protagonist (akin to the live-action star system) rather than a recurring theme or collection of one-off films. [16] Literature continued to provide useful material for long-running series in need of new plots but remained largely overshadowed by the personalities of the leading characters. Coincidentally, Disney released an adaptation of *Gulliver's Travels* starring Mickey Mouse, *Gulliver Mickey* (1934), while the Fleischer Studio produced *Snow-White* (1933) with Betty Boop in the title role.

Gulliver Mickey begins with the Mouse reading *Gulliver's Travels*, and then retelling the tale to a group of children under the pretense that it is his own life story. The imagined sequence sees Mickey washed up on the island of Lilliput, and taken prisoner by the diminutive residents. This is followed, somewhat bizarrely, by the Mouse fighting a giant spider that terrorizes the town: a potential, if oblique, reference to the second part of Swift's text, wherein Gulliver encounters several large animals on the island of Brobdingnag. The film concludes in the "present-day," with the Mouse continuing to exaggerate these "heroic" tales, only to jump in fright when one of the children dangles a rubber spider on a string in front of his face. The Lilliputian tale remains unresolved, and Mickey gamely laughs at his own comeuppance.

The Fleischers' *Snow-White* condenses the plot—perhaps taking the title too literally—by having Betty accidentally fall down a snow-laden hill into an icy "coffin," rather than being deliberately poisoned by the queen. The Dwarfs barely appear, serving only to transport the already comatose character to a cave, where the narrative reaches its climax. This final section deviates entirely from the source text, including an extended musical number featuring Koko the Clown (a protagonist from an earlier Fleischer series, *Out of the Inkwell*) with the singing voice of jazz musician Cab Calloway. The magic mirror betrays the queen, turning her into a dragon-like creature, and revives Snow White. A brief chase sequence occurs until another of Betty's co-stars, Bimbo the Dog, defeats the queen by literally pulling her body inside out. While the surprising grotesqueness of this action may seem worthy of the Brothers Grimm, despite being unique to the film, this cartoon mostly presents variations of formulas associated with the Boop series rather than the plot of "Snow White."

The seven-minute running times of these films may have limited the potential for complexity, but the lengthy comedic digressions within this already-economical structure indicate a conscious decision to privilege humor over faithfulness to the originals. Disney's *Snow White* took a different approach by overtly stressing fidelity (even if, as noted above, its own adaptive processes are ultimately rather complicated). The film aims to present itself as a respectful—and, by extension, *respectable*—work in contrast to the narrative "poaching" and deviation of many earlier cartoons. As Michael Barrier notes, that Disney ultimately chose *not* to produce his first feature starring Mickey Mouse, a seemingly obvious choice for a sure-fire hit, is revealing.[17] *Snow White* was a project designed to bring prestige to the studio and not just commercial success.

SNOW WHITE AND THE SILLY SYMPHONIES

The trajectory of Disney's feature was heavily influenced by developments in his series of *Silly Symphonies* shorts, which had already broken from wider traditions within the animation industry by largely avoiding recurring characters, overt slapstick humor, and repetitive chase formulas. As production of *Snow White* began, the *Symphonies* became increasingly experimental, employing innovative techniques and technologies to evoke tone and mood, as well as sophisticated, often three-dimensional effects. *The Old Mill* (1937) debuted the studio's multiplane camera, soon used for a number of extended scenes in *Snow White*. For instance, the heroine's traumatic descent into the forest is dealt with in a few short sentences in the Grimms' text.[18] In the Disney adaptation, the sequence lasts over a minute, emphasizing her vulnerability by revealing the ominous, seemingly inescapable depth of the woodland, and subjectively imagining the trees and foliage transforming into monsters. The sequence remains broadly faithful to the original tale, but elaborates upon the source material to provide a showcase for the evolving Disney Studio aesthetic.

While the earliest film of the *Silly Symphonies* series, *The Skeleton Dance* (1929), foregrounded the synchronicity between characters' movements and musical effects, later instalments experimented with music as an additional means of developing emotion. The songs in *Snow White* further the narrative, but once again go beyond the relative economy of the Grimms' version. "Some Day My Prince Will Come" expands upon and foreshadows the romantic union of the heroine and her beau. Even a comedic sequence such as "Whistle While You Work," which develops a brief mention of housework in the original text into a full musical number, emphasizes the change brought about by Snow White's presence.[19] The song also attempts to integrate the humorous business of her cute animal helpers within a wider dramatic narrative, as opposed to the "comedy-for-its-own-sake" mentality that drove a significant proportion of short cartoon production.

Another breakthrough of the *Symphonies* series occurred in personality animation. For instance, the porcine stars of *The Three Little Pigs* (1933) are very similar in appearance, but each crucially has a recognizable and unique personality. This approach was subsequently incorporated into the *Snow White* feature. The brevity of the Grimms' text means that the Dwarfs are not articulated outside of their collective group identity, and the Fleischer cartoon adaptation simply reproduces the same character design seven times. The Braham White play preceded Disney's film in naming the characters—dubbing them Blick, Flick, Glick, Snick, Plick, Whick, and Quee—but did not distinguish specific characteristics beyond a few comedic sequences with Quee (whose antics may be seen as a partial inspiration for Dopey).[20] Disney developed his own names in a lengthy period of brainstorming before finalizing them as Doc, Grumpy, Happy, Sleepy, Bashful, Sneezy, and Dopey.[21] While identifying the Dwarfs in relation to a singular, dominant trait may seem reductive, it marks a significant departure from presenting such figures as a homogenous group. Furthermore, the sight of the Dwarfs, including Grumpy, shedding a tear at Snow White's apparent demise hints at a deeper psychological complexity than is suggested by their names. The film generally does not attempt to sustain the audience's attention by adding further plot complications. Rather, it employs the spine of the existing story as a means of creating extended sequences driven by the studio's experimentations with animation and sound.

ADAPTING DISNEY'S SUCCESS

Alan Bryman argues that "so successful is the Disney company at what it does, namely applying a distinctive template to stories and legends . . . that its style is frequently copied. As a result, audiences are sometimes unsure about what is and is not a Disney film."[22] *Snow White* is perceived to have influenced a wave of Hollywood movies attempting to match its appeal.[23] MGM's *The Wizard of Oz* (1939) shares many aesthetic qualities, including the narrative of a young woman's quest in a fantasy environment, emphasized by the use of Technicolor, and the presence of witches, humorous companions, and memorable original songs. The live-action screwball comedy *Ball of Fire* (1941) also presents a variation of the *Snow White* tale, in which a gangster's moll (Barbara Stanwyck) on the run from the law seeks refuge with eight professors (one of whom, played by Gary Cooper, ultimately assumes the "prince" role as her virtuous love interest.)

Many cartoon producers attempted to launch their own features, although only the Fleischers proceeded beyond the planning stages. The impetus came from their distributor, Paramount, which offered significant investment to relocate the studio from its New York base to Florida.[24] Following the move, it appears that the unit was increasingly pressured by Paramount to align itself more closely to the Disney model. The jazz soundtrack of earlier Fleischer shorts, such as Betty Boop's *Snow-White*, is replaced in *Gulliver* with more mainstream "crooning," and character designs tend toward cuteness rather than humorous grotesque. In particular, there is a strong similarity between the bluebirds in the forest during *Snow White*'s "With a Smile and a Song" sequence and the bluebirds that watch the princess serenade the prince with the song "Faithful" in *Gulliver*.

The adaptation of the source text also mimics Disney's approach in taking key plot points and employing them to showcase animation techniques. Scenes from the book, such as the villagers discovering Gulliver washed up on the beach and tethering him down, are turned into extended sequences full of visual spectacle. Compared to *Snow White*, however, *Gulliver* departs widely from the literary material. As noted, Disney had the opportunity to elaborate and expand upon a relatively simple story that already had a history of being retold by new authors in new contexts. Swift's book is not only considerably longer, but also more complex in its parody of the travel writing genre and its satiric parallels to then-contemporary English aristocracy. According to the credits, the Fleischer film is "Based on Jonathan Swift's Immortal Tale": a statement which attempts to make a claim for the continued relevance of the story to new audiences, although the links between page and screen are in fact relatively few. Some changes are, again, "common sense," or at least partially justifiable against wider adaptation traditions. Notably, the film is based solely upon the first (and relatively self-contained) part of the novel, the voyage to Lilliput—a decision shared with most earlier (and, in fact, subsequent) cinematic versions. In addition to this tighter focus, the residents of Lilliput speak English, allowing them to converse freely with Gulliver, eliminating "communication problems" found in the original novel. Furthermore, given the targeted family audience and content restrictions imposed by the Production Code Administration, the filmmakers perhaps wisely choose not to visualize Swift's description of Gulliver defecating, or finding a "unique" way to extinguish a fire through urination.

Like Disney's *Snow White*, the Fleischers' *Gulliver's Travels* begins with a text-based prologue, implicitly presented as an extract from the novel, but actually written specifically for this production. It mimics the first-person narration of Swift's text before the film (perhaps unavoidably) switches to an objective third-person approach. In the original book, aspects of the story which the narrator did not experience firsthand are retrospectively described through "translated" documents that he later acquires. By contrast, the film spends considerable time in the company of two squabbling kings, which is largely a new addition to the story. In the novel, Gulliver ultimately refuses to assist the king of Lilliput's plans to overthrow the neighboring Blefuscu. In the film, the son and daughter of the respective kings are due to wed, but war erupts over which of the provinces' anthems to play at the ceremony. Gulliver creates a happy ending by showing how the harmonies fit together when sung in unison.

Many original aspects of the Fleischers' version of *Gulliver* are designed to push the narrative toward a more conventional romantic plot, coupled with a sense of the fantastic. The villagers' fascination with the seemingly "giant" Gulliver echoes the interaction between Snow White and the Dwarfs, and both films conclude with the union of a prince and his bride. It is possible, therefore, to read the Fleischer film not only as an adaptation of Swift but as a direct response to, perhaps even adaptation of, Disney's *Snow White*.[25] The process of translating a book to the screen does not only engage with the histories of that particular text but rather draws upon a larger series of inter-texts, including, in this case, Disney's film.

EXTENDING (AND DENYING?) ADAPTATION

Disney resisted the temptation to capitalize on the success of *Snow White* by establishing an ongoing movie series featuring its popular characters. However, recent research indicates that a sequel—albeit a short rather than a second feature—was contemplated.[26] The proposed storyline would have incorporated two sequences partially completed (but deleted) from the original film, recontextualized to take place during a subsequent "annual visit" to the Dwarfs' cottage by Snow White. The official reasons for cancellation remain unclear, but may reflect Disney's approach to the *Symphonies*, which had largely avoided follow-ups. Having experienced a significant audience response to *The Three Little Pigs*, the studio produced three further cartoons featuring the characters, but Disney later expressed disappointment with the results, noting that "I could not see how we could possibly top pigs with pigs. But we tried, and I doubt any one of you reading this can name the other cartoons in which the pigs appeared."[27] During Walt's lifetime, no direct sequels were produced to any of the studio's animated features.[28] Nonetheless, the inclusion of Snow White and the Dwarfs into the "official" Disney roster, alongside characters originated entirely by the studio, has served to complicate issues surrounding adaptation and ownership. The television series *House of Mouse* (2001–2003) features a nightclub hosted by Mickey, with guests ranging from Donald Duck and Goofy to Snow White, the Dwarfs, Hercules, and Winnie the Pooh. Similarly, patrons can "meet" Snow White at Disney theme parks, together with many representative "stars" from the studio's other franchises. Snow White has also been inducted into the Disney Princess marketing brand, which includes characters such as Cinderella, Mulan, and Pocahontas, each originating from stories and folklore that predate the Disney versions.[29] Such extensions create significant links between otherwise separate texts. Characters are removed from their respective literary universes and coexist under an all-encompassing Disney umbrella.

Merchandising of *Snow White* further extends audience engagement predominantly with the Disney versions of the protagonists. As J. P. Telotte notes,

> on the day that Snow White opened, [Disney's product licensing office] had in place a complete merchandising campaign that involved agreements with over seventy companies, thereby marking the start of an elaborate nexus of entertainment and advertisement that would eventually become a model for the American marketplace.[30]

Alongside toys and musical scores, the studio also released several storybook adaptations, each presenting the film's events, including elements that deviate from earlier versions of the tale.[31] The pervasiveness of the Disney branding—to the point of extending back into print—can potentially serve to diminish knowledge of the original adapted work(s).

A raft of merchandise similarly accompanied the initial release of the Fleischers' *Gulliver's Travels*, again including a children's storybook. As with the Disney novelizations, the text recalls the film's narrative instead of reproducing or abridging Swift.[32] Between 1940 and 1941, the Fleischers also released three sets of short films showcasing characters created for the *Gulliver* feature. These reflect the earlier "star-led" traditions of animation rather than continuing the "prestige" adaptive processes of *Snow White* and *Gulliver*. Although nominally set on the isles of Lilliput and Blefuscu and broadly maintaining a "period" setting, the events of the spin-off films are dictated by generic comedic formulas and do not explicitly adhere to Swift (or even reference the source novel in the credits).[33] Many elements hark back to the animated feature—returning characters, the reprise of its music, and so on—but there remains an implicit resistance to acknowledge a wider history of adaptation. The authorship of these short films appears entirely subsumed by the Fleischer Studio.

Ultimately, none of the Fleischers' spin-offs were particularly successful. Even Gabby, widely touted by the studio as the breakout star of the feature, failed to make a significant impression in his own cartoons. Today, these are largely forgotten, and the Fleischers' storybook version of *Gulliver's Travels* is out of print. Having fallen into the public domain in recent decades, the feature itself has had a multitude of home video releases, mostly from low-quality duplicated prints. There is no "official" version of the film currently available.[34] Part of the uniqueness of Disney, then, is the level of control it retains and exerts on its properties. As Rudy Behlmer notes, "the Disney policy carefully allows for full-scale theatrical reissue of most of their features approximately every seven years. *Snow White* was reissued in 1944, 1952, 1958, 1967, and 1975."[35] Subsequent releases of the film on VHS, DVD, and most recently Blu-ray, have continued this practice, with each product only available for a limited period before, in the studio's terminology, going back to the "Vault." The removal of *Snow White* from circulation posits each cyclical reissue as an "event," often accompanied by a new range of tie-in merchandising. Through this marketing strategy, the film is simultaneously presented as both timeless and of renewed relevance to each subsequent generation.

Disney's absorption of preexisting texts into its own studio portfolio clearly polarizes critical response. There is validity to arguments that the continued prominence of the *Snow White* film, now nearly eighty years old, can at least partially sever the earlier traditions of the text, and complicate audience expectations in terms of other adaptations which deviate from Disney's version of the story. In some ways, however, this tradition echoes the Grimms' own process of collecting and retelling folklore, which similarly has become canonized, and at times mistaken as the sole origin. While it is tempting to read Disney's film—and particularly its associated merchandise—as devouring and destroying all that came before (and others, like the Fleischers, at least attempting to do the same), there exists a strong historical precedent for authors placing their own distinctive mark upon an enduring and ever-evolving text.

NOTES

1. Limited experiments with feature animation had occurred previously in other countries. Lotte Reiniger's German film *The Adventures of Prince Achmed* (1926) is the oldest surviving animated feature, and some evidence suggests that Italian-born Quirino Cristiani may have set an earlier precedent in Argentina in 1917. See Giannalberto Bendazzi, *Cartoons: One Hundred Years of Cinema Animation* (London: John Libbey, 1994), 49–52.

2. Brothers Grimm, "Snow White," in *The Complete Fairy Tales*, ed. and trans. Jack Zipes (London: Vintage Books, 2007), 237–46.

3. Richard Hollis and Brian Sibley, *Walt Disney's Snow White and the Seven Dwarfs and the Making of the Classic Film* (New York: Simon & Schuster, 1987), 33–35.

4. Jonathan Swift, *Gulliver's Travels*, ed. Albert J. Rivero (New York: W. W. Norton, 2002).

5. At least one Disney storybook adaptation has subsequently reproduced (and expanded beyond) the text found in the film's prologue. See *Walt Disney's Snow White and the Seven Dwarfs* (New York: Viking, 1979).

6. For an evaluative summary of various critical objections to the film, see Lucy Rollin, "Fear of Faerie: Disney and the Elitist Critics," *Children's Literature Association Quarterly* 12, no. 2 (1987): 90–93.

7. Richard Schickel, *The Disney Version: The Life, Times, Art and Commerce of Walt Disney* (Chicago: Ivan R. Dee, 1997), 225.

8. M. Thomas Inge, "Walt Disney's Snow White and the Seven Dwarfs: Art, Adaptation, and Ideology," *Journal of Popular Film and Television* 32, no. 3 (2004): 137–42.

9. Jack Zipes, *The Brothers Grimm: From Enchanted Forests to the Modern World* (Basingstoke, UK: Palgrave Macmillan, 2002), 31; Jack Zipes, *Fairy Tales and the Art of Subversion: The Classical Genre for Children and the Process of Civilization*, 2nd ed. (London: Routledge, 2006), 67.

10. Jack Zipes, *Fairy Tale as Myth/Myth as Fairy Tale* (Lexington: University Press of Kentucky, 1994), 72.

11. Zipes, *Brothers Grimm*, 59.

12. David R. Williams, "Extracts from Story Conference Notes Relating to 'Snow White and the Seven Dwarfs' in the Disney Archives, Burbank, California," 1987, Snow White and the Seven Dwarfs Collection, British Film Institute Library Special Collections, London.

13. Walt Disney, "Why I Chose Snow White," *Photoplay Studies* 3, no. 10 (1937): 7.

14. Karen Merritt, "Marguerite Clark as America's Snow White: The Resourceful Orphan Who Inspired Walt Disney," *Griffithiana* 64 (1998): 5, 17.

15. Merritt, "Marguerite Clark," 19.

16. Donald Crafton, *Before Mickey: The Animated Film, 1898–1928* (Chicago: University of Chicago Press, 1993), 271–97.

17. Michael Barrier, *The Animated Man: A Life of Walt Disney* (Berkeley: University of California Press, 2008), 101.

18. Grimm, "Snow White," 238–39.

19. The messy living habits of Disney's Dwarfs deviates from the Grimms' tale, which describes the cottage as already "indescribably dainty and neat" when Snow White arrives. In the original story, the household duties occur as part of her agreement to continue living with the Dwarfs after she is discovered sleeping in the bedroom (Grimm, "Snow White," 239–40).

20. Jessie Braham White, *Snow White and the Seven Dwarfs: A Fairy Tale Play Based on the Story of the Brothers Grimm* (New York: Dodd, Mead & Company, 1913).

21. Names that were ultimately rejected include Practical, Jumpy, Baldy, Hickey, Nifty, Sniffy, Stubby, Lazy, Puffy, Stuffy, Shorty, Wheezy, Burpy, Dizzy, Tubby, Deafy, Hoppy, Weepy, Dirty, Hungry, Thrifty, Shifty, Woeful, Doleful, Soulful, Awful, Snoopy, Blabby, Neurtsy, Gloomy, Daffy, Gaspy, Hotsy, Jaunty, Biggy, Biggy-Wiggy, and Biggo-Eggo. The name Gabby, subsequently used by the Fleischers for a character in Gulliver's Travels, was coincidentally also touted as a potential moniker for one of Disney's Dwarfs. See Williams, "Extracts"; Rudy Behlmer, *America's Favorite Movies: Behind the Scenes* (New York: Frederick Ungar, 1982), 42.

22. Alan Bryman, *The Disneyization of Society* (London: Sage, 2004), 5–6.

23. Aljean Harmetz, *The Making of The Wizard of Oz* (London: Pavilion Books, 1989), 3–4.

24. Leslie Cabarga, *The Fleischer Story*, rev. ed. (New York: DaCapo Press, 1988), 144.

25. It should nonetheless be reiterated that the Fleischer Studio was one of the most distinctive cartoon producers for much of the 1930s, and pioneered a number of animation techniques that predated similar approaches by Disney. Indeed, Mark Langer suggests that the major technological innovations of this period—including several of the advances ultimately integrated into *Snow White*—were "motivated chiefly by competition" specifically between Fleischer and Disney ("The Disney-Fleischer Dilemma: Product Differentiation and Technological Innovation," *Screen* 33, no. 4 [Winter 1992]: 351). Although the critical and commercial success of *Snow White* made it an unavoidable point of reference for the Fleischers' *Gulliver's Travels*,

this should not undermine the important contributions made by *both* studios in the lead-up to feature production.

26. See the documentary "Snow White Returns," *Snow White and the Seven Dwarfs: Platinum Edition*, DVD (Walt Disney Studios Home Entertainment, 2009).

27. Walt Disney, quoted in Schickel, *The Disney Version*, 156.

28. Between the mid-1990s and 2000s, the Disney Studio embarked upon a number of (predominantly direct-to-video) follow-ups to their earlier features, including *Cinderella II: Dreams Come True* (2002) and *Bambi II* (2006). These sequels have at times been accused of profiteering from, and sullying, the "classic" status of the original films and, following the Disney merger with Pixar in 2006, production was discontinued (Joe Strike, "Disney DTV Sequels: End of the Line," *Animation World Network*, March 28, 2007, http://www.awn.com/animationworld/disney-dtv-sequels-end-line). There were no plans announced for a *Snow White* sequel ahead of this cancellation. The Dwarfs admittedly did return in a number of government-funded cartoons—such as *Seven Wise Dwarfs* (1941) and *The Winged Scourge* (1943)—during the Second World War, but these were produced for propaganda and/or educational, rather than entertainment, purposes.

29. For an analysis of the Disney Princess brand, see Marc DiPaolo, "Mass-Marketing 'Beauty': How a Feminist Heroine Became an Insipid Disney Princess," in *Beyond Adaptation: Essays on Radical Transformations of Original Works*, ed. Phyllis Frus and Christy Williams (Jefferson, NC: McFarland, 2010), 168–80. With reference to *Beauty and the Beast* (1991), he argues that the subsequent marketing distilled the strength of Belle's character as presented in the film in order to make her conform to a generic princess stereotype.

30. J.P. Telotte, *The Mouse Machine: Disney and Technology* (Urbana: University of Illinois Press, 2008), 98–99.

31. For a comprehensive overview of Disney's *Snow White* merchandising, see Hollis and Sibley, *Walt Disney's Snow White*, 73–87. Over the years, the studio has continued to publish storybook tie-ins for its movies based upon folklore and fairy tales, including further versions of *Snow White*. See Jane Yolen for an analysis of two Disney books based on their film version of *Cinderella* (1950). She argues that "the story in the mass market has not been the same" since the release of Disney's film and its associated merchandise, although arguably overstates her own subjective case for the "true meaning" of the original text ("America's Cinderella," in *Cinderella: A Folklore Casebook*, ed. Alan Dundes [New York: Garland, 1982], 302–03).

32. *The Story of Gulliver's Travels: Authorized Edition, as Adapted from Paramount's Full-Length Feature in Technicolor* (London: Birn Brothers, 1939).

33. The three instalments featuring Twinkletoes, the incompetent carrier pigeon, are based around disastrous postal deliveries. The two films starring the assassins Sneak, Snoop, and Snitch focus on their continued criminal mishaps. Gabby, the town crier, appeared in eight cartoons, and was permitted the most variation in terms of narrative, ranging from being appointed King of Lilliput after an assassination threat, in *King for a Day* (1940), to simply attempting to change the diaper of a mischievous baby, in *All's Well* (1941). Each cartoon establishes a broad slapstick routine around Gabby's bumbling, know–it–all personality. There is no direct reference to Gulliver in any of the films.

34. A recent "unofficial" release from the independent studio Thunderbean has finally made a high-quality version of the film available for home audiences. See *Fleischer Classics Featuring Gulliver's Travels*, Blu-ray/DVD (Thunderbean, 2014).

35. Behlmer, *America's Favorite Movies*, 59–60.

Chapter Two

The Perils of a Masculine Upbringing

Pinocchio, from Carlo Collodi to Walt Disney

Jean-Marie Apostolidès

Any comparison of Collodi's version of *The Adventures of Pinocchio*, originally published in the initial issue of the *Giornali per i Bambini* in July 1881 as *Story of a Marionette*, and Disney's 1940 film reveals much about the adaptation of literary works to cinema. Though the narrative through line remains essentially intact, key changes from book to movie, in this tale of the eponymous wooden character's desire to behave like "a regular little boy," imply a great deal about the upbringing of children, specifically boys, during the six decades between publication of the literary piece and the film's release, allowing us to comprehend the evolution of children's roles in society.

COLLODI'S ORIGINAL MARIONETTE

Pinocchio is a marionette without strings, a puppet who has broken his ties, or rather never had ties, though that was the intention of Geppetto, his father and creator, when he visited Master Cherry to procure a log.[1] Geppetto's desire to have a child by himself, without feminine intervention—a son he could hold and manipulate at will—is answered by Pinocchio's opposite desire to break free. While still a roughed-out log, Collodi's puppet makes himself heard. He resists being worked and polished and is repeatedly insolent toward his creator. His strangest impertinence is the exaggerated growth of his nose, which Geppetto interprets as an act of boyish rebellion that the man tries in vain to squelch: "Poor Geppetto kept struggling to cut it back; the more he cut, the longer that impudent nose became" (99).

13

Each organ, each member fabricated for Pinocchio, determines his peculiar relationship to the world. His hands finished, Pinocchio uses them for new insults. He appropriates his father's wig, transforming himself into a grotesque mirror image of the old man. In the face of his son's disobedience, a serious transgression in a patriarchal society of the type that existed in Italy during the latter half of the nineteenth century, poor Geppetto can do nothing but rail: "Scamp of a child, you aren't even finished and you're already beginning to lack respect for your father!" (101). Early impertinence marks the beginning of a long series of separations, leading finally to Pinocchio's roaming the world in search of his fortune. Actually, Pinocchio rebels as much against Geppetto's advice as against his wretched social condition. Until he discovers the means of escaping from his poverty, the marionette is content to dream, at one point picturing himself as a rich lord.

Pinocchio can be seen as the adolescent representative of the character type Marthe Robert defines as "bastard."[2] Collodi's fantastical "hero" rejects having been born of an ordinary father.[3] As far as his mother is concerned, she—appearing in the guise of a fairy—is no ordinary woman. Pinocchio himself possesses a dual nature: he is a boy and simultaneously a marionette. This second identity is a source of humiliations and anxieties but offers numerous advantages as well, constituting a carapace or shell that the child employs to protect himself from the outside world. His body of wood takes beating better than would human flesh; it also provides Pinocchio with an unbearable lightness of being, allowing him to escape tight spots. The author self-consciously associates this with the animal world: Pinocchio leaps like a hare, climbs over hedges like a goat, and swims in the sea like a fish. His metamorphosis into a donkey is but the ultimate manifestation of an animal nature Pinocchio possesses from the outset. During the era in which this tale was conceived, childhood constituted a radically different world from that of the adult. To bridge this gap, any child had to be trained in the manner of an animal, controlled in every particular like a puppet by any concerned parent.

In 1848, then again in 1859, Tuscany rebelled against the Hapsburgs. These were events in which Collodi was closely involved. In addition to political upheavals, others arising from differences of social class exerted great influence. While revealing sympathy for his puppet's impertinence, Collodi was nevertheless writing a novel of formation (*Bildungsroman*),[4] a pedagogical intent of the author that is clear in every chapter. With Italy's unification, the need emerged for a form of education common to children of all classes—those of the bourgeoisie as well as the working class.[5] Hence, Pinocchio must attend school to be able to provide for his family's needs. Geppetto, who has no money and for whom the daily need for food is a source of constant concern, sacrifices his overcoat to buy his "son" an alphabet book. Pinocchio thus finds himself caught, from his conception, in a network of inescapable obligations. Early on, he becomes conscious of his responsibility to "produce": "Today, at school, I'll learn how to read right away, tomorrow I'll learn how to write, and the day after tomorrow, I'll learn arithmetic. Then with my skill I'll make lots of money, and with the first money that I get I'll buy my father a beautiful woolen jacket" (137).

Pinocchio, as a meaningful work that (if through a fairy-tale-like narrative) presents a unified approach to education, is split between two value systems that are essentially mutually exclusive. On the one hand, there's the system of traditional underprivileged classes, for whom school and the prolongation of childhood constitute a luxury they cannot afford. Geppetto, a proponent of such an approach, wants to impose adult behavior on his son immediately; the book is haunted by their continuous search for food. On the other hand, Pinocchio's story is based on the new bourgeois set of values, dictating that a child does not possess the same status as in earlier/traditional society. From this perspective, having recently emerged as that era's "new normal," Pinocchio is relieved of adult responsibilities: less expected to produce than to conform to moral precepts. However, he is constantly confronted by immense challenges in which cruelty is never absent. He is successively hung, locked in jail for months, forced to confront a giant snake, arrested by police, and swallowed by a shark before his education is complete, all before finally obtaining the right to experience a normal boy's life. Little more than a monstrous inventory of punishments recalcitrant children might then undergo, this book may be read, at least in retrospect, as a historical representative of nineteenth-century boyhood life experiences.[6]

Pinocchio flees from the adult role his father wants to circumscribe the puppet/son within, attempting to find refuge in a transitional world. The latter, not realistic to its time period, might be characterized as foreshadowing a modern adolescence even then emerging. All the while, Pinocchio never ceases to dream. He hesitates between the conquest of the world and its wealth and the safe return into the arms of a mother for whom he becomes the child-phallus. The Blue Fairy first appears in the guise of a distant sister, then a typical fairy of the literary tradition.[7] Following Pinocchio's betrayal by robbers, she rescues him, bringing Pinocchio back to a child's world—one that is the opposite of Geppetto's. From being a provider of food in his father's universe, Pinocchio becomes the pampered center of a cosmos (created for him by his mother) structured around oral drives. The fairy sends for him in a carriage that is "covered with whipped cream and ladyfingers in custard" (195).[8] Under her guidance, Pinocchio enacts the essential steps of a bourgeois upbringing. She reeducates him according to the family values of a different class, much as Oliver Twist is treated by Mr. Brownlow and his housekeeper, Mrs. Bedwin, in Dickens's in some ways parallel classic about the terrors of male childhood. In *Pinocchio*, the opposition between paternal and maternal space is matched by a second opposition between working class and middle class (Geppetto is not a proletarian: he retains the tools of his trade). Behavior that represented a source of pride in the father's world becomes ground for reproach in the mother's. When, after a lie to the fairy, the marionette's nose grows out of proportion, Pinocchio is overcome with shame. Moreover, he must submit to the demands of the familial world: obey, be reliable, take his medicine, and work hard at school.

However, his return to his mother's bosom is not without problems. The fairy is ambivalent toward this stubborn son whom she raises without a father. When Pinocchio refuses a laxative and announces that he'd rather "die than drink," she summons four black rabbits carrying a coffin in which he will be placed. When the marionette's nose grows, she does not return it to its normal size immediately, only "when she saw him disfigured and with eyes popping out of his head in wild despair" (213). When Pinocchio returns to the fairy after leaving prison, she causes him to believe she has died of sorrow. However, he finds her again on the island of the Busy Bees, where the fairy reappears in a new form: as a middle-class woman, the first step toward her final disappearance from the masculine world. Having lost some of her magical attributes, she leaves him with his foot caught in the front door for a whole night because "she was sleeping, did not want to be awakened" (341). Shortly before the Blue Fairy disappears entirely, she plays another cruel trick on the poor marionette, making believe she has been reduced to poverty and now lies in a hospital.

Clearly, Collodi's text functions as a fictional yet ideological response to tensions running through Italian society at century's end, calling into question the assumption that progress can be achieved through reform of the educational system. Pinocchio struggles to become a man because he does not have a male role model. His father belongs to a traditional world and to an impecunious class from which the puppet longs to flee. Still, he cannot escape responsibilities. His flight, then, can be interpreted as a search for a more relevant father figure. Such an image can be located only through an excursion into the feminine world, excluded from the traditional patriarchal society. For this reason, Pinocchio's mother and father inhabit different spheres. These parents never meet, their son providing their only link. The then-emergent feminine world in the social order is characterized not only by ambivalence but also its manifestation through the imaginary, which in literature engenders the marvelous. Childhood fears, fantasies of being eaten or castrated, are projected onto the external world, mostly through the aforementioned mythical/monstrous figures.

At a key turning point, Pinocchio undergoes a transformation into a donkey following his stay in Funland. Reduced to animality, sold to a circus, then to a peasant who plans to make a drum from his skin, Pinocchio would die without the fairy's intervention. Barely escaping death, he takes advantage of his metamorphosis from donkey into marionette to, finally, fully arc into personhood. His acceptance of reality (an important step from boyhood to manhood) marks the beginning of the book's final act, allowing for the unique solution that Pinocchio discovers for escaping from contradictions in his world. From that moment, he accepts the laws of society and the male role implicitly hoped for by his father. Now in accord with Geppetto's desires, Pinocchio searches for him, landing in the stomach of a shark. Having survived this test, the marionette goes to work. The family achieves stability and unity around the son, who has become responsible. It is not a retro-traditional family, in which the links of solidarity extend to kin or to the village community. When Pinocchio encounters the Fox and the Cat in dire straits, he refuses to come to their rescue because of their negative role in his past life. He is a different person; he has grown, matured, learned, become humanized.

This new family is organized around the father's role, which passes from father to son without permanent attachment to one or the other. To become a young man is to become a productive adult, that is, to share equally in the role of father. Family structure is reproduced, at the fantasy level, without the intervention of women—a legacy transmitted directly from one generation to the next. This does not imply that, in the novel's narrative, passage through the mother's world was pointless. To the contrary, it is what allowed Pinocchio to transform his family, to move up in social status, to change their class standing. The strict imitation of Geppetto's example would only have prolonged poverty. The fairy's final intervention makes Pinocchio rich. She gives Pinocchio gold coins, and, thanks to this treasure, Pinocchio and Geppetto escape from the hell of daily poverty to enter the middle class of a reunified Italy.

WALT'S (RE-)CREATION

In September 1937, during production of *Snow White and the Seven Dwarfs*, Disney decided that his studio's next project would be an Americanized version of *Pinocchio*. An important step was taken with Walt's decision to create an essential role for (Jiminy) Cricket, a minor figure in Collodi. This Disney Version did not entail a total eradication of European aspects, rather their transformation into "cultural signs" within a global/American frame of reference. Still, changes to Collodi's puppet were drastic enough that the animated version was coolly received in Italy at its time of release. [9]

In Disney, Pinocchio emerges as an American child masked by Bavarian costume. [10] Disney's story is narrated by the talking cricket, here given the name Jiminy. One small voice among others in Collodi, the cricket has been promoted to the stature of official conscience. In the novel, the marionette heard a multitude of external voices communicating advice drawn from popular wisdom in the form of proverbs. This concert, played by animals—the cricket, the slug, the pigeon, the parrot, and so on—echoed the parental voice. To Pinocchio, all of nature united to indicate the proper path to follow. In Disney, Jiminy becomes an interiorized conscience, endowed with Protestant values: the puppet's superego, solemnly knighted by the Blue Fairy. In passing from Collodi to Disney, Pinocchio changes from an old-fashioned outer-directed to a contemporary inner-directed personality.[11] This new Pinocchio does not exhibit any rebelliousness toward the adult world, rather impulsively attempting to take advantage of what that world offers him, if initially unable to distinguish what is good from what is detrimental. His misfortunes are partly due to his conscience's own uncertainty since once more we are located in a period of changing values—here the specific social situation during which Disney's film was produced.

The story has been rewritten in terms of the American values of the late thirties. Geppetto is no longer a starving woodcarver but a comfortable craftsman who makes clocks and toys for children. When the fairy grants his wish to see his marionette come to life, she simply says: "Kind Geppetto, you have given so much happiness to others that you deserve to be rewarded." The Blue Fairy enters at this narrative's opening, whereas she first appeared in Collodi's chapter 15. When the audience initially views Pinocchio, Geppetto is adding the finishing touch: a wide smile on his wooden face. Consequently, the marionnette does not come to life by himself; Disney's "boy" requires *both* parents, precisely as real children did during the America of the 1930s. The primary issue here: conformism that turns Pinocchio into a well-adjusted child. His father gives him form, his external appearance; his mother endows Pinocchio with soul, bringing him into existence. The Disney mother's psychological and moral approach to child raising replaces the father's mechanical alternative. There is no ambivalence in Disney's fairy; she is endowed with the same physical and moral characteristics one finds in the American master's other princesses of dreams: Snow White and Cinderella. Her behavior with Geppetto is that of a younger bride, kind if a bit cool, reserved. She speaks to him as she would to a normal child, playing the role of a protective, upright mother. When Pinocchio asks what he has to do to become an actual boy, she recites the moral commonplaces of American middle-class life: "Be courageous, reliable and generous. Be a good son to your father, so he can be proud of you! Learn to distinguish evil from good, and one day, when you wake up, you will discover that you are a regular boy."[12]

Like the parental figures, values here presented to Pinocchio are not ambivalent. The good guys are easily distinguishable from the bad; they dressed in rags. Honest John (the Fox) and Gideon (the Cat) provide examples of misfits, excluded from middle-class society. This holds true for the rowdies of Pleasure Island: a close-up of their shoes reveals they all hail from a poorer class. Their transformation into donkeys becomes a metaphor, indicating all they had to sell was their ability to do manual labor. As a boy from the middle class, Pinocchio's predicament is that, as a result of associating with such boys, he risks ending up like them, an animalistic member of the proletariat.

In Disney, ambiguous characters like the puppeteer Mangefeu lose some of their complexity. In Collodi, this character shares features with Bluebeard. When Pinocchio arrives in the theater, he is welcomed by the marionettes of the Commedia dell'Arte as a liberator. Thanks to him, they are freed from traditional roles and shower Pinocchio with praise. After considering using him as a fireplace log, Mangefeu forgives Pinocchio and sends him home with five gold coins. In Disney, the puppet master, renamed Stromboli, becomes an old accomplice of Fox and Cat. Sold to Stromboli by Honest John and Gideon for a fast buck, Pinocchio becomes the main attraction. The arising problem is that of the child star created by 1930s Hollywood. Pinocchio is no longer a child, let alone a puppet, yet cannot be considered an adult. If on the one hand he is gainfully employed, on the other he's cheated. Stromboli exploits him shamelessly, threatening to destroy Pinocchio when his success inevitably declines.

The clash of values in Disney's work occurs between the world of the traditional craftsman and large-scale industry, between Geppetto's little work-ethic world and that of Pleasure Island's coachman, who transforms children into animals. At the inn, this coachman enlists Honest John and Gideon to help him lure wayward boys, ultimately turning them into donkeys. Pinocchio would not consider leaving his father's home if the external world didn't present him with such continuous temptations, not limited to traditional entertainments like Stromboli's puppet show; they are concentrated in the amusement park. There are not only merry-go-rounds and games but adult activities, forbidden to American children: smoking, drinking, gambling, fighting. The park was designed for boys to "make jackasses of themselves." With such an absence of authority figures, children transgress all rules, vandalizing everything, to Jiminy's dismay.

On Pleasure Island, children wreak havoc on the essential values of the Western world—the tradition of literature and the arts that affluent American culture of the mid-twentieth century considered necessary for boys to learn if they were to live out the American Dream and continuously, gradually rise in status and wealth. Torn-up books lie strewn about; a palace is offered up for destruction. As Lampwick, a juvenile delinquent, and Pinocchio enter, a vandal chops a grand piano to pieces. While Lampwick lights his cigar by striking matches on the Mona Lisa, his friend gleefully breaks a cathedral stained-glass window. In 1940, these scenes could have been interpreted as allusions to the book burnings during immediately preceding years in Nazi Germany. Today, they can equally well be interpreted as an allegory for the society of consumption, developing in the United States even as the film was produced and, consciously or unconscously, absorbed by Disney's team, relocated from reality to their cinematic version of *Pinocchio*.

Disney's Americanized Geppetto projects a traditional Protestant mentality, belonging socially to an endangered economic world. He doesn't have much leverage when it comes to keeping his son at home. It isn't surprising, then, that Pinocchio turns toward the outer/larger world, its deceivingly colorful images filling the void of his private, middle-class, unexciting existence. Ultimately, the marionette is reborn as a real (human) boy, thanks to the fairy, she judging that he has proven himself brave, truthful, unselfish. He finds his specific place in society after confronting different challenges, culminating in a heroic rescue of his father. Pinocchio's place is neither in the upper class, among capitalists, nor in the working class, with poor street rebels. He belongs to the middle class, its values incarnated from the beginning by Jiminy. At the end, the cricket steps outside to thank the fairy for such a happy ending and is rewarded with a solid-gold badge, certifying him as an official conscience. Nicolas Sammond argues that the film serves as "an apt metaphor for the metaphysics of midcentury American child-rearing," the film "ultimately an assimilationist fable." *Pinocchio* thus emerges as the central Disney film, the most strongly middle class in orientation, conveying a message that indulging in "the pleasures of the working class, of vaudeville, or of pool halls and amusement parks, led to a life as a beast of burden."[13]

THE PSYCHOLOGY OF DISNEY'S *PINOCCHIO*

From a psychological point of view, Pinocchio is torn between the traditional inner-directed model and a new emergent template, the latter encouraging imitation and identification with one's peer group; Pinocchio is eager to be like his peers because his marionette's nature sets him apart from the perceived norm. Another reason for his quest for a masculine role model relates to Geppetto's age and personality. He a good man but old, as much Pinocchio's companion as father. Gepetto plays and dances with the child but provides no role model. Nor is he a husband to the Blue Fairy, who floats above the masculine world, a protective though distant "Mom." If she has no intimate relation with Geppetto, she nevertheless grants his wish, magically appearing in his workshop, endowing his puppet with life. The only way Pinocchio can resolve these contradictions is by becoming a hero—essentially, by escaping into the "extraordinary." In saving Geppetto's life and then devoting himself to Gepetto, Pinocchio assumes the role of absent-father. The fairy-mother acknowledges this substitution by accelerating the child's accession to manhood, declaring him a real (American!) boy. This acknowledgment is represented in typical Disney's iconography: Pinocchio receives a new finger on each hand. Indeed, whereas the marionette created by Geppetto had only four fingers (the convention in Hollywood animation), the first thing Pinocchio notices when he wakes up after his transformation is his acquisition of a human hand.

The problem facing Collodi's Pinocchio was passage from a bankrupt world of the artisan to the middle class, refusing the strings of the traditional marionette because he felt driven by an inner will that expressed itself through acts of insolence and rebellion, gradually discovering a transitional world in which he learned of the joys of freedom and individuality, and of serious responsibilities, that is, how to distinguish the real from the imaginary. For Disney's Pinocchio, the essential problem is not a challenge to achieving individuality nor arrival at self-knowledge; instead, it is a matter of *avoiding* these issues and accepting the suburban-style conformity that would flourish in America during the twentieth century's second half. Psychic processes, therefore, are no longer represented through confrontations with monsters, which now remain at the level of the Freudian unconscious. The love between Pinocchio and the fairy has no expression outside these characters' unconscious minds. She only/specifically appears to embody the force of Goodness in contrast to Evil, symbolized by Stomboli. Likewise, the ambivalence of the parental couple toward their child is discarded in favor of total transparence of family relationships. The numerous mediating beings that populated Collodi's world are absent from Disney. By bringing them into play, the film could have explored either phantasmatically or intellectually the characters' unconscious, which the film attempts to deny and relegate to nonexistence. Even Collodi's shark is stripped by Disney of its connotations of the fantastic. In the place of a voracious mother-monster, the filmmaker elaborates variations on the myth of Moby-Dick, that great whale that structures the conscious sensibility of America since its creation in the mid-nineteenth century. By escaping Monstro's violence, Pinocchio becomes identified with an American legend, Ishmael, narrator of Herman Melville's story.[14] Pinocchio not only becomes a regular boy but attains the status of the exemplary child others (those making up the child audience) must, after leaving the theater, imitate. Collodi's call for Italian children of his own transitional era to achieve individuality has been replaced by Disney's insistence on the mid-twentieth-century need for American children to accept conformism to societal roles while striving after the success-oriented American Dream that Walt, in his own lifetime, lived out and, on film, consistently projected as "the right approach" to life.

CONCLUSION

In 1940, Pleasure Island, its appearance inspired by the Luna Parks, remained an ambiguous place for lower-class entertainment. People encountered there were not always respectable. Years later, when the consumer society had established its system of values, Disney transformed Pleasure Island into Disneyland. Cleansed of its lower-class odor, Disney's own amusement park became morally acceptable, an expression and embodiment of middle-class values. Accompanied by his parents, each American child makes the required pilgrimage there, in the footsteps of Pinocchio, if he is ever to discover that he is a *regular* boy.

NOTES

1. Carlo Collodi, *The Adventures of Pinocchio, Story of a Puppet*, translated with an introductory essay and notes by Nicolas J. Perella (Berkeley: University of California Press, 1986), 89. Subsequent citations of Collodi's text are given parentheticaly in the text.
   2. Marthe Robert, *Origins of the Novel* (Bloomington: Indiana University Press, 1980).
   3. "During the period I have mentioned, the child's imagination becomes engaged in the task of achieving freedom from parents, of whom he now has such a low opinion and of replacing them by others, occupying, as a rule, a higher social station." Sigmund Freud, *Collected Papers*, (New York : Basic Books, 1959). Cf. vol.5, p. 76.
   4. A novel of formation or education is a literary genre focusing on the psychological and moral growth of the protagonist from youth to adulthood, with a character arc essential. In English literature, *Great Expectations* by Charles Dickens (1861) is one of the most famous examples, in American literature, *The Adventures of Huckleberry Finn* by Mark Twain (1884).
   5. Concerning the context of Pinocchio's creation, see Nicolas J. Perella's introduction to his translation of *Pinocchio*.
   6. See Pierre Lambert, *Pinocchio* [1995], translated from French by Jeanine Herman (New York: Hyperion, 1997), 14.
   7. Collodi translated and adapted Perrault's tales, as well as those of Madame d'Aulnoy and Madame Leprince de Beaumont. Numerous allusions to French fairy tales can be found in his works.
   8. This carriage seems to be a reference to a popular song known to French children as "Dame Tartine."
   9. See Valentino Balducci and Andrea Rauch, *Pinocchio, Image d'une marionnette* (Paris: Gallimard, 1982), 90.
   10. We never know exactly where the story takes place, although the spectator could easily imagine that it is located in Tuscany. In his article "The Nostalgic Builder," Bruno Girveau says, "The small Bavarian town of Rothenburg ob der Tauber was the main source of inspiration for the village in *Pinocchio*" (in *Once Upon a Time: Walt Disney, the Source of Inspiration for the Disney Studios* [Munich: Prestel, 2007], 228).
   11. See David Riesman, *The Lonely Crowd* (New Haven, CT: Yale University Press, 1950).
   12. "Prove yourself brave, truthful and unselfish. Be a good son to Geppetto—make him proud of you! Learn to tell right from wrong. Then, some day, you will wake up and find yourself a real boy" (*Walt Disney's Pinocchio* [Racine, WI: Whitman, 1940], unpaginated edition).
   13. Susan Honeyman, *Consuming Agency in Fairy Tales, Childlore, and Folkliterature* (New York: Routledge, 2013), 29.
   14. Ishmael is the oldest son of Abraham, by the Egyptian Hagar, servant to his then-barren wife Sarah. As such, he is an outcast from a great family.

Chapter Three

Here Be Gay Dragons

Queer Allegory and Disney's
The Reluctant Dragon *(1941)*

Tison Pugh

"Hic sunt dracones" translates as "Here are dragons." Within the cultural imaginary, a more common translation features an archaic flair: "Here *be* dragons." We moderns can confidently declare that yesteryear's explorers would have encountered exciting discoveries, yet a dragon would not have been among them. And so the paradox of "hic sunt dracones": a cartographer supposedly plots out an unknown region with that phrase invoking a mythic monster. But is the idiom "hic sunt dracones" nothing more than a myth itself? According to Simon Garfield:

> The phrase "Here Be Dragons" has never actually appeared on a historic map. There have been lots of ironic, nostalgic and fearful uses in literature, but try finding those three words on a map from the medieval or golden ages . . . and you'll look in vain. [1]

Questing for dragons, even with a map, leads the adventurer to discover only the unknowability of certain territories. These cartographic issues parallel the challenges of queer cinematic interpretation, in which a film's audience must leave its surface level of narration and explore unmarked depths. This endeavor runs into greater travails while investigating children's media, owing to the genre's presumed off-limits innocence.

Disney's *The Reluctant Dragon* (1941) exemplifies these difficulties: it has been interpreted as a queer allegory as its eponymous beast shatters expectations of normative dragon behavior. Yet this puzzling character concomitantly fractures the possibility that one could ever define "normative dragon behavior." In this light, medieval maps with their dragons, as well as the vagaries of interpreting uncharted territories, serve as a hermeneutic model for reading Disney films queerly. Such viewers must strike off on their own, with few clearly marked signposts to guide their way. What is normative, what is queer, one might well wonder, when the map—the surface narrative and standard interpretive praxes of it—introduces dragons who flaunt codes of gendered conduct within the general parameters of children's entertainments?

Most Disney films are insistently heterosexual in their surface level of narration. The "Someday My Prince Will Come" theme seemingly leaves little room for depictions of gay desires. Still, in their critical reception, several Disney productions have elicited queer-friendly interpretations, with viewers identifying allegories of submerged homoeroticism. Various characters assume a dual layer of signification that includes potential queerness. The close friendships of Timon and Pumba in *The Lion King* (1994) and of Hugo and Djali in *The Hunchback of Notre Dame* (1996) resemble romantic pairings. In a similar vein, since Mulan of *Mulan* (1998) and Merida of *Brave* (2012) resist cultural constructions of femininity, their films can be read as queer coming-of-age narratives. In another such rewriting of female agency, *Frozen* (2013) upends the standard marriage plot in its storyline of sororal affection triumphing over adversity—with no prince necessary to achieve this desired end. Many of Disney's male villains, including Captain Hook in *Peter Pan* (1953), Prince John in *Robin Hood* (1973), and Jafar in *Aladdin* (1992), act foppishly, imbuing their portrayals with an artily effeminate edge. Also, gay and lesbian actors often lend their voices to Disney characters, allowing these roles to be read as gay too, including Rosie O'Donnell's Terk in *Tarzan* (1999), Nathan Lane's Timon in *The Lion King*, and David Ogden Stiers's many parts, including Cogsworth in *Beauty and the Beast* (1991), Governor Ratcliffe in *Pocahontas* (1995), and Dr. Jumba Jookiba in *Lilo & Stitch* (2002). In contrast to such queer-friendly interpretations, some conservative commentators rail against potential gay subtexts. From their perspective, the introduction of queer storylines into children's media upsets the genre's presumed foundation of innocence. In all such instances, though, it must be admitted that the evidence for queer readings depends on allegorical interpretations of films predominantly normative in their gendered and sexual orientation: Timon and Pumba never kiss, so to interpret them as gay depends on conjecturing from the clear referents of the cinematic text to its potential allegorical registers and, as a result, finding queerness therein.

But the fact that some interpretations lie hidden from view does not invalidate them; many texts and films play with multiple layers of signification, and much of the pleasure of interpretation arises in decoding how an allegory conveys various, even contradictory, meanings simultaneously.

Summarizing allegory's polyvocality, Matt Bergbusch proposes that the form illuminates meanings potentially lost in time:

> Allegory redeems the dead matter of history into (new, revolutionary) meaning . . . by dislodging "sign systems" from "the historical maps commissioned by the dominant classes"; moments of "revolutionary promise" are thereby saved by allegory from "stagnation and death in history."[2]

Interpreting narratives queerly entails determining the significance of moments in the margins.

Queer allegories subvert the ideological construction of children as the preferred consumers of children's media, claiming a space for adult enjoyment of youth-oriented entertainments while subverting the presumption that youthful innocence stands as these narratives' de facto sensibility. In regard to the title character of *The Reluctant Dragon*, such a perspective gives credence to the possibility he should be read as gay.[3] Prominent Disney scholar Douglas Brode describes the dragon as "flamboyantly gay" and notes that, while this portrayal is certainly a "caricature," it is "hardly vicious" in its intent; Brode points out as well that it is "those who do not understand and accept the dragon (in the film, and in the audience watching) who are chastised."[4] Sean Griffin agrees, suggesting that *The Reluctant Dragon* "presents an easily read gay character under the guise of fantasy and shows (normal) characters accepting him as he is."[5] With this film's didactic call to appreciate difference and put aside prejudices, Brode and Griffin conclude that *Dragon*'s allegorical register imbues its narrative level with an affirmation of homosexuality.

Still, Brode and Griffin focus their analysis chiefly on the animated short that concludes *The Reluctant Dragon*. Actually, the film tells a more expansive tale and announces its irregular ambitions prior to its narrative action: "This picture is made in answer to the many requests to show the backstage life of animated cartoons. P.S. Any resemblance to a regular motion picture is purely coincidental." With this tongue-in-cheek admission that it is more concerned with the mechanics of animation than some standard plot, *Dragon* begins its loose frame narrative: humorist and actor Robert Benchley (playing himself) has been ordered by his wife (Nana Bryant) to sell the movie rights for "The Reluctant Dragon" to Walt Disney. Benchley resists, Mrs. Benchley insists, and so Benchley journeys to the Disney studio, where he learns about the intricate processes of creating an animated film. Along the way, he views several shorts, including "Casey, Jr." (the tale of a train's travels, used to explain sound effects), "Baby Weems," (an infant genius, illustrating the storyboarding process), and Goofy's "How to Ride a Horse." Then Benchley finally meets Disney, who invites him to a screening of the

animated short of "The Reluctant Dragon"; after watching it, Benchley and
Mrs. Benchley drive home.

Numerous themes connect *Dragon*'s frame narrative to its animated sequence, with muted issues of queerness similarly arising. The film encourages viewers to see Benchley's likeness to the Reluctant Dragon: at the
Disney compound's gates, a security guard requests of Benchley, "Name,
please," and Benchley replies "The Reluctant Dra—." Building from this
misidentification, Benchley reveals another similarity in his own reluctance:
he does not want to obey his wife's demands, and so continually attempts to
elude humorless Humphrey, his tour guide. Benchley proves as reluctant to
venture upon his quest—to find Walt and cinch the sale—as the Reluctant
Dragon is to adhere to the expected codes of gender. Benchley's reluctance
to obey his wife's authority underscores his beleaguered performance of
masculinity as a henpecked husband, allowing queer potential to emerge.

Significantly, Benchley and Mrs. Benchley's relationship is shown unflat-
teringly. She shrewishly bosses him about; he candidly regrets their union:
Mrs. Benchley observes, "Well, you hardly knew me when you suggested
marriage," to which Benchley mumbles in reply, "Yeah, look at the trouble I
got now." She seems as much his chastising mother as his wife. Assuming a
maternal stance, she reads Kenneth Grahame's "The Reluctant Dragon"
aloud in the film's opening, then scolds him because he hesitates to approach
Disney—"You'd think you were going to the dentist!" He prefers to play
with his popgun, but she upbraids him: "Get your things on. And stop shilly-
shallying." As this scene closes, Benchley throws a temper tantrum, shout-
ing, "I am not shillying, and I am not shallying. But once and for all, I will
not go to the studio. I will not make myself ridiculous." He falls into the pool
and adds, in a Donald Duck voice, "And that's final!" The irony of this
statement is that Benchley declares an end to the film's narrative action just
as it has begun. Viewers realize that, this outburst notwithstanding, Mrs.
Benchley rules their marriage. With husbandly masculinity under duress,
Benchley reverts to childhood.

A slightly odd aspect of *Dragon* involves a plot point that makes little
sense narratively but deepens the film's investment in depicting Benchley as
a reluctant, even petulant, child: his wife leaves to go shopping, not accompanying her husband. Her absence is critical to the portrayal both of Benchley's reluctance—presumably, he could not "shilly-shally" if she, like humorless Humphrey, escorted him—and of his continued rejuvenation. Disney
has long predicated its allure on bringing forth adults' inner children; Benchley becomes similarly revived through his tour. A key contrast in the film's
frame narrative guides viewers' perspective on the intersecting meanings of
masculinity and childhood: Mrs. Benchley infantilizes her husband into a
petulant boy; Disney rejuvenates him into a happy, contented kid. Along
these lines, the security guard issues him a pass to the compound—similar to

a hall pass in elementary school—while Benchley carries his copy of "The Reluctant Dragon" in a schoolboy's posture. At one point, the P.A. system calls for him—"Mr. Benchley, you're wanted in Walt's office"—as if he were an errant youngster summoned to the principal. After watching "Baby Weems," an artist presents a caricature of Benchley in the style of this infant toon. Benchley says approvingly: "That's a pip. That's taken years off my life." In a similar moment, Benchley presumes that an array of ceramic figures, which the artists use as models for their drawings, must be for sale; Doris, his escort, replies that they are not. Benchley asks, "Well, if they're not for sale, what are they for? Or am I too young to know?" Jovially casting himself as an innocent curious about taboo knowledge, Benchley assumes the position of a child, establishing childhood innocence as the desired destination of this middle-aged man's journey while undermining any coherency to the governing image of childhood.

Despite the emphasis on Benchley's marital discontents and status as a rejuvenated youngster, which bear queer potential in deconstructing the presumed privileges of 1940s-era adult masculinity, clearly his amatory interests remain heterosexual in orientation, complicating efforts to read *Dragon*'s frame-narrative as a gay allegory. After Benchley eludes Humphrey's control, he sees an attractive female model, covered modestly if suggestively in a robe, entering the art studio, presumably to pose; Benchley spies through the window—obviously trying to catch a glimpse of her naked. The scene proceeds with an ironic reversal. Benchley sneaks into the drawing studio and overhears the instructor's suggestive directions to his pupils: "Remember, curves are the important thing in a model of this type. Be sure and bring out the sweep of her torso and the modeling of those hips." The joke is soon evident—the class is sketching an elephant, not the attractive young woman—yet the humor does not overwrite Benchley's heteroerotic attractions. As Benchley enters, several drawings of nude females hang in the background, indicating that his hope to see a naked woman was reasonable, even amid the general milieu of Disney "innocence."

These heteroerotic dynamics continue. Benchley meets the various artists in training, providing the opportunity for a quick flirtation. "Hey, here's something pretty cute over here," he states, meeting Lotus, an Asian American illustrator. Benchley admires her efforts, but the instructor, to enhance the elephant's comedic appeal, exaggerates its belly in her sketch. Benchley consoles Lotus—"What a shame"—offering his support to her artistic vision. She counters, "Oh, no, I think round tummy kind of cute," hinting that she finds Benchley attractive, notwithstanding his middle-aged girth. He later meets Doris, who teaches him about sound effects; again, it's clear that he finds her attractive. "Don't be afraid, I'm only the train whistle," she declares. He responds approvingly, "Well, they certainly have improved the looks of them since I was a boy." At another point, she holds up a cel drawing of Bambi through which she is visible, as she explains that she will find an appropriate background for the image; Benchley compliments her— "Nothing wrong with the one I just saw"—in appreciation of her beauty. Clearly, to interpret Benchley as a queer figure necessitates overlooking his heterosexual interests by focusing instead on the way his marital discontents undermine his masculinity. Again, the surface narrative hides what its queer allegory otherwise allows.

Benchley's anti-quest ends as he finally meets Walt, the man he has avoided for the film's duration. About to watch Disney's already-produced film of Grahame's story, Benchley cannot sell what already exists and so sits down to enjoy the cartoon. Throughout the frame, viewers have seen marriage debased but heterosexual attractions exalted. Reluctance, as Benchley's own key trait, has accomplished little yet defines resistance to other's calls to action as a necessary step for simple pleasures. As Benchley soon realizes, Disney's "The Reluctant Dragon" is loosely based on Grahame's short story. The work tells of a peaceful creature and the combat he fakes with St. George to appease bloodthirsty townsfolk. Grahame's story encourages readers to free themselves of bias—"So they must make friends, and not be prejudiced, and go about fancying they knew everything there was to be known, because they didn't, not by a long way."[6] With this gentle admonition against prejudice, the story can be read as an allegory of accepting otherness, although little in the surface narration indicates that this Reluctant Dragon is *sexually* other. Grahame directed his readers *away* from sexual interpretations of his works, notably *The Wind in the Willows*, declaring they contained "no problems, no sex, no second meaning," that they were "clear of the clash of sex."[7] Despite this caveat, his canon, like Disney's, has inspired spirited discussion concerning gay themes, particularly due to its preference for male homosociality. Wynn Yarbrough uncovers a "tradition of bachelor and homo-social manhood" in Grahame's stories;[8] Sandra Schwab argues that the characterization of St. George mocks Victorian chivalric ideals by deflating his masculinity.[9] Queer possibilities emerge from Grahame's text, with the questioning of traditional masculinities conducive to a queer reimagining, Grahame's own statement notwithstanding.

Disney's version begins with a voiceover highlighting its fairy-tale origins: "Long, long ago there lived a little boy who considered himself quite an authority on brave, fearless knights and their mortal enemies, the horrible fire-breathing dragons that daily terrorized the countryside": The boy's father, in terror, tells him of a nearby dragon. But the boy finds the beast singing merrily; he interrupts his song to greet him, as the dragon fends off any possible attack: "Oh, oh! Now, boy, don't you bung stones at me or squirt water or anything. I won't have it!" Barnett Parker, the Dragon's voice, speaks with an arch, feminized flair, squealing off the "Oh, Oh," prissily accentuating the "I won't have it!" The boy asks if the dragon has been "devouring fair damsels" over the countryside.

DRAGON: Scourging? Devouring? Good heavens, no.

BOY: But don't you ever do anything desperate?

DRAGON: Well, yes, I—I do make up poetry.

Following the Dragon's confession of an effete pastime, the boy peers down to consult his guidebook, which contains an illustration of a fierce dragon, then glances up at this dragon, surprised by the contrast. The Dragon is also modest: while showering, he requests, "But if you don't mind, the other way, please." This scene tacitly raises the question of a dragon's genitalia—what indeed would they look like?—but his desire for privacy forecloses the issue. Certainly, poetry and modesty would not be the stereotypical traits one associates with 1940s American masculinity, with the nation about to enter World War II. Yet neither are they recognized as exclusively feminine traits and, often in old films, are associated with apparently gay males.

Through the freedoms of animation, cartoonists can fracture and reconfigure viewers' expectations of mythological creatures. Notably, the Dragon has purple coloring over his eyes; it's unclear if this is part of his "natural" reptilian skin tone or if he has applied eyeshadow to enhance the appeal of his long, fluttery eyelashes. Grahame refers to the Dragon as a "he," yet confusion resulted about this core aspect of the dragon's identity for many viewers of the Disney Version. The *New York Times* critic perceived the Dragon as female, as evident in the pronouns used: "Whatever the villagers think, she is nonetheless just a harmless old biddy forever drinking tea."[10] The reviewer for *Variety* likewise believed this, referring to "a pleasant old girl."[11] These gender assumptions are incorrect. At one point Sir Giles says, "He doesn't seem right"—a telling assessment of the beast's nonconformity to a range of expected behaviors, gendered and otherwise. In describing the Dragon as female, those reviewers misidentified his sex by rightfully noting the gender play in his portrayal. Other critics presented the dragon's homosexuality as a foregone conclusion: *Commonweal* refers to it as a "swishy dragon," a telling adjective then used disparagingly for gay men;[12] *Newsweek* calls the dragon a "pacifist of the lisp-and-swish variety," an unsubtle swipe at both pacifists and gays.[13] With this panoply of identifications, the Dragon demolishes the ability of viewers to define his gender or sexual orientation conclusively, leaving only a sense of his radical "overall" queerness (he certainly doesn't act "normal") intact.

Sir Giles is also regendered, although his transformation oscillates not between male and female but between poles of knightly masculinity. In

Grahame's tale, he is the archetypal figure of British bravery, St. George; in
the film, redubbed Giles, he's drawn as old and doddering. From St. George
to Sir Giles bespeaks a comic devolution of heroism. The queer connections
between Giles and the Dragon, presumably adversaries, come into focus. The
boy first encounters Giles as he splashes in his bathtub, recalling the boy's
initial encounter with the showering dragon. Giles and the Dragon are also
linked through their genders—a parodic masculinity for the former, an ambiguous sex and sexual orientation for the latter. Giles similarly admits his
poetic predilections—"I'm a bit of a bard myself, you know." Disney repeats
the sequence of the boy turning to his book, comparing its vision of knightly
romance with reality. Once again, the boy becomes befuddled that his book
has led him astray, disproving the utility of books, maps, and guides when
confronting unexpected gender performances.

But the world's most authoritative English language dictionary fails out-
Whereas both the Dragon and Giles are effeminized, it is the dragon
whose characterization skirts with homosexuality—as Brode, Griffin, and the
reviewers for *Commonweal* and *Newsweek* observe. Both the boy and Giles
refer to the Reluctant Dragon with terms denoting queerness. The boy, disap-
pointed by the dragon's refusal to fight, states, "Too bad you're not a real
dragon instead of a *punk* poet." The dragon takes offense; the two repeat the
term eight times in their escalating conflict. Yet *punk* bears so many denotations it's difficult to ascertain which is in play in this line. The *Oxford
English Dictionary* includes in the word's many definitions "A person of no
account; a despicable or contemptible person." Yet *punk* in the 1940s also
denoted "a man who is made use of as a sexual partner by another man."[14] In
another telling instance of language with queer connotations, when the Dragon and Giles pretend to fight in the cave, they enjoy tea. Giles shouts out,
"Oh, you bugger!" for the benefit of the nearby crowd. He clearly employs
an opprobrious term for an adversary—one that must be convincing for the
bloodthirsty audience enjoying their battle. The *Oxford Dictionary* dates the
denotations of *bugger* and *buggery* as indicative of sodomy from the mid-
sixteenth century. Both *punk* and *bugger* represent light insults about the
dragon's reluctance or aggressive slurs against his sexuality.

But the world's most authoritative English language dictionary fails outright when considering the dragon's doggerel verse "To an Upside-Down
Cake." This poem teeters confusingly between children's innocence and
queer eroticism. The Dragon begins his recitation, "Sweet little upside-down
cake / Cares and woes, you've got 'em, / Poor little upside-down cake." He
then pauses to kiss the cake, concluding his quatrain, "Your top is on your
bottom." He recites a few more lines, with the following quatrain concluding
inversely, "Your bottom's on your top." Could these be whispered allusions
to anal sex in the Dragon's ode celebrating cake? *Top* and *bottom* have a long
history of sexual meaning, though not exclusively to refer to homosexual
intercourse. *Oxford* dates *bottom* as meaning the "sitting part of a man, the

posteriors" to the late eighteenth century; Shakespeare uses *top* as the equivalent of *screw* in *Othello*—"Cassio did top her. Ask thy husband else."[15] But simply because *top* and *bottom*, common words, bear possible sexual connotations does not mean these connotations are in play every time they are used. A blatantly queer interpretation of "To an Upside-Down Cake" daringly subverts the standard hetero-erotics of the Disney canon, yet stretches one's imagination to think that this was the screenwriters' intention. Several noted dictionaries of slang—including Eric Partridge's *A Dictionary of Slang* and John Ayto's *The Oxford Dictionary of Slang*—omit the queer meanings of *top* and *bottom*, leaving attempts to pin down such a possibility within this 1940s context unfulfilled.[16]

At the same time, "To an Upside-Down Cake" need not address sexuality in its subtext. It *does* absolutely addresses inversion in its text, so at what point should inversion's interpretive echoes cease? That is to say, the Reluctant Dragon, "The Reluctant Dragon," and *The Reluctant Dragon* all reassess the prevailing social order and endorse laxer codes of gender, so it makes little sense to cordon off its gender play as separate from its play with sexuality. As "The Reluctant Dragon" concludes, the frame narrative returns with Benchley and Mrs. Benchley driving home. She again berates him for "shilly-shallying," sharply demanding, "Why don't you *say* something?" Benchley, again approximating Donald Duck's voice, spits out, "Ah, phooey." Here is a remarkably ambiguous ending: Benchley speaks back to his wife in a spirit of resistance, intoning in an irreverently Disney spirit of childish rebellion. Yet he did so at the film's beginning as well, with little indication his words carried any consequence. Reluctant at the film's beginning, he is reluctant at its end. If Benchley models queerness in his antimarital and Disney-inspired juvenility, he also models its limits in prevailing against the dominant order of uxorial and matriarchal authority.

In sum, Disney's *The Reluctant Dragon* casts adult heterosexuality as undesirable and celebrates children's sexuality as the innocence of unfulfilled expectations—with the Dragon mediating between these viewpoints in a gender performance of baffling complexity. Both asexual and sexualized, normative and queer, this dragon erodes rigid binaries of desire in pursuit of poetry and interspecies fellowship that the film endorses in its quiet call to appreciate differences. As "The Reluctant Dragon" concludes with the townsfolk toasting their new friend with "For He's a Jolly Good Fellow," it celebrates the integration of the queer into the society. On the other hand, as *The Reluctant Dragon* concludes with a marital spat, it adumbrates the limits of reluctance in advancing the childish aims of an otherwise normative, heterosexual white man.

There be maps with territories unmarked and unexplored, and there be gay dragons in Disney's realm. If you use the maps effectively—and sense when to look away from them, when necessary—you might indeed find queer beasts overlooked while roaming in plain sight.

NOTES

1. Simon Garfield, *On the Map: Why the World Looks the Way It Does* (London: Profile Books, 2012), 72.

2. Matt Bergbusch, "Additional Dialogue: William Shakespeare, Queer Allegory, and *My Own Private Idaho*," in *Shakespeare without Class: Misappropriations of Cultural Capital*, ed. Donald Hedrick and Bryan Reynolds (New York: Palgrave, 2000), 209–25, at 219–20. Bergbusch builds his definition from the work of Walter Benjamin, *The Origin of German Tragic Drama*; Azade Seyhan, "Allegories of History: The Politics of Representation in Walter Benjamin"; and Terry Eagleton, *Walter Benjamin: Or, Towards a Revolutionary Criticism*.

3. Given the multiple dragons of *The Reluctant Dragon*, I refer to the character as the Reluctant Dragon, to the animated short as "The Reluctant Dragon," and to the film and its frame narrative as *The Reluctant Dragon*.

4. Douglas Brode, *Multiculturalism and the Mouse: Race and Sex in Disney Entertainment* (Austin: University of Texas Press, 2005), 246.

5. Sean Griffin, *Tinker Belles and Evil Queens: The Walt Disney Company from the Inside Out* (New York: New York University Press, 2000), 66.

6. Kenneth Grahame, *The Reluctant Dragon* (1898; New York: Holiday House, 1938), unnumbered page.

7. Lois Kuznets, "Kenneth Grahame and Father Nature, or Whither Blows *The Wind in the Willows*?" *Children's Literature* 16 (1988): 175–81, at 175.

8. Wynn Yarbrough, *Masculinity in Children's Animal Stories, 1888–1928* (Jefferson, NC: McFarland, 2011), 177.

9. Sandra Schwab, "What Is a Man? The Refuting of the Chivalric Ideal," in *Beyond Arthurian Romances*, ed. Loretta Holloway and Jennifer Palmgren (New York: Palgrave, 2005), 217–31.

10. T.S., "*The Reluctant Dragon*, a Walt Disney Compound of Fact and Fancy," *New York Times*, July 25, 1941.

11. "Review: *The Reluctant Dragon*," *Variety*, June 11, 1941, 14.

12. Philip Hartung, "The Screen: Stars, Strikes, and Dragons," *Commonweal*, August 8, 1941, 376–77, at 377. The *Oxford English Dictionary* defines "swishy" as "characteristic of a male homosexual; effeminate."

13. "Benchley in Disneyland: Flesh-and-Blood Tour of Studio Bares Pen-and-Ink Technique," *Newsweek*, June 30, 1941, 55–56, at 56.

14. See also Brode, *Multiculturalism*, 246.

15. William Shakespeare, *Othello*, in *The Norton Shakespeare: Tragedies*, ed. Stephen Greenblatt (New York: W. W. Norton), 389–427, at 5.2.145.

16. See Eric Partridge, *A Dictionary of Slang and Unconventional English*, ed. Paul Beale (London: Routledge, 2002), and John Ayto, ed., *The Oxford Dictionary of Slang* (Oxford: Oxford University Press, 1998).

Chapter Four

Zip-a-Dee-Doo-Dah

The Re-enslavement of Uncle Remus

Peggy A. Russo

Books can disappear in a variety of ways. They can be burned, banned, censored, locked away in rare-book rooms; they can also be replaced by bogus visual versions. This is particularly true of Uncle Remus. That title character, now a mere specter of the original conception, has haunted popular culture for the last seventy years. He calls himself Uncle Remus and purports to be the creation of Joel Chandler Harris. In fact, he is a simulacrum created by Walt Disney, foisted upon an unsuspecting public with *Song of the South* (1946). Disney not only tampered with the Harris text but literally replaced it with his own distorted version.

Fletch Lives, the 1989 film starring Chevy Chase, illustrates the pervasiveness of Disney's Remus. Chase plays California-based reporter I. M. Fletcher, who has inherited a Southern plantation. En route to Louisiana, he falls asleep on the plane, dreaming of a beautiful Old South mansion and relaxing on the veranda as slaves approach to serenade him at day's end. "Uncle Frank," says Fletch "you know my favorite tune." "Sure do, Colonel," the slave replies. Informed that field hands want to dance for him, Fletch says: "Dance for me? Why, I'll dance for *them*." With that, he and the African Americans break into a full-scale production number. "Zip-a-Dee-Doo-Dah" is the tune; it comes complete with a Disney bluebird on Chase's shoulder. Admittedly, this dream sequence is designed to call up Old Hollywood stereotypical images of an idyllic plantation world, which are overturned when Fletch discovers the comic reality of a ruined mansion with a single African American caretaker (actually an FBI agent).[1]

Nonetheless, the stereotype, as envisioned not only by Fletch but by those viewers who have seen *Song of the South* follows the Disney Version. An-

33

other variation appears in *The Bourne Ultimatum*, Robert Ludlum's 1990 spy novel. In trouble and desperate, white hero Jason Bourne seeks out a friend, an elderly African American affectionately nicknamed Uncle Remus. This Remus is humorous, wise, successful—a retired expert in the creation of forged documents. He calls Bourne "Brer Rabbit."[2] Clearly, Ludlum had Harris's Remus in mind. But owing to Disney's dominance, most readers fail to fully understand Ludlum's sophisticated literary rather than obvious cinematic allusion.

The foreword to the Golden Book edition of *Walt Disney's Uncle Remus Stories*, published in 1946, reveals the genesis of Disney's Uncle Remus: "The Disney studio became interested in presenting [the Harris stories] on the screen" because of their "universal appeal . . . and their place in the heritage of this country." The stated purpose for subsequent publication sounds similarly selfless and positive: "Though these adaptations cannot take the place of the originals, it was hoped that a representative selection might help to introduce new readers to the stories of Uncle Remus."[3] Following the financial failure of *Fantasia* (1940) and large expenses incurred by building a new studio, Disney felt compelled to announce, "We're through with caviar. . . . From now on, it's mashed potatoes and gravy."[4] Disney purchased the rights to the Harris canon in 1939, the price a then-reasonable $10,000. But the original plan, calling for full animation, was replaced by Disney's earlier technique of combining the cartoon process with live action. Owing to its dual nature, Harris's property seemed well suited for such treatment. As mashed potatoes and gravy became all important, the "caviar" of "universal appeal" and "heritage" diminished. Biographer Richard Schickel believes that Disney did not possess the "intellectual and artistic . . . tools" needed to be "faithful . . . to [the] true . . . animating spirit" of the materials translated: "He could make something his own . . . but that process nearly always robbed the work of its uniqueness, of its soul."[5]

Such negative criticism of Disney was, back in 1969, rare. As film historian Jack Nachbar says, "It's hard to get a really organized campaign going against Uncle Walt."[6] But Schickel's opinion had one notable precedent. In a 1965 letter to the *Los Angeles Times*, Frances Clark Sayers criticized Disney "for his debasement of the traditional literature of childhood." Sayers accused him of (1) lack of respect for the "integrity of original creations"; (2) "manipulation and vulgarization" of texts for his own ends; (3) lack of regard for the "anthropological, spiritual, or psychological truths" of folklore; (4) "fixing his mutilated film versions in books which are cut to a fraction of their original forms"; and (5) "illustration of those books with garish pictures." Sayers laments Disney's "tendency to take over a . . . work and make it his own without any regard for the original author or to the original book."[7]

Disney's approach to *Song of the South* underscores Sayers's point: in Disneyfying Harris's work, Walt ignored much of the text. Credit for the film's "original story" went to Dalton Raymond, his narrative merely "based on Uncle Remus Tales by Joel Chandler Harris."[8] The credits might have contained an additional word: "loosely." The work does indeed deserve to be called an "original story," though at least two people who saw the script did not believe that it represented an improvement. African American actor Clarence Muse, hired to help with the writing project, made "suggestions for upgrading the image" of the black characters. When those suggestions were rejected, he resigned, stating that he believed the movie would be "detrimental to the cultural advancement of the Negro people." Following suit, actor Rex Ingram turned down the Uncle Remus role, reasoning that the film would "set back my people many years."[9] But what image needed "upgrading"? Were Muse and Ingram objecting to Harris's characters or to those from Raymond's "original" story?

The finished product—for a *product* it is!—reveals much about Disney; contemplating the contrast between film and book sheds new light on the original. Changes in plot and Remus's character constitute the most obvious differences. Harris's tale involves initiation and coming of age. In *Told by Uncle Remus*, the relationship between Remus and the boy is highly involved and thoroughly explored, effectively exemplifying Harris's revelation of the possibilities of mutual love and respect between man and boy, old and young, country and city, black and white, old South and new. This boy represents the next generation; he is the grandson of Miss Sally and son of the boy who interacted with Remus in earlier volumes. The new boy is serious, frail, and dominated by a strict, overprotective, highly prejudiced mother. Miss Sally disapproves of her daughter-in-law's approach to child rearing but fears to interfere. Remus also disapproves but, unlike Miss Sally, sets out to make things right even if it means teaching the mother the fine art of parenting. In an early chapter, learning that the mother has imprisoned the boy in the parlor for wiping his mouth on his sleeve, Remus intervenes. Certain that the mother can hear, Remus visits the boy, telling him he has probably learned that as he can be punished for nothing, he might as well commit far worse crimes in the future. Warned by the boy of the mother's presence, Remus claims he does not care; he wishes, in fact, that the father were there so that he could tell him "what fer." The mother, shamed by Remus's remarks, hurries to undo her error in judgment.[10]

Remus grasps that the boy has not enjoyed a "normal" childhood. He doesn't know how to laugh; he has been taught not to ask questions; and though he possesses imagination, he has no illusions. Gradually, through the tales, Remus teaches the boy the value of wonder, of questioning, and of laughter. Most importantly, he initiates the boy into life's dark secrets. There is, for example, the terrible lesson in Remus's tale of Wiley Wolf, son of Brer Wolf, who comes to a sad end because he minds his father's command to tie up his friend Riley Rab in a bag so Brer Wolf can cook him for supper. Brer

Rabbit protects his son Riley by outsmarting Brer Wolf; Wiley ends up in the bag, put in a pot of boiling water by his own father.[11] The symbolic significance of the tale is not lost on the boy; sixty-eight pages further, he says to Remus, "You think Mother is queer; Grandmother thinks so too." Remus asks, "How come you ter be so wise, honey?" The boy answers, "I know by the way you talk, and by the way Grandmother looks sometimes."[12] "Wise" is the correct term here. The boy realizes that unquestioning obedience to authority may not always be wise—one can wind up in the soup like Wiley.

Disney would hardly include the "dark night of the soul" represented by this tale since undermining parental authority would likely displease the adult moviegoer. Nor would he depict Remus as a Virgil guiding the boy through such a night. Disney's Remus is neither Socratic nor Virgilian.

Meanwhile, the boy in the film resembles the boy in the book solely because he is the visiting grandson of the plantation owner. The film's conflict, however, does not reflect the book's more intense drama. Disney modernized his property by inserting a moral imperative against divorce or separation (a popular topic in 1946 owing to the rising divorce rate). The film depicts Johnny's arrival at Grandmother's plantation amid a distressing farewell scene with his father, leading to Johnny's decision to run away. Instead, he encounters Remus, who changes Johnny's mind with a Brer Rabbit story. Its moral: one cannot run away from trouble. Johnny decides to return home; because of his absence, the worried mother blames Remus, ultimately commanding Remus not to speak to Johnny again. Unlike Harris's Remus, Disney's passively accepts the mother's value system and, convinced of his own worthlessness, leaves. Running after Remus across a pasture, Johnny is attacked by a bull and badly gored. When, as a last resort, Remus is brought to the boy's bedside, Johnny recovers; his parents reconcile. In this way, the film's cause/effect relationship—divorce/damage to children—becomes clear in the most maudlin manner. Disney substitutes a dramatic but emotionally trite conflict, reducing Remus's character to the Hollywood image of an "oldtime darky" who takes care of his master's child. Disney sought to entertain an adult audience and so made his Remus an entertainer. Harris, however, wanted to pass on the inherent wisdom of the folktales; he made his Remus a teacher.

A more subtle difference between book and film appears in the ratio of folktale to frame. Those who have read the original know the tales themselves take center stage. The dialogue often begins with the boy asking Remus a questions, which triggers the tale; Remus then returns to the question after the tale end for him. This emphasis lends credence to Harris's claim that he always wrote with an audience of children in mind. Mark Twain considered such fables "alligator pears," secondary to the "dressing" of the frame.[13] An estimate of the average ratio of tales to frame in the books is seven to three. The ratio of tales to frame in the film, on the other hand, is roughly the reverse. The ninety-four-minute movie contains only three cartoon sequences plus several scenes that blend animation and live action. According to Leonard Maltin, "more than one critic wondered why Disney didn't make total use of [the] tales." But Disney had no wish to translate the tales to film. "He was looking for a new kind of entertainment form," says Maltin, "and believed *Song of the South* was it."[14] A more obvious reason is the cost of producing animated sequences. Still another suggests itself in Sayers's claim that "Disney . . . never addressed himself to children once in his life; [his] material is made to reach an adult audience."[15] This suggestion is supported by obvious pandering to the white adult moviegoer. Disney's formula: figure out what had sold before and repeat it—only bigger and better. The attempt to follow successful models seems apparent in shades of *Gone with the Wind* (the Tara-like plantation, Hattie McDaniel's Aunt Tempy, the premiere in Atlanta); in mimicry of Shirley Temple's successful team ventures with black dancer Bill "Bojangles" Robinson, particularly *The Littlest Rebel* (incarnating the image of a white girl-child dancing with her adult male slave); and minstrel show echoes in the casting of James Baskett, a regular on radio's *Amos 'n' Andy*, in the role of Uncle Remus.[16]

Even if Disney had employed folktales more prominently, it remains doubtful he would have included any that suggested full tragedy. The film lacks tension even in the scenes designed to represent reality. In translating book to film, Disney deliberately tried to make the frame part of the fantasy, achieving his goal via admittedly admirable technique. By filming the frame against backdrops painted to resemble those used for cartoon sequences, Remus could meld with the animation. The result: the live Remus resembles a cartoon character, as when he and a frog share a pipe smoking scene, or Remus cavorts with adorable animals, singing "Zip-a-Dee-Doo-Dah" with cute birds. As with any of Disney's treatments of folktales, the Brer Rabbit sequences become as precious as possible. In Disney's version of the tar baby tale, Brer Rabbit is cute and sassy—a sort of grown up, good ol' boy version of the Thumper character in *Bambi*. Brer Fox is skinny, sly, but not very smart. In addition, he has a partner, Brer Bear (not included in the original tale), who, though bigger, is no smarter. Bear and Fox come across as inept bullies picking on the smart little kid on the block, so Brer Rabbit never seems in much danger. As a result, Disney's version teaches nothing of tragic significance. Instead, he transforms the frame into a package that pretends to teach. Disney sacrifices Harris's original juxtaposition of illusion in the tales and the relative realism of the frame as well as the tales' beauty, wonder, and terror.

We do learn something about what Harris succeeded in doing from Disney's errors in adaptation: The tales, wonderful and terrible as they are, must remain fantasies. Harris's Remus tells the boy there is a difference between men and "creeturs." In *Uncle Remus and His Friends*, he relates the story of

"The Man and His Boots": a man tries to play a Brer Rabbit trick on another man with disastrous results. Remus's moral: "Creeturs kin take what ain't dern, en tel fibs, en dey don't no harm come fum it; but when folks tries it dey er bleedzd ter come ter some bad een."[17] Again, Remus employs a tale to *teach*. Unlike the film's frame, Harris's frame takes us back to the "real" world, a world that holds the comforting presence of Remus to mitigate the terror and frequent cruelty of the tales. Remus not only comforts; he demonstrates the difference between illusion and reality. Harris's Remus is no Bojangles; he embodies much more than a child's playmate, confidant, and entertainer. Harris's Remus embodies the wisdom of the folk; it is his purpose to pass that wisdom on to the young.

Despite the film's two Academy Awards—one for best song, one to Baskett for his portrayal of Remus—critical opinion split in a clear pattern: praise for the animation process and rejection of the rest. *Newsweek*, for example, called the story "irritatingly inconsequential."[18] *Variety*'s reviewer complained that the story of the "confused and insufficiently explained estrangement of the parents overbalances the cartoon sequences."[19] The *New York Times*' Bosley Crowther called Disney's writers "just a lot of conventional hacks." While responding positively to the cartoon segments, Crowther asserted that actors in the film "behave like characters in a travesty on the ante bellum South."[20] The National Urban League objected, citing "another . . . perpetuation of the stereotype casting of the Negro in the servant role, depicting him as indolent, one who handles the truth lightly."[21] Moreover, Walter F. White, executive secretary of the NAACP, protested the perpetuation of "a dangerously glorified picture of slavery." While recognizing the film's "artistic merit," White regretted that Disney had made use of what he called the "beautiful Uncle Remus folklore" to give the impression of an idyllic master-slave relationship, which is a distortion of the facts.[22] Neither film critics nor social critics, however, mentioned the "distortion" of Harris's work. Nor did they object to the warping of folktales and image of Harris's Remus. The original became lost in the film's image, described in an *Ebony* editorial as an "Uncle Tom-Aunt Jemima caricature complete with all the fawning standard equipment thereof: the toothy smile, battered hat, grey beard, and a profusion of 'dis and 'dat talk."[23] Reacting to such criticism, a Disney spokesman claimed Walt "was not trying to put across any message, but, was making a sincere effort to depict American folklore, to put the Uncle Remus stories into pictures"[24] According to reporter Frederick Mullaly, Disney himself "denied that there would be any real antagonism toward the film, went on to assert that the criticism came from the radicals 'who just love stirring up trouble whenever they can.'"[25] Since Disney had not created this film with a black audience in mind, his depiction of Remus as a negative stereotype made no claim on his conscience.

Song of the South might have disappeared into the vaults after 1946, in which case Disney's Remus image might have been forgotten. Two things prevented that: the publication of the Golden Book edition of Disney's film, which became a popular replacement for Harris's text, and many rereleases of the film. Reissued in 1956, it was again attacked at the national level by black critics and picketed at the local level by black political groups. After that, it remained out of circulation until 1972, when, released again, it grossed twice as much as it had in the two previous releases. It has reappeared twice since: in 1980 and 1986. The latter rerelease led *Newsweek* reviewer Barbara Kantrowitz to warn parents that the film was "unfit for the kids" due to negative racial stereotyping.[26] However, to Maltin, *Song of the South* had become a classic: "Accusations of Uncle Tomisms and quibbles over its syrupy storyline are ultimately defeated by the film's sheer entertainment value."[27]

After 1946, Disney's Uncle Remus supplanted Harris's original. As early as 1948, Peter Noble's *The Negro in Films* includes the following description of the character as "that beloved menial figure of early American fiction, Uncle Remus, the superstitious, dialect-speaking, lovable [n-word]."[28] All later African American film histories assign Remus a prominent place in their books. He figures, for example, in Edward Mapp's *Blacks in American Films: Today and Yesterday* (1972), Daniel J. Leab's *From Sambo to Superspade* (1975), and James R. Nesteby's *Black Images in American Films, 1896–1954* (1982). Each cites Remus as a prime example of a black stereotype.[29] By 1973, in Donald Bogle's *Toms, Coons, Mulattoes, Mammies, and Bucks*, the name "Remus" becomes the label for a category of stereotyping:

> Harmless and congenial, he is a first cousin to the tom, yet he distinguishes himself by his quaint, naive, and comic philosophizing. . . . Remus's mirth, like tom's contentment and the coon's antics, has always been used to indicate the black man's satisfaction with the system and his place in it.[30]

The Disney image carried over into comments of scholars involved in children's literature. In *Images of the Black in Children's Fiction* (1972), Dorothy M. Broderick includes Harris's *The Complete Tales of Uncle Remus* in a list of texts guilty of "role-assigning," part of a discussion wherein Broderick asserts that the "characters do not develop," and "blacks [are] important only as workers."[31] Broderick discusses Harris's text, but the Remus she describes belongs to Disney.

Joining film historians and critics of children's literature, literary critics also swallow the Disney Version. In 1950, African American writer Sterling Brown noted that "Uncle Remus and his Brer Rabbit tales [no longer] stood for the Negro folk and their lore"; *Song of the South* had revealed that Remus "belonged to white people rather than to Negroes."[32] Prior to 1946, however,

Brown had described Harris's Uncle Remus as "one of the best characters in American fiction."[33] In 1949, Bernard Wolfe described Uncle Remus as "'an Uncle Tom' Negro telling amusing stories for the little white boy, son of the plantation owners. . . . This painful reminder of slavery times in which a grown Negro man is depicted as the playmate or nursemaid of a 'boy,' is offensive to contemporary American Negroes and some whites."[34] Clearly, this is Disney's Remus. By 1975, Robert Bone could sum up the then current view of Harris's work thusly:

> Joel Chandler Harris is in bad odor among the younger generation of literary men. The blacks, who tend to equate Uncle Remus with Uncle Tom—sometimes, one suspects, without having read either Harris or Stowe—reject the Uncle Remus books out of hand. And sympathetic whites, who hope thereby to ingratiate themselves with the black militants, are fond of giving Harris a gratuitous kick in the shins.[35]

A key phrase here is the parenthetical, which suggests some of the negative criticism results from unfamiliarity with the originals. If Uncle Remus is equated with Uncle Tom, that surely comes from familiarity with Disney rather than Harris's text.

Disney did American popular culture a great disservice when he produced *Song of the South*. Viewing the Harris canon through the prism of that film, critics have since been unable or unwilling to see Harris's work without bias. This has often resulted in condemnation of Harris as a singer of stolen slave songs, a creator of stereotypes, a perpetrator of plantation myths. Such condemnation has affected and continues to affect generations of readers, especially African Americans, many of whom eschew the original printed text because, based on Disney, they see it only as an example of black stereotyping. Novelist Alice Walker, for example, grew up hearing the folktales from her parents; disgusted at what they saw in the film, her parents stopped telling the tales after seeing *Song of the South*, and she and her siblings no longer wished to hear them.[36] Such negative responses dissuaded publishers from gambling on new editions of Harris's text. This led to a publishing trend that translates the language into a facsimile of standard English, removing the frame completely, erasing from the tales any "taint" of slavery. Three such editions have appeared including Julius Lester's *The Tales of Uncle Remus: The Adventures of Brer Rabbit* (1987), a commendable attempt to salvage the originals from oblivion.

Lester writes in his preface that his purpose is "to make the tales accessible again," especially to African Americans since the tales belong to their heritage. However, Lester apologetically tells us he cannot include Remus in his book, despite his statement that "there are no inaccuracies in Harris's characterization . . . the most cursory reading of the slave narratives collected by the Federal Writer's Project of the 1930s reveals that there were many slaves who fit the Uncle Remus mold." Remus represents an accurate representation, but, says Lester, "He became a stereotype and therefore negative."[37] What Lester fails to mention is that Remus became a negative stereotype only *after* the release of Disney's *Song of the South*. John Cech, writing in *USA Today*, applauded Lester:

> In recent decades, it has been difficult for writers or editors to touch the Uncle Remus stories without somehow reviving the racial stereotypes that generations of Americans have struggled to dispel . . . But Julius Lester's new collection . . . has returned them to today's audience.[38]

June Jordan, however, reviewing Lester's book in the *New York Times Book Review*, oppositionally argued that "elimination of the Uncle Remus factor" fails to salvage Harris's work because the tales themselves are tainted by the "specifics of his fiction." She was particularly negative about Brer Rabbit's "chicanery" and the "homicidal humor of the material." Her final word: "This misbegotten resurrection is a terrible waste of . . . talents."[39] Obviously, both Cech and Jordan substituted Disney's Remus for Harris's in their minds, attesting to how powerful (if not in a "good" sense) any Disney film can be. We need to take a closer look at the relationship between singer and song as well as singer and listener. Kenneth Lynn has suggested that Harris and Twain shared a desire for "a quality of experience they could not find in their white lives; both men sent their boy heroes in search of the companionship and understanding of the black man."[40] Twain's description of his boyhood experiences with a black storyteller named Uncle Dan'l supports this theory:

> the look of Uncle Dan'l's kitchen as it was on the privileged nights when I was a child. . . . I can see the white and black children grouped on the hearth. . . . I can hear Uncle Dan'l telling the immortal tales which Uncle Remus Harris was to gather into his book.[41]

Of course, the storyteller need not be black. In a 1991 televised interview, Chilean novelist Isabel Allende described similar childhood experiences. In her family's home, which she called "cold and dark," her favorite place was the kitchen, full of light, warmth, music, good smells, and stories told by family servants. It became not only her safe place but one that introduced her to the magic of the imagination.[42] Uncle Dan'l's kitchen and Allende's childhood retreat echo Harris's description of Uncle Remus's "laughing place." All three writers were exposed to the oral tradition that reflects the warmth of humanity and magic of imagination. The experience changed their lives; they too became storytellers.

We need now to return to the original image of Remus as storyteller. Instead of viewing the Harris canon through the prism of Disney's film and our biases, we should perceive it through the prism of humanistic and imaginative values. In that light, we would treasure these works for capturing man's ability to preserve his basic humanity in the midst of adversity. Rather than accuse Harris of plagiarism as well as closet racism, we ought to praise him for trying to preserve black folktales for both their particular and their universal value, for people of all races. Disney may have believed that he was doing the right thing when he produced *Song of the South*, but he succeeded primarily in robbing us of folktales and a folk hero descended from Africa. Remus and his tales became enslaved in a cartoon image. It would probably take a new film version to change his popularly held false image. Perhaps WDC should sell Uncle Remus to Spike Lee; he could then set the old man free.

NOTES

This chapter is based on my earlier article, "Uncle Walt's Uncle Remus: Disney's Distortion of Harris's Hero," *Southern Literary Journal* 25, no. 1 (1992): 19–32.

1. In his review of *Fletch Lives*, *Newsweek*'s David Ansen makes no mention of the dream sequence but refers to the film setting as "the kind of Deep South that only exists in the minds of middle-aged liberal Hollywood screenwriters complete with clumsy Ku Klux Klanners, TV evangelists, moss-laden mansions, biker gangs, and courtly Southern gentlemen who dress up in confederate costumes." David Ansen, "Muddling Through March," *Newsweek*, March 20, 1989, 83.
2. Robert Ludlum, *The Bourne Ultimatum* (New York: Random House, 1990), 53–55.
3. Marion Palmer, *Walt Disney's Uncle Remus Stories* (New York: Golden Press, 1946), 7.
4. Richard Schickel, *The Disney Version: The Life, Times, Art and Commerce of Walt Disney* (Chicago: Ivan R. Dee, 1997), 226.
5. Ibid., 227.
6. Quoted in Barbara Kantrowitz, "A Film Unfit for the Kids?," *Newsweek*, December 22, 1986.
7. Frances Clark Sayers, "Walt Disney Accused," *Horn Book Magazine*, December 1965, 602–11.
8. Leonard Maltin, *The Disney Films*, 4th ed. (New York: Disney Editions, 2000), 73.
9. Quoted in Daniel J. Leab, *From Sambo to Superspade: The Black Experience in Motion Ppictures* (Boston: Houghton Mifflin, 1975), 137.
10. Joel Chandler Harris, *The Complete Tales of Uncle Remus*, compiled by Richard Chase (Boston: Houghton Mifflin, 1955), 588–89. All subsequent citations are to this edition.
11. Ibid., 603–4.
12. Ibid., 672.
13. Quoted in Julia Collier Harris, ed., *Joel Chandler Harris, Editor and Essayist* (Chapel Hill: University of North Carolina Press, 1931), 170.
14. Maltin, *Disney Films*, 78.
15. Sayers, "Walt Disney Accused," 607.
16. Another parallel with *Gone with the Wind*: Hattie McDaniel could not attend the premieres of either film (nor, of course, could any of the other black cast members). Although James Baskett finally received a special Academy Award, it was only after actor Jean Hersholt insisted and threatened the academy with public disclosure of the disgraceful way that Baskett's work had been ignored because of his race. See Frank Thompson, "Animating the South," *Storyline*, November 12, 1986.
17. Harris, *Complete Tales*, 563.

18. "Disney's Uncle Remus," *Newsweek*, December 2, 1946.

19. "Song of the South," *Variety*, November 16, 1948, 18.

20. Bosley Crowther, "'Song of the South,' Disney Film Combining Cartoons and Life," *New York Times*, November 28, 1946.

21. Quoted in Maltin, *Disney Films*, 78.

22. Quoted in "White Regrets Film," *New York Times*, November 28, 1946.

23. Quoted in Leab, *From Sambo to Superspade*, 137.

24. Quoted in Maltin, *Disney Films*, 78.

25. Quoted in Peter Noble, *The Negro in Films* (London: Skelton Robinson, 1948), 219.

26. Kantrowitz, "Film Unfit for the Kids?," 63.

27. Maltin, *Disney Films*, 78.

28. Noble, *Negro in Films*, 218–19.

29. See Edward Mapp, *Blacks in American Films: Today and Yesterday* (Metuchen, NJ: Scarecrow Press, 1972), 43–44; Leab, *From Sambo to Superspade*, 136–37; James R. Nesteby, *Black Images in American Films, 1896–1954: The Interplay between Civil Rights and Film Culture* (Lanham, MD: University Press of America, 1982), 228–29.

30. Donald Bogle, *Toms, Coons, Mulattoes, Mammies, and Bucks: An Interpretive History of Blacks in American Films* (New York: Viking Press, 1973), 8.

31. Dorothy M. Broderick, *Images of the Black in Children's Fiction* (New York: R. R. Bowker, 1973), 178.

32. Quoted in R. Bruce Bickley, *Joel Chandler Harris: A Reference Guide* (Boston: G. K. Hall, 1978), 217.

33. Quoted in Bickley, *Joel Chandler Harris*, 178.

34. Bernard Wolfe, "Uncle Remus and the Malevolent Rabbit," *Commentary*, July 1949, 42.

35. Robert Bone, *Down Home: A History of Afro-American Short Fiction from Its Beginnings to the End of the Harlem Renaissance* (New York: G. P. Putnam's Sons, 1975), 19.

36. Alice Walker, *Living by the Word: Essays* (New York: Harcourt Brace Jovanovich, 1988), 26.

37. Julius Lester, *The Tales of Uncle Remus: The Adventures of Brer Rabbit* (Harmondsworth, UK: Puffin Books, 1987), xiii–xxi.

38. John Cech, "A Child's Midsummer Selection of Tales," *USA Today*, July 3, 1987, 37.

39. June Jordan, "A Truly Bad Rabbit," *New York Times Book Review*, May 17, 1987, 32.

40. Kenneth Lynn, *Mark Twain and Southwestern Humor* (Boston: Little, Brown, 1960), 242.

41. Quoted in Lynn, *Mark Twain*, 242.

42. Isabel Allende, interview by Lewis Lapham, *Bookmark*, PBS, September 9, 1991.

Chapter Five

"Glory in the Flower"

Disneyfying Bambi

David Payne

"Now is the hour / Of splendor in the grass, / Glory in the flower . . ."
—William Wordsworth, 1804

In the foreword to the 1929 English translation of *Bambi*, English novelist and PEN founder John Galsworthy pronounces the book "a little master-piece." Felix Salten (1869–1945) "feels nature deeply," says Galsworthy, praising his "delicacy of perception and essential truth," testifying that "be-hind the conversation" of the animals, "one feels the real sensations of the creatures who speak." Galsworthy, who four years later would win the Nobel Prize for literature, states simply: "Salten is a poet."[1]

In a world where Walt Disney had not yet made *Dumbo* (1940) or movies from two later Salten books, *Perri* (1957) and *The Shaggy Dog* (1959; from *The Hound of Florence*), Austrian writer Salten's ability to capture the ani-mals' point of view by allowing them human speech must have woven a compelling illusion. If, like Dr. Dolittle, we could "talk to the animals," we would learn they have so much to say about the pains and joys of life in nature. They would articulate the things we humans would say, feel the things we feel, only with an elegance and charm—even humanism—that somehow escapes people, trapped in our opposition to nature and insulation from the pains we inflict on other animals.

Despite the illusion, Salten's poetics do not capture what the individual species of the forest do in fact feel. They instead converse about the joys and pains of parenting, their anxiety and awe of Man; social propriety, the foibles of youth, the wisdom of old age; about the authority of the male, the role of women, and why men ignore their wives. These are things they would feel if

45

they were indeed humans, navigating this startlingly anthropocentric idea of nature. The deer call each other "people," yet all the forest animals share the same basic character, despite predation, and are unified in their fear of and godlike reverence for "Him." In the book, a whole chapter is devoted to two leaves discussing the mysterious coming of winter, ending tragically with one falling to the ground. The very human (i.e., Western) idea of the deer's patriarchal social structure helps create the conviction that animals must feel what we feel.[2] Those who decry the "Bambi Syndrome" are justified in their criticism that Disney's film is magically effective in seducing us into treating animals as though they were the nicest and most noble humans in a world where humans are themselves malicious, full of betrayal, motivated only by the desire to kill.[3]

Disney may have himself harbored similar feelings about hunting and animals. One story is told that when his family moved to a farm overrun by rabbits, young Walt spent days drawing them in playful romping pose and was filled with horror when his brother Roy shot a large buck. Walt refused to eat the rabbit stew their mother then cooked.[4] One journalist reports that Walt never intentionally killed an animal and was haunted by his accidental killing of an owl.[5]

Whatever the mature Disney felt about killing animals, he no doubt was swept up by the ethos of Salten's book as a profound representation of nature's "essential truth." *Bambi*'s mission became an obsession to let "nature tell her own story."[6] Animators attended night classes on drawing animals; rabbits and fawns were brought to the studio to study; the animator in charge of the skunks was reassigned because he just couldn't "love" the animal in the way required to render Flower with fidelity.[7] Begun in 1937, work on "the most monumental undertaking of animation in its day" stretched out over four years, not ready for release until 1942.[8] *Bambi* is widely reported to have been Walt's favorite of his animated films.

If Salten's poetics revealed nature's "essential truth," then Disney revealed the majesty and awe of nature in lyricism by capturing the animals' graceful movements. "Revelation" is the right word for how the animators here tell "nature's story." The opening immerses the viewer in the dense forest, accompanied by a chorale of human voices, delivering us to the magical birth scene of the "new Prince." Here is animation serving spiritual animism—the grandeur and awe of nature is thus *revealed*. Our senses are awakened to the shattering power of lightning, the sounds of raindrops and silent grace of birds' flight.

In the book, we overhear the animal's fear and reverence for the godlike mystery of an all-powerful but vengeful "Him" (especially in story lines deleted from the film). In the movie, we experience a dramatic climax where these episodes merge into a crescendo of image, music, and event unlike anything possible on the written page. The lyrical poetry of *Bambi* the film gives way to the dialectics of drama as the Disney version resolves into agonistic crisis: Disney condenses the stark events of Man's armed invasion of the forest, Bambi's being shot, and the forest fire consuming the animal's world in apocalypse. Amid this frenzy, Disney depicts Bambi's heroic defense of Faline, his battle with vicious dogs, and his near death and struggle to survive with the loving insistence of his father, the Great Stag. For the second time, the film brings the drama to a powerful and tragic climax, fades, then the lyrical magic of nature returns to displace the drama with the music, flowers, and cheerful animals of spring.

Other than cinematic dramaturgy and spectacular animation, what else does Disney bring to the piece? There are three key components to the film: the story of Bambi from birth, maturation, to his ascension as the new Prince; the troupe of animated supporting cast members that provide "cartoon relief" from the somber/tragic elements; and the secular metaphysics of nature that the visual medium of film accomplishes in ways not possible in print.

As for the basic story line, Disney's *Bambi* is remarkably faithful to the book's narrative. At 293 pages (first edition), Salten is more detailed and elaborate in some of the telling, and several elements were eliminated for the movie. But virtually every plot element in the film can be found in the book. Both book and film are organized according to the cycles of the season, from the early summer of Bambi's birth to the early summer of Bambi observing the birth of his own children; from his first encounter with his father, the Great Stag, to his own detached appraisal of his offspring with Faline. In both book and movie, Bambi's mother is killed during his first winter, while he is yet a fawn, and spring comes with the sprouting of his antlers, an awakened desire for romance, and a willingness to do battle for the affections of Faline.

Some of the film's more brilliant elements derive from how the animators chose to interpret and depict several of the book's scenes. One of the key resources of film—animated or otherwise—is that we can be shown rather than told what is happening (the final film script contains less than on thousand words of dialogue). In the opening sequence, for instance, we are visually drawn through the dense forest to settle our gaze on the little fawn nestled against his mother. This is a direct visual rendering of how Salten verbally begins his story, the author's words entirely replaced by the auteur's perfectly corresponding images. Disney's animators also seize the opportunity for a pageant of stunning sights that only photography or realistic art could provide. These clear translations of descriptive details into image can be found throughout book and film: the Old Prince inspecting the youth; the deer's romp in the meadow; the dramatic appearance of the young bucks en masse; deer racing away from gunshots in the meadow; the silhouetted fight between Bambi and the buck who would take Faline. One sequence is surprising as to its fidelity to the book's depiction: the neurotically anxious pheasant, heart pounding at the approach of "Him" and his weapons, repeats over and over "don't fly, don't fly"; then, unable to contain its fear and instincts, the pheasant erupts into flight only to be shot midair, crumpling to the ground. So intense and vivid is this personification of the hunted bird's rupture into flight—from the pheasant's point of view—one would suspect it to be the creation of cartoonists. Yet it is moment to moment, image for word, a scene Salten himself crafted.

The most significant example of the cinematic adaptation of Salten's narration—also the one with the most enduring effects—involves Bambi's mother, killed by hunters. As in the book, they are in the meadow, realizing "He" is in the forest. Mother has instructed Bambi to run and keep running even as shots ring out. Once in the thicket, huge snowflakes falling, Bambi calls mournfully, "Mother, Mother." The shadowy huge stag appears, saying only, "Your mother can't be with you anymore"; Bambi sadly realizes what has happened and drops a tear. The stag says, "Come . . . my son," and slowly struts off with the fawn reluctantly following. Fade to black. None of this happens in such a fashion in the book: Bambi runs away, finds himself with Faline and *her* mother, and asks, the next day, if anyone has seen his mother. The book's narrator informs us that "Bambi never saw his mother again."

While story elements are here eliminated from the film script, this is true of virtually any cinematic adaptation—particularly those that significantly alter or expand on what is found or even possible in the book. The opening sequence, again, is protracted, remarkable, and stunning in a way chirographic marks could never achieve. The meadow scenes, the battles, the fire, are all exaggerated because of the animation's majesty and the power of the musical score. When "He" first appears, the simultaneous percussion of strings and the sharp reactions of the deer do not merely alert the audience to the hunters' presence but startles viewers with the intense danger and drama of the event the deer experience. Being told of the reactions and danger cannot produce the same emotional reaction as do these sensational cinematic cues.

The most common criticism of *Bambi*, book and film, addresses the tone of the animals' lives and their struggle to survive—in this case against Man and hunting, not against the travails of nature. Story editor Perce Pearce pronounced that "all predators other than Homo sapiens had to be excised from the script," adding, "There's nobody swooping down and eating someone else and their one common enemy is Man."⁹ The book's tragic cast is offset by the Disneyfication of the story in two distinct ways: first, through the musical productions of nature and the animals sequenced throughout the film; second, in the troupe of cartoon characters that accompany Bambi—Thumper, Flower, and the Old Owl. Besides life, laughter, and lovability, the theme of both these elements is the celebration of the fecundity and essentially comic elements of nature. Memorable episodes are marked by powerful musical interpretations: the chorale that accompanies our immersion into the forest and thicket where Bambi is born, the powerful march of the young bucks displaying their prowess, the moving condensation of the fire and the reunion with "Love Is a Song." *Bambi* earned three Academy Award nominations: Best Sound, Best Score, and Best Song (for "Love Is a Song"). There are also punctuated moments: after the wintery scene where Bambi learns of his mother's death, we are greeted by birds relishing, musically, in the advent of spring. Some of the music is purely celebration of nature because Disney can achieve this: some nineteen minutes into the film, Disney artists insert a rain and lightning storm that is purely their own invention, accompanied by "Little April Shower." The choreography of animation with music, revealing how all forest creatures endure and respond to the dramatic event, is as artful as any four minutes in the contemporaneous *Fantasia*.

Most of the musical numbers provide emotional relief from the tragic script, helping to celebrate the wonder of nature as a counterpoint to the evil of Man. But the supporting animal characters offer "cartoon relief" in episodes that are pure Disney. In the book, there is a hare and a screech owl, but no Thumper and Flower, as Bambi's childhood friends who also undergo puberty and the perils of romance. The book's Owl is not Disney's wise Old Owl, who supervises the birth scene and later schools the teenagers in "Twitterpation." These characters, their stories, their role as a supporting ensemble, and their delightful romantic interludes constitute "cartoon relief" typical of Disney's use of animals. We do notice that Disney's animation of these characters, especially the females who seduce our fellows, follows standard Disney animation idioms—rounded bodies, big eyes, and so on—whereas the animation of the deer required Disney artists to develop new realistic drawing conventions to allow them "the potential for tragedy."[10]

The American Film Institute's 2008 rankings list *Bambi* as the number three animated film of all time, behind *Snow White* and *Pinocchio* and just ahead of *The Lion King* and *Fantasia*. Whatever the fifteen hundred voters counted as the "best" animated film, it is difficult to imagine that animation itself was the chief criterion for ranking *Snow White* and *Pinocchio* above *Bambi*, among the most criticized and controversial of Disney's films. *Bambi* is also ranked in the top twenty horror films for the indelible "primal" impact of his mother's death and is called out as "the most effective piece of anti-hunting propaganda ever made."[11]

Bambi is a work of art. In the final analysis, it is not merely the animation, both different and brilliant; or the music, which like the drama is powerful; or the poetry, which is considerable; or the propaganda, which is pronounced, that make *Bambi* the film a work of art that reaches far beyond the book that inspired it. The metaphysical quest of realism that guided Disney and his artists to push animation to its limits and use of animals in a new direction conspired with other studio innovations developing at the same time. In *Fantasia* (1940) we find the synchronizing of music with images consummated in ways that make the musical scenes of *Bambi* appear profound. In *Dumbo* (1941) we discover the anthropomorphism and power of tragic loss infused into animals' stories. In *Pinnochio* (1940) we witness the willingness to use animation to tell a classic children's story with a terrifying side. During *all* of the years Disney studios were starting and completing these projects, artists, editors, and musicians were working on *Bambi* with a keen sense that here was an ultimate test of the animated arts, Walt's favorite project, and a special homage to nature and her story. That quest in and of itself provides the synergy for all elements to make *Bambi* a notable moment in filmmaking history while causing most of us to forget that it began with Salten's worthy little book.

How disappointing it must have been, then, that the initial theatrical release was not a financial success, representing an end to the era where animated spectaculars were the central mission of Disney and his artists. Notably, four of the five of AFI's top animated films of all time come from this era—and the fifth, *The Lion King*, can be seen as an attempt to recapture the message, spirituality, and spectacle of *Bambi* during a new age of computer animation.[12]

NOTES

1. Felix Salten, *Bambi*, trans. Whittaker Chambers (New York: Simon and Schuster, 1929).

2. David Payne, "Bambi," in *From Mouse to Mermaid: The Politics of Film, Gender, and Culture*, ed. E. Bell, L. Haas, and L. Sells (Bloomington: Indiana University Press, 1995), 137–147.

3. See Matt Carmill, "The Bambi Syndrome," *Natural History* 102 (June 1993): 6–12.

4. Ibid., 7–8.

5. Janet Martin, "Bringing Bambi to the Screen," *Nature Magazine* 35 (1942): 353.

6. Robert D. Field, *The Art of Walt Disney* (New York: Macmillan, 1942), 197.

7. Martin, "Bringing Bambi to the Screen," 352.

8. John Grant, *Encyclopedia of Walt Disney's Animated Characters*, 2nd ed. (New York: Hyperion, 1993), 189.

9. Carmill, "Bambi Syndrome," 8–9.

10. Ibid., 8.

11. Ibid., 6.

12. There are several strong parallels between *Bambi* and *The Lion King*. Both are spectacles of animation, with *Lion King* bedazzling us with computer animation as *Bambi* had done with traditional animation; both were exceptional with music, with *The Lion King* winning Academy Awards for Best Score and Best Song; both were tragic stories mollified only by the comedy of cartoon characters and nature's continuity; and both superimpose human sociopolitical hierarchy onto the animal kingdom and show its natural integration with the seasonal and cyclical powers of nature. See Payne, "Bambi."

Chapter Six

Through the Cinematic Looking Glass

*Walt Disney's 1951 Animated Version and
Tim Burton's 2010 Film*

Sarah Boslaugh

When Lewis Carroll (1832–1898), aka Charles Lutwidge Dodgson, published *Alice's Adventures in Wonderland*[1] in 1865, he could hardly have anticipated the influence his book, and its central character, would exert on popular culture, nor how long lasting that influence would be. One hundred and fifty years later, *Alice's Adventures* and Carroll's follow-up, *Through the Looking Glass*[2] (1871), remain popular among children and adults alike. Both have been adapted for other media, including television, theater, and film. The Internet Movie Database lists eighty-two films and television productions in which Alice appears, from the 1903 Georges Méliès short *Alice in Wonderland* to the 2016 feature film *Alice Through the Looking Glass* directed by James Bobin.[3] Among the best known are two feature films produced by Disney, both titled *Alice in Wonderland*. The first is the 1951 animated film[4] directed by Clyde Geronimi, Wilfred Jackson, and Hamilton Luske, featuring the voices of Kathryn Beaumont (Alice), Ed Wynn (the Mad Hatter), Richard Haydn (the Caterpillar), and Verna Felton (the Queen of Hearts). The second is the 2010 live-action film[5] directed by Tim Burton, starring Mia Wasikowska (Alice), Johnny Depp (the Mad Hatter), and Helena Bonham Carter (the Red Queen).

While the films share common elements, many drawn from Carroll's texts, they are notably different in theme, tone, and other aesthetic aspects. In particular, they differ in their presentation of Alice's character and the manner in which her journey through Wonderland ("Underland" in Burton's film) relates to Alice's life above ground.

THE ANIMATED *ALICE*

Disney's interest in *Alice* dates back to at least the 1920s, when he produced a series of "Alice comedies" mixing live action and animation. Elements from Carroll's texts were incorporated into the 1937 Mickey Mouse "Thru the Mirror."[6] Disney twice considered feature-length, live-action versions, initially with Mary Pickford and later Ginger Rogers potentially assuming the role.[7] Neither project came to fruition, partly because, according to Disney, "Practically everyone who has read and loved the book of necessity sees the Tenniel Alice, and no matter how closely we approximate her with a living Alice, I feel the result would be a disappointment."[8]

In 1946, Disney decided to produce an animated adaptation. The studio considered basing its visual style on the illustrations by Sir John Tenniel included in the first edition of Carroll's *Alice* but abandoned this approach as impractical.[9] Nonetheless, the spirit of Tenniel is evident in the completed film's title sequence, which includes artwork resembling colored versions of some of Tenniel's illustrations. Both story development and animation proceeded slowly. According to Bob Thomas, "Everyone felt relief when *Alice in Wonderland* was finished. Especially Walt. He vowed never again to undertake a tamper-proof classic."[10]

Disney's *Alice* was released by RKO Radio Pictures on July 28, 1951. Like other Disney features, many individuals worked on the key elements, including ten animating directors and thirteen people credited as contributing to the story.[11] This collaborative process, standard for Disney animated features, caused problems during this film's creation. One of the animating directors, Ward Kimball, said that directors working on the project competed with each other, "trying to top the other guys and make his sequences the biggest and craziest in the show"; as a result, the film "degenerated into a loud-mouthed vaudeville show."[12]

This version is, above all, an animated Disney film. It draws on elements of both *Alice* and *Through the Looking Glass* but transforms many of Carroll's original concepts to render them more typical of other Disney films. For instance, the White Rabbit is a key character in both the Carroll novels and Disney's version. But in the film, he has become a comical bunny with a hugely oversized watch, rather than the dignified, rather stern-looking rabbit featured in woodcuts by Tenniel.[13] Other characters, such as the talking doorknob, do not derive from Carroll, added to facilitate comic bits clearly in the Disney spirit. Simply put, this is not just an animated presentation of Lewis Carroll's *Alice* but truly the Disney Version, that is, a film made by Disney and company for their loyal ongoing audience—for better or worse.

A musical, Disney's film includes numerous original songs and musical settings of some of Carroll's poems, including "Old Father William" and "'Twas Brillig" (the latter with lyrics adapted from the poem "Jabberwocky," which appears in *Through the Looking Glass*). Disney employed a variety of pop music and film industry veterans, including Bob Hilliard, Sammy Fain, Oliver Wallace, and Ted Sears.[14] In keeping with the Disney process of making the story "theirs," such tunes are typical of and reminiscent to songs in other popular Disney films, rather than intended to create a musical match for the spirit of Carroll's texts.

Whereas most Disney animated projects feature a singular look the team appropriated for their take on a particular classic, several different visual styles are here employed. Most obviously, the framing story is animated in a semirealistic manner, similar to that employed for Disney's *Bambi*, with depth suggested through use of the multiplane camera. In contrast, the Wonderland scenes are replete with comical exaggerations and talking animals reminiscent of short cartoons such as Disney's ambitious Silly Symphonies.[15] Some episodes in Wonderland are more adventurous: the influence of Salvador Dali can be seen in the final chase sequence before Alice awakens.[16] This belies any question of whether the supposedly old-fashioned Disney was aware, and open to the influence of, experimental forms of modern art.

Upon release, *Alice* proved neither a critical nor popular success. The Disney Company lost an estimated one million dollars on the project.[17] Contemporary critics did not greet *Alice* with the same enthusiasm as other Disney films, dismissing it with phrases that complained of Disney's film "owing more to the culture of popcorn and bubble gum than to the genius of either Dodgson or Tenniel," while criticizing the songs as "cheaply pretty."[18] Contemporary scholars and academics also criticize *Alice*: Leonard Maltin finds it "flash and generally entertaining" but lacking in "that essential thread that made Disney's best features hang together."[19] Maltin also notes that the film "has trouble maintaining pace and continuity,"[20] while an anonymous critic writing in *Sight and Sound* in 2010 called it "a Tex Avery-style parade of diverting, cute, instantly forgotten cartoon gags."[21] Interestingly, *Alice* enjoyed a resurgence of interest in the 1960s and 1970s due to its drug references (the Caterpillar does smoke a hookah, after all) and the psychedelic, countercultural vibe many college-age viewers found in the Wonderland episodes.[22] These connections were played up in a 1974 promotional campaign for the theatrical rerelease, claiming the film offered "visual euphoria" and referencing the Jefferson Airplane song "White Rabbit" with the slogan, "Should you go see it? Go ask Alice."[23]

ANIMATED ALICE'S WONDROUS JOURNEY

The animated *Alice* is an episodic film, a quality it shares with Carroll's *Alice's Adventures* as well as with many other popular children's books, including Frank Baum's Oz novels. Disney adopted Carroll's framing story of Alice becoming bored in the company of her older sister, falling asleep by a riverbank, and experiencing her adventures as a dream that Alice relates to the older sister when she awakens. In the film, Alice's sister tries to teach her a history lesson; the sister's role as a representative of the sensible adult world is emphasized, in contrast to Alice's imagined world in which animals can talk and books can be made up entirely of pictures. However much this varies from Carroll's brief setup, the approach is in line with what Disney does with the successive anecdotes.

Disney employs familiar comic devices such as the enormous, shrewish wife and the tiny, meek husband (the King and Queen of Hearts).[24] Disney also creates visual gags by transforming familiar objects into surreal projections: flowers become musical instruments while the oysters appear to be humanlike babies, their upper shells serving as bonnets, their lower shells as cribs.

When we first meet the animated Alice, she is a girl in the care of her older sister, preferring the world of her individual imagination to school lessons. When Alice returns from Wonderland, she is very much the same person. Her experiences are clearly presented as having taken place within a dream; thus, when Alice wakes, she tries to tell her older sister about it. But her sensible sibling will have none of this, instead declaring it's time for tea. Many critics have commented on Alice's lack of transformation, the absence of any tangible arc, as a result of her adventures. M. Keith Booker notes that *Alice* "seem[s] to celebrate the individual imagination only ultimately to advise individuals to accept the status quo"[25] as Alice is compelled to return to the sensible world of her older sister, where wild flights of imagination have no place. William Verrone notes that Alice may actually be more of a conformist when she returns than before, since at the film's start she at least rebelled against a boring lesson, whereas at the end she seems submissive and accepting.[26]

In contrast, when Carroll's Alice wakes and at once returns to the normal world, her sister takes the time to listen to the girl's story before sending her in to have her tea. More remarkably, the sister stays in the meadow, falling into her own waking dream in which she sees many of the characters described by Alice. While the older sister knows none of this is real—the sound of the teacups is only sheep bells; the wind, not the White Rabbit, rustles the grass—she too is reluctant to give up this imaginary world. In the final paragraph she imagines Alice grown up, but keeping "the simple and loving heart of her childhood" and how she would hence "gather about her other little children, and make THEIR eyes bright and eager with many a strange tale, perhaps even with the dream of Wonderland."[27] With this paragraph, Carroll underlines his respect for the beneficial powers of the imagination, a point omitted from Disney's animated *Alice*.

In the final analysis, Disney's 1951 *Alice* is a conventional Disney film that includes some beautiful animation but remains too tame to do justice to Carroll's anarchic world and too episodic and stylistically inconsistent to satisfy as a feature-length project. It's worth noting that the character of Alice was something of an anomaly in a Disney film of the time: as Amy Davis notes, in the period from 1937 to 1967, only *Alice* and *Peter Pan* had female leads, and only Alice and Wendy "ever enjoy real adventures in new, strange worlds."[28] However, there is no sense that Alice has had a true hero's journey, returning transformed by it; instead, she is oddly, perhaps surprisingly passive even during her adventures.[29] Also, Alice is constantly pressured to behave like a conventional Victorian English girl even in a world populated with talking rabbits and humanized playing cards.[30] Most important, the post-adventures Alice does nothing to challenge the existing social order—instead, she fits into it perhaps even better than she did before her unrewarding journey.

TIM BURTON'S 2010 *ALICE IN WONDERLAND*

Tim Burton's 2010 *Alice* departs much further from Carroll's *Alice* than did the 1951 film. Burton's most significant changes are replacing Carroll's simple framing device with a wholly original, much more developed story line, while making Alice a young lady of marriageable age (nineteen years) rather than a prepubescent girl. The Underland section also departs from Carroll; traditional characters and story elements are used within a new story of a sibling rivalry leading to a war between the Red Queen (a figure analogous to the Queen of Hearts in Carroll's text) and the White Queen. References to Carroll's books are salted throughout, though assigned to different characters and employed in other contexts, creating alternative meanings for the repeated phrases. The importance of the characters are also altered, the Mad Hatter elevated almost to a co-leading role in the Underland sequences; Johnny Depp, who plays that character, received over-the-title billing in publicity materials.[31] The decision to emphasize Depp's role may have been due to his status as an established star, whereas Mia Wasikowska (Alice) was considerably less well known.

Burton's film freely mixes live action and CGI (computer-generated imagery) in the Underland sequences, while the frame story remains primarily live action. Critical response was mixed, with *Alice* praised for visual inventiveness (Oscar winner for Best Art Direction and Best Costume Design, also nominated for Best Visual Effects) while criticized for narrative incoherence in Underland as well as for changes made to Carroll's text. Owen Gleiberman called the film "a strange brew indeed: murky, diffuse, and meandering," criticizing the decision to transform Alice from "the spunky girl we

remember" to "a rather stern 19-year-old Victorian ingénue."[32] Todd
McCarthy noted that the "design, effects, makeup and technical work is of a
high order" but criticized the "formulaic" plot written to unify the Underland
episodes, as well as poorly done 3D filming for the frame story.[33] However,
Burton's *Alice* was a financial success, opening in the United States as the
number one film for the weekend of March 5–7, 2010.[34]

If the 1951 *Alice* is best characterized as having at least as much in
common with other Disney films as with Carroll's text, it's even more true
that the 2010 film draws on Carroll's text almost entirely in the service of
creating a Tim Burton film. Gleiberman notes Burton's previous fondness for
setting his films in alternative worlds (e.g., *Beetlejuice*), using "oddballs" as
central characters (e.g., *Edward Scissorhands*), and adapting children's stories (*Charlie and the Chocolate Factory*), all these previous elements present
again in *Alice*.[35] Jeffrey Andrew Weinstock notes the similarity between
Alice's rejection of societal limitations and her need to overcome monsters,
which he finds analogous to that of Victor in Burton's *Frankenweenie*; her
entry into an "other world" populated with fantastic creatures he likens to the
chocolate factory in Burton's *Charlie and the Chocolate Factory*. Weinstock
notes Alice's similarities to Edward Scissorhands, Batman, and Barnabas
Collins in that she must renew a world (Underland) controlled by a stifling
force (the Red Queen).[36] Catherine Spooner notes that, as in other Burton
films, the visual components of Alice are stronger than the storytelling,[37]
calling *Alice* "a kind of apotheosis of Burton's use of costume" in which "the
outsider protagonist's journey of maturation is expressed through clothes."[38]
There is no question that in this case, Burton plays the role of auteur while
Lewis Carroll, once the author, has become merely a source that can be
drawn from or ignored, portrayed faithfully when it serves Burton's purposes
or betrayed when it does not.

THE WONDROUS JOURNEY OF BURTON'S ALICE

Burton's *Alice* opens and closes in a realistic nineteenth-century London. In
the prologue, set in 1855, Alice's father, Charles Kingsleigh, proposes to a
group of businessmen that they should expand trade routes to the Far East.
When one, Lord Ascot, declares this impossible, Kingsleigh replies, "The
only way to achieve the impossible is to believe that it is possible." They are
interrupted by nine-year-old Alice, who has had a bad dream involving falling down a dark hole and seeing strange creatures, including a smiling cat, a
blue caterpillar, and a rabbit wearing a waistcoat. She asks her father if she
has gone mad; he assures her that she is in fact "Bonkers. Off your head," but
that "all the best people are." Here, notably, the element of madness, so
prevalent in Carroll's text (if only indirectly addressed in the Disney Ver-

sion) becomes prominent as soon as possible; madness does after all underline virtually all works in the Burton oeuvre in a way it does not figure prominently for Walt's own earlier films.

The main section is set ten years later, after Charles Kingsleigh's death. The teenage Alice displays her dislike of conformity by failing to wear a corset or stockings to a garden party. When challenged by her mother, Alice defends her nonconformity with: "What if it was agreed that 'proper' was wearing a codfish on your head? Would you wear it?" At the garden party, Alice spots several characters representing unfortunate aspects of the adult world she is expected to join, including her sister's cheating husband and Aunt Imogene, an aging spinster who harbors the belief that she has a noble suitor. During the party, Alice catches glimpses of a rabbit in a waistcoat, but the other guests do not. When Hamish proposes, Alice excuses herself and runs after the rabbit, who leads her into the woods—dark and scraggly in contrast to the sunny, manicured garden depicted in Disney's less edgy frame.

In keeping with the by-now-mythic notion of Down the Rabbit Hole, Alice falls in, landing in a dark, decaying room, part of Underland. Though she doesn't realize it yet, in Burton's version, this is the same place she visited in her childhood dreams. The white rabbit and other fantastic characters debate whether she is the "right Alice" because she doesn't seem to remember being there before, also since she appears to have lost the pluck and courage of her childhood self. Although not explicitly stated, this idea draws on research by Brown and Gilligan, demonstrating that many girls lose their sense of self in adolescence as they are pressured to conform to societal norms of femininity and female behavior.[39] Burton's creation of such an Alice reveals as much about his sensibility and social concerns as Disney's supremely self-sufficient Alice did about that man and his vision.

Unlike either Carroll's Alice or the 1951 animated Alice, Burton's Alice here embarks on a true hero's journey worthy of classical myth as defined in the writings of Joseph Campbell. Her task is to slay the Jabberwocky, a fire-breathing dragon; remove the oppressive Red Queen from power; and restore the White Queen to her rightful place as ruler of Underland. Initially, Alice rejects such a call to action, claiming that "I don't slay" and "I couldn't if I wanted to." However, she grows into her task, the turning point occurring when she recovers her childhood memories of Underland and regains the confidence of her girlhood. She is aided in this character arc by the blue caterpillar, Absolem, himself about to undergo transformation into a butterfly. So encouraged to embrace her own transformation, Alice steals the Vorpal Sword from the Red Queen's castle, employing it to slay the Jabberwocky, thereby freeing inhabitants of Underland. Although the Mad Hatter entreats her to remain, Alice realizes she must return to the aboveground world because she has "questions I have to answer. Things I have to do." She drinks a vial of the Jabberwocky's blood, allowing her to return to the garden part, with but a short period of time having elapsed.

Burton's transformed Alice now (as a direct result of what may or may not have been "only a dream") knows her own mind and is not afraid to speak it. She declines Hamish's proposal ("I'm sorry Hamish, I can't marry you. You're not the right man for me"). She asserts her new identity by delivering confident statements to each of the principal characters, including her sister Margaret: "I love you Margaret. But this is my life. I'll decide what to do with it"; and her mother: "Don't worry, mother. I'll find something useful to do with my life." She then proposes to Lord Ascot that he should expand his trade routes to China, furthering her father's proposal from the opening segment. Ascot offers her a counter-position, reasoning that "since you're not going to be my daughter-in-law, perhaps you'd consider becoming an apprentice with the company." In the finale, Alice is on deck of a trading ship, the *Wonder*, preparing to depart for China. The sequence's visual splendor, and Alice's self-confidence, as well as the appearance of Absolem in the form of a blue butterfly, all signify that Alice's transformation is complete: she has not rejected adulthood but has found an adult role that allows her to express her best qualities rather than conforming to a predetermined and limited view of what a woman's life should be.

NOTES

1. Lewis Carroll, *Alice's Adventures in Wonderland* (Millennium Fulcrum Edition 3.0, Project Gutenberg EBook 11, 2008), http://www.gutenberg.org/cache/epub/11/pg11.txt.

2. Lewis Carroll, *Through the Looking-Glass* (Project Gutenberg EBook 12, 2009), http://www.gutenberg.org/cache/epub/12/pg12.txt.

3. "Alice (Character)," Internet Movie Database, http://www.imdb.com/character/ch0408645/?ref_=tt_cl_t1.

4. *Alice in Wonderland*, directed by Clyde Geronimi, Wilfred Jackson, and Hamilton Luske (1951; Burbank, CA: Walt Disney Home Video, 2004), DVD.

5. *Alice in Wonderland*, directed by Tim Burton (2010; Burbank, CA: Walt Disney Studios Home Entertainment, 2010), DVD.

6. Leonard Maltin, *The Disney Films*, 4th ed. (New York: Disney Editions, 2000), 101.

7. Bob Thomas, *Walt Disney: An American Original* (New York: Hyperion, 1994), 220–21.

8. Quoted in ibid., 221.

9. John Tenniel, *The Tenniel Illustrations for Carroll's Wonderland* (Project Gutenberg EBook 114, 2008), http://www.gutenberg.org/files/114/114-h/114-h.htm.

10. Thomas, *Walt Disney*, 221.

11. Maltin, *Disney Films*, 101.

12. Quoted in ibid., 103.

13. Tenniel, *Tenniel Illustrations*, illustration 2.

14. Maltin, *Disney Films*, 101.

15. "Alice Through the Lens," *Sight and Sound* 20, no. 4 (April 2010): 36.

16. Will Brooker, *Alice's Adventures: Lewis Carroll in Popular Culture* (New York: Continuum, 2004), 207.

17. Thomas, *Walt Disney*, 221.

18. Both quoted in Brooker, *Alice's Adventures*, 206.

19. Maltin, *Disney Films*, 103.
20. Ibid., 102.
21. "Alice Through the Lens," 37.
22. William Verrone, "Is Disney Avante-Garde? A Comparative Analysis of *Alice in Wonderland* (1951) and Jan Svankmajer's *Alice* (1989)," in *Diversity in Disney Films: Critical Essays on Race, Ethnicity, Gender, Sexuality and Disability*, ed. Johnson Cheu (Jefferson, NC: McFarland, 2013), 209.
23. Brooker, *Alice's Adventures*, 208.
24. Mark I. Pinsky, *The Gospel according to Disney: Faith, Trust, and Pixie Dust* (Louisville, KY: Westminster John Knox Press, 2004), 59.
25. M. Keith Booker, *Disney, Pixar, and the Hidden Messages of Children's Films* (Santa Barbara, CA: Praeger, 2010), 23.
26. Verrone, "Is Disney Avante-Garde?," 217.
27. Carroll, *Alice's Adventures*, 60.
28. Amy M. Davis, *Good Girls and Wicked Witches: Women in Disney's Feature Animation* (Eastleigh, UK: John Libbey, 2006), 104–5.
29. Verrone, "Is Disney Avante-Garde?," 215.
30. Pinsky, *The Gospel according to Disney*, 58–60.
31. "Alice (Character)," Internet Movie Database.
32. Owen Gleiberman, "Alice in Wonderland," *Entertainment Weekly*, March 3, 2010, http://www.ew.com/article/2010/03/03/alice-wonderland.
33. Todd McCarthy, "Review: 'Alice in Wonderland,'" *Variety*, February 25, 2010, http://variety.com/2010/film/features/alice-in-wonderland-1117942306/.
34. "Alice in Wonderland (2010)," *Box Office Mojo*, http://www.boxofficemojo.com/movies/?id=aliceinwonderland10.htm.
35. Gleiberman, "Alice in Wonderland."
36. Jeffrey Andrew Weinstock, "Mainstream Outsider: Burton Adapts Burton," in *The Works of Tim Burton: Margins to Mainstream*, ed. Jeffrey Andrew Weinstock (New York: Palgrave Macmillan, 2013), 21.
37. Catherine Spooner, "Costuming the Outsider in Tim Burton's Cinema, or, Why a Corset Is Like a Codfish," in *The Works of Tim Burton: Margins to Mainstream*, ed. Jeffrey Andrew Weinstock (New York: Palgrave Macmillan, 2013), 48.
38. Ibid., 58.
39. Lyn Mikel Brown and Carol Gilligan, *Meeting at the Crossroads: Women's Psychology and Girls' Development* (New York: Ballantine Books, 1992), 2.

Chapter Seven

Walt Disney and Robert Louis Stevenson

Haskin's Treasure Island *or Stevenson's* Kidnapped?

Scott Allen Nollen

Born in Edinburgh, Scotland, Robert Louis Stevenson (1850–1894) remains one of the most prolific and acclaimed authors in the English language. Known primarily for historical and horror novels (including *The Strange Case of Dr. Jekyll and Mr. Hyde*, 1885), he suffered from a tubercular-like condition that often confined him to bed. Among his many adventure tales, *Treasure Island* (1883), graced with multigenerational appeal and brimming with rousing lore of the sea, remains the perfect adventure-tale blueprint. In August 1881, Stevenson first conceived of "The Sea Cook: A Story for Boys" in a cottage at Braemar, Scotland. Troubled by wet, windy weather exacerbating his poor health, he remained indoors. His stepson, Lloyd Osbourne, experimented with a box of paints, sketching a map of an imaginary island, which provided the inspiration.

One month later, serialized chapters appeared in *Young Folks* magazine. The entire novel ran in seventeen weekly installments, Stevenson declining to use his real name, titling the serialization "Treasure Island, or, The Mutiny of the Hispaniola. By Captain George North." On November 14, 1883, Cassell and Company published it in book form; British critics were nearly unanimous in their praise. Stevenson's short sentences allow a reader to see the landscape, feel the atmosphere: "Not a man, not a sail, upon the sea, the very largeness of the view increased the sense of solitude." Distinct dialects for various characters further distinguished the piece. A receiver experiences not only the formal English of Squire Trelawney but the metaphorical and rhythmic jargon of Long John Silver. Although he is larger than life, this iconic fictional pirate, nicknamed "Barbecue" by his shipmates, was inspired by Stevenson's colleague and friend W. E. Henley. Having lost one of his legs, Henley's physical disability became an eternal part of buccaneer lore.

Treasure Island offers a prime example of Stevenson's refusal to champion any particular moral or social code. Evil is as resourceful, even likeable, as good; both can be found in the character of Silver. His personality confuses the "good" characters but seems clear-cut to the pirates: While they observe the same ambivalence in his nature, these scurvy shipmates know that obedience is necessary in any chain of command, particularly toward a man at once resourceful and brutal. Considering their captain to be preternatural, the pirates fear and obey him until late in the story, when they hand him the black spot. Even then, Silver gains the upper hand by calling attention to their desecration of a Bible.

Treasure Island has been praised for Stevenson's depiction of Jim Hawkins, a boy forced to grow up quickly owing to extraordinary circumstances. After efforts by his adult mentors prove ineffectual, Jim saves the ship and, with marooned Ben Gunn's help, the treasure. This may account for the novel's reputation as a children's favorite. Stevenson himself referred to *Treasure Island* as a boys' adventure tale. Unfortunately, its subsequent reputation as a children's novel has damaged its credibility as a major nineteenth-century work.

Graced by Stevenson's "visual" style, the novel would seem ideally suited to cinematic adaptation. Yet, as the record shows, it has been botched nearly every time. It took eighty-two years and eight major attempts before a satisfying and faithful treatment appeared. Writer-director Fraser Heston's 1990 version starred his father, Charlton, and was produced for Turner Network Television.

The ongoing misconception that this was a children's novel can be attributed, at least in part, to Disney's $1.8 million 1950 film. Like Metro-Goldwyn-Mayer's 1934 adaptation, Disney abandons plot exposition and detail for an abridged narrative, simplistic characterizations, and fabricated dialogue. The visual style, rendered by director Byron Haskin and cinematographer F. A. Young, is often cramped and static, relying primarily on the medium two shot. While these are augmented by striking silhouette images (depicting men, horses, and ships' riggings against the night sky), the latter do little to balance an artificial atmosphere.

Prior to this, Disney never had produced a live-action film, which may account for the cartoonlike screenplay and performances. To utilize frozen British revenues, he shot in England and, together with RKO Radio, maintained a sound commercial strategy by treading close to the puerile content of his animated productions. Catering to popular taste, Disney unwisely cast twelve-year-old Iowa-born Bobby Driscoll as Jim Hawkins (with dubious "period" clothing and a thick Midwestern U.S. accent) alongside a company of English character actors.

Lawrence Watkin's script follows the novel's basic outline, but many specific incidents, most of the colorful period dialogue, and, disastrously, Jim's first-person narration are eliminated. As the film begins, Billy Bones (called "Captain" Bones [Finlay Currie]) is at the Admiral Benbow, lying near death. Stevenson's fascinating Bones becomes inconsequential. Currie's characterization is neither menacing nor capable of arousing much sympathy. Mrs. Hawkins and Jim's ailing (or deceased) father are eliminated. Apparently, the wee lad has been operating the Benbow alone! Watkin's characters telegraph results of events beforehand, a narrative blunder worsened by Haskin's frenetic pacing. Before Long John (Robert Newton) is introduced, Jim, Dr. Livesey (Denis O'Dea), and Squire Trelawney (Walter Fitzgerald) here stroll into the Spy-Glass Inn and discuss the apples they will take on the voyage. Following Silver's initial appearance, he and Jim, facing each other in the back room, eagerly shake hands "as shipmates." When the *Hispaniola* reaches the island, Jim escapes Silver's clutches and, pursued by pirates, immediately runs into Ben Gunn (Geoffrey Wilkinson), who leaps down from a crag.

Such action sequences pale in comparison to those in the 1934 MGM version. The mutiny aboard the *Hispaniola* amounts to little (land is sighted as Jim, hiding in the apple barrel, overhears Silver's plans); the battle at the stockade culminates in a montage of close-ups alternating between Captain Smollett's (Basil Sydney) men and Silver's cutthroats. The Disney Version of Jim's recapture of the *Hispaniola* proves worse still. Jim does send Israel Hands (Geoffrey Keen) to Davy Jones's Locker. But instead of sailing the ship to the northern inlet, he beaches her on the sand, in plain sight of the pirates. Remarkably, he strikes the Jolly Roger and raises the Union Jack before returning to the stockade.

The pirates' mutiny against Silver is one of the film's better sequences, although much of Stevenson's rich dialogue is discarded. The majority of this sequence is well staged, but the childish impotence of Driscoll (and Watkin's script) mars the overall effect. After Silver barks his resignation, he turns and winks at Jim, apparently too stupid to understand the proceedings. When they reach the looted treasure spot (the hunt lasts exactly two minutes), the villains are dispatched and Jim pleads for Silver's life. Soon Jim and Dr. Livesey state that they will testify at his "fair trial in England."

The most satisfying moments (as in the 1934 version) are supplied by supporting actors. The two featured performances, however, fail to capture much of the Silver–Hawkins rapport. While Driscoll's Jim appears lethargic, Newton's Silver is too blustery and overblown. His bizarre pronunciations, coupled with eye-rolling and incessant grimaces, add to the unconvincing atmosphere. Newton, more subdued in some scenes, is limited by the script.

Silver and Jim have no relationship, merely exchanging starchy dialogue. The cartoonlike style is reinforced by Clifton Parker's musical score, particularly in scenes featuring Ben Gunn: each time the marooned sailor leaps into Jim's path, he is accompanied by an absurd xylophone flourish. Haskin and Watkin's shallow presentation offers select events from the novel, animated by actors blurting out stale approximations of Stevenson's dialogue without motivation.

Disney's *Treasure Island* appeals primarily to children below age twelve, for whom it provides a pleasant diversion. Past (Disney-inclined) critics have praised this adaptation as a great adventure film, but their assessments suggest that none has read the novel. Some critical remarks actually blame *Stevenson* for Newton's histrionic caricature of Silver. Newton's cardboard pirate possesses none of the admirable moral ambiguity of the author's creation. A talented cinematographer and special effects artist, Haskin was technically adept but poorly qualified to direct a literary piece. The general quality of *Treasure Island* can be attributed to his oblivious misinterpretation that "the film was a children's story, told by Stevenson to children. Kids don't go in much for subtleties."[1] Considering Haskin's attitude, it's no wonder Jim Hawkins appears so dense in the film.

Several of Haskin's technical choices can be criticized. Though the static visual style is occasionally broken by silhouette shots, his one attempt at a picturesque long shot, depicting a sweeping vista, is framed from the *wrong* perspective: rather than showing the island from the point of view of a character onboard the *Hispaniola*, Haskin reveals the ship from the viewpoint of the island! Since Ben Gunn has yet to be introduced, his point of view (never once employed as a visual or narrative device) hardly rates as a logical choice. Disney allowed Haskin and Watkin free reign during filming, on location and at Denham Studios in England. Critical reaction to release on July 19, 1950, proved negative on both sides of the Atlantic. Box office receipts were far below what Disney had anticipated. Due to lukewarm reception, *Treasure Island* was not reissued, though it was later broadcast on Disney's weekly television program. (An edited version was released to theaters in 1975.)

A decade would pass before Disney produced another Stevenson adaptation, *Kidnapped* (1960), based on the sweeping historical novel published in *Young Folks* magazine, and in book form by Cassell and Company during the summer of 1886. By combining the excitement and imagery of *Treasure Island* with a specific historical environment, detailed geography, and character psychology contrasting the Lowland and Highland cultures, Stevenson demonstrated enormous growth as a novelist. Unlike other authors who tackled Scottish history, he used actual events as a backdrop for the conflicts experienced by people in various cultural settings. The esteemed Henry James, for one, considered *Kidnapped* to be Stevenson's finest book.

In this novel, Stevenson explores the duality that contributed to his home-land's turbulent past. Through the eyes of a Jacobite fighter and a Whig youth, he vividly examines emotions experienced by Highlanders and Low-landers five years after the appalling butchery at the battle of Culloden in April 1746. As a political movement, Jacobitism had been initiated in late 1688 by Scots and English who supported the main line of the Stewart dynasty. Upon gaining the throne in 1685, the Stewart king, James II of England and VII of Scotland, intended to restore Catholicism throughout both kingdoms. A vast majority opposed this development; in November 1688, James was overthrown by his Dutch son-in-law, Prince William of Orange, who reigned until his death in 1702.

In 1700, James died in exile. In Scotland, the Williamite government passed the Act of Settlement in 1700, declaring that future monarchs must be Protestant supporters of the Church of England. The Westminster govern-ment became even less popular with Jacobites after the Scottish Parliament ratified the Act of Union on January 16, 1707, merging Scotland and Eng-land into one nation, Great Britain, thereby abolishing Scottish sovereignty. Following disastrous rebellions in 1715 and 1745, the Jacobites' last hope, Charles Edward Stuart, known as "Bonnie Prince Charlie," fled from the Culloden battlefield, aided by faithful Jacobites and others who respected his royal lineage. Hanoverian troops burned homes, stole and killed livestock, and plundered the belongings of rebels and nonrebels alike. The government instituted a series of measures that literally destroyed the Highland way of life. Traditional dress, including the kilt, was outlawed, the speaking of Gael-ic discouraged.

In *Kidnapped*, David Balfour and Alan Breck Stewart display their differ-ent impressions of Jacobitism. While Alan clings to an anachronistic past so as to make sense of Highland life, David supports the modern Whig heritage that supplanted it. Stevenson adapted facts about the historical Allan Breck's exploits, along with those of his kinsman, James Stewart; both served in the Jacobite army during 1745–1746. Specifically, Stevenson incorporated the infamous Appin Murder of Colin Roy Campbell of Glenure, a crown factor (land agent) known as the Red Fox. During the afternoon of May 14, 1752, Campbell, braced with a legal precept to evict five Stewart tenants from Ardshiel, was shot. Five days later, James Stewart was arrested, although Breck evaded capture. Convicted of the crime, James was sentenced to death; protesting his innocence, he was hanged at Ballachulish on November 8. Allan Breck had last been seen at Invernahadden, Rannoch, in late May.

As Stevenson mentions in the dedication, his version of the Appin Murder occurs in 1751, a year before the historical incident. The episode is witnessed by David, but the lad doesn't see who fires the fatal shot. (This device remains consistent with the historical evidence; no one has positively iden-tified the actual murderer.) Like the historical Allan Breck, Stevenson's character, Alan, is glimpsed on a hill (in this instance, in the Wood of Letter-more), by David. It is he who questions Alan before taking flight in the heather. In the novel, Alan tells David of the eviction of Ardshiel tenants and appointment of Colin Campbell. This factual material lends *Kidnapped* a darker tone than *Treasure Island* by drawing on social distinctions that separate Stevenson's two main characters, ultimately spurring David to defend James Stewart on his return to Edinburgh.

The historical accuracy does not end there. When David reaches the Western Highlands, he witnesses severe poverty. Stevenson depicts the sorrow people experienced when forced to immigrate to the New World. The novel follows David's account of the dispirited scene with a terse, one-sentence paragraph directly identifying the ship and its cargo. Stevenson's juxtaposition of the passengers' tear-covered faces with "Lochaber No More," a song attributed to Allan Ramsay, is an example of understated literary power. Such a passage could provide a talented filmmaker with a vivid sequence. No dialogue would be needed to convey their sad plight. Stevenson's approach, combining a visual image with deeply moving background music, provides a literary precursor of cinematic style, revealing Stevenson's protomodernity.

Since *Kidnapped* is narrated by David, the reader experiences Breck's behavior through the lad's eyes: Highland attitudes, filtered through a Lowland sensibility. When the two part at novel's end, one of Stevenson's basic points is demonstrated clearly: though David and Alan hail from different cultures and their respective ideologies are opposed, they overlook these differences and remain friends. Neither character alters his opinions, but each realizes that he has survived with the other's help.

In his best moments, Breck is charming and courageous; in his worst, pompous and childish. Unlike the split personalities of earlier Stevenson characters, including the Jekyll–Hyde dichotomy, Alan's behavior is complex. This is often demonstrated through his use of humor, sometimes in dangerous and desperate situations. Humor serves as a bridge between good and evil, blurring distinctions that separate these traits. This links the fictional Alan with the historical Bonnie Prince Charlie, who jested during his harrowing flight.

Many uninformed readers categorize *Kidnapped* as a children's story or boys' adventure tale. But the historical aspects and rich characterizations allow Stevenson's novel to work on many levels. The author's incorporation of clan warfare in eighteenth-century Scotland allows knowledgeable adults to appreciate the complexity of the history, while his ingenious style permits younger readers to enjoy the adventure plot without needing to understand the Caledonian past.

Prior to Disney's adaptation, three film versions were produced: a 1917 silent condensation released by Forum/Edison (and now lost); 20th Century

Fox's unfaithful 1938 travesty starring Warner Baxter and Freddie Bartholomew; and the occasionally striking and well-acted (by Dan O'Herlihy and Roddy McDowall), medium-budget 1948 production, directed by William Beaudine for Monogram. Although Fox and Monogram advertised their films as "Robert Louis Stevenson's *Kidnapped*," Disney's 1960 production was the first to merit such a claim. Containing none of the scenery-chewing melodramatics of 1950's *Treasure Island*, *Kidnapped* is the better of Disney's two Stevenson adaptations, and an entertaining film in its own right.

During preproduction, Disney screened the 1938 and 1948 releases, noting their weaknesses and deviations from the novel. Wisely, he chose London-born Robert Stevenson (no relation to R.L.S.) to write and direct the most faithful visualization that his tight budget would allow. Disney's publicity department issued an article titled "*Kidnapped* Author and Its Director Have More in Common Than Name" to suggest both had experienced similar lifestyles: "The two Stevensons share the same young-in-heart approach to all facets of life . . . the same stimulating and lively imagination which colors their creative work."[2]

Educated at Cambridge, the latter Stevenson began writing screenplays in 1930. Two years later, he was directing for Germany's UFA and Gainsborough in England. Eventually, Stevenson began helming fantasy classics for Gaumont-British: *The Man Who Changed His Mind* (1936, Boris Karloff) and *King Solomon's Mines* (1937, Paul Robeson). In 1939, after signing with Hollywood's David O. Selznick, Stevenson became noted for his technical prowess and elegant visual style. He directed several major films, including an adaptation of Charlotte Brontë's *Jane Eyre* (1944) starring Joan Fontaine and Orson Welles and, in 1957, the Revolutionary War tale *Johnny Tremain* for Disney, spending the next twenty years working for that studio. Stevenson helmed such hits as *Old Yeller* (1957), *Darby O'Gill and the Little People* (1959), *The Absent-Minded Professor* (1961), *Son of Flubber* (1963), *Mary Poppins* (1964), and *Blackbeard's Ghost* (1968).

While Stevenson completed the *Kidnapped* screenplay, Disney searched for actual sites depicted in the novel. His decision to base production in Great Britain gave the cast and crew the luxury of proper dramatic and geographic atmosphere. In early 1959, shooting commenced at London's Pinewood Studios, where interior scenes and special effects sequences were completed. In April, relevant cast members and eighty-five technicians trekked to Scotland to shoot all exterior scenes on location. From Ardgour, equipment was carried by pack ponies to Lettermore Wood, where the murder of Colin Campbell was re-created. Other scenes were filmed at Ganavan Sands, Loch Nell, Easdale, Glen Nevis, Creagon, Onich Falls, Oban, and Ballachulish. One of the film's most powerful images is a beautifully composed long shot of Glencoe, where Alan (Peter Finch) and David (James MacArthur) stop for a brief rest.

The narrative closely follows the novel, covering every incident except David's experiences on the Isle of Earraid (this material is replaced by his meeting with a sinister Highlander) and the heroic effort of Alison Hastie (unnamed in *Kidnapped*, revealed in its sequel, *Catriona*) on the Forth. Instead, Alan's hoodwinking of an old woman allows them to cross the guarded Stirling Bridge. The flight in the heather is abridged but well represented by sections lifted verbatim from the novel. Most importantly, unlike earlier film adaptations, there is no female love interest to slow the pace and interrupt the tale's adventurous and political aspects. All major characters depicted resemble their literary counterparts. The fusion of Robert Stevenson's screenplay and Disney's casting present careful re-creations that are exciting yet restrained. After a brief session in Hollywood, Disney had selected the majority of his actors at Pinewood. A young Peter O'Toole, born in Connemara, Ireland, turns in a brief but memorable performance as Robin Oig MacGregor. Scottish actors include Shakespearean-trained John Laurie as David's unscrupulous uncle, Ebenezer Balfour; eighty-one-year-old Finlay Currie as fearless Cluny MacPherson (Laurie and Currie also appear in Disney's *Treasure Island*); Andrew Cruikshank as a pompous and painted Colin Roy Campbell; and Duncan MacRae as the murderous Highlander.

As David, twenty-two-year-old MacArthur is too obviously American. But as Alan, Peter Finch gives *Kidnapped* a Stevenson-based performance equal to those of Fredric March in *Dr. Jekyll and Mr. Hyde* (1931), Boris Karloff in *The Body Snatcher* (1945), and Charlton Heston in *Treasure Island* (1990). Born in London, raised in Australia, he eventually became Laurence Olivier's protégé. During the 1950s, he emerged as one of Great Britain's top stars and won the British Film Academy (BFA) best actor award four times. Before *Kidnapped* was released on March 25, 1960, Finch called Breck "a role of tremendous power and by far the most exciting thing I've ever done."[3] To prepare, Finch, aided by dialect adviser John Breslin, worked for six weeks to acquire a passable Highland brogue. He then left for Scotland, spending three weeks in the Western Highlands familiarizing himself with the geography and customs.

Finch impeccably captures Alan's personality, especially his resourcefulness, intelligence in battle, and tempered bravado. In the seafaring scenes aboard the *Covenant*, Finch precisely conveys entire dialogue passages from the novel. When he describes his hatred for the Campbells, the battle at Culloden, and activities of the Red Fox, the film effectively captures the powerful drama of Stevenson's prose. Finch is particularly striking during the battle in the roundhouse. As in the novel, Alan plans his strategy beforehand: with David positioned at the window, he stands before the open door, awaiting his enemies. The inexperienced lad expresses concern. Alan replies, "Ye see, I have but one face; but so long as that door is open and my face to it, the best part of my enemies will be in front of me, where I would aye wish to find them." After the battle is won, Alan presents David with a silver button from his French greatcoat, qualifying this as the only film version to include this key symbol of Alan's ongoing friendship. During the heather sequence, R.L.S.'s political argument is, perhaps surprisingly, emphasized. When the exhausted David loses his temper and draws his sword, Alan refuses to fight.

Alan's meeting with Robin Oig MacGregor proves a dramatic highlight. When an argument escalates into armed conflict, Donald Dhu MacLaren (Abe Barker) suggests that they prove their mettle with the Highland bagpipes. Alan swaggers around the room as he plays "The White Cockade." His bravado ends when Robin skirls into a superior performance. Finch and O'Toole are flawless, with the latter (in one of his first screen appearances) manipulating the pipes in a relaxed, effortless style. When Alan becomes visibly irritated, Robin mimics his swaggering march. Inclusion of this sequence adds an important element to the cinematic Breck, again aiding in his complexity.

As David and Alan bid each other farewell, Disney's film alters R.L.S.'s ending. Though the two men are not hampered by the presence of other characters (as they are in earlier adaptations), Alan prepares to board a French ship in the Forth. Apparently, director Stevenson chose not to worry about the price on Alan's head (the ship is anchored in open water) or David's uncertainty about his feelings for his Jacobite friend. Stewart is mentioned (David asks Colin Campbell about the home of "James of the Glens"), but his part in the Appin incident is omitted. During their flight, Alan and David do not visit James's home nor cite his name. When they part, Alan is free to go where he pleases and David has received his inheritance.

Technically speaking, Paul Beeson's cinematography often fails to take advantage of the Scottish locations Disney and his crew so diligently located. Other than the magnificent image of Glencoe and a few shots of lochs and mountains, the visual style is marred by an overabundance of close-ups. During the Highland scenes, the viewer is allowed little of the geographic detail that distinguishes the novel, so the picturesque grandeur of the area is often lost. The scenes aboard the *Covenant* also are cramped, the miniatures and back-screen projection effects doing nothing to improve the claustrophobic atmosphere.

As in other Disney films, the mood often is dependent on music. Cedric Thorpe Davie's thunderous and syrupy score, conducted by Muir Mathieson, contains little traditional material. But "The White Cockade," a tune commemorating the white rosette worn by the Jacobite army during the 1745 rebellion, can be heard in several scenes.

One interesting component is Disney's subtle inclusion of his own moral message. In the novel, David thinks about the men he has killed in the roundhouse but is interested primarily in matching Alan's military prowess.

By contrast, Disney's David expresses dismay after killing a man. In a contemporary review, Arthur Knight praised the film because it "takes a forthright stand against killing, drinking and gambling without ever being mealy-mouthed or self-conscious about it."[4] Throughout the novel, Stevenson maintained his emblematic ambiguity toward these practices.

Ironically (but perhaps not surprisingly), the qualities that make Disney's *Kidnapped* a worthy Stevenson adaptation actually sealed the film's box office failure. While most British critics praised the work for its fidelity to the novel, many American reviewers disliked it for the same reason. Ironically, of Disney's two Stevenson adaptations, the faithful, history-laden *Kidnapped* is the better film, while the more simplistic, even cartoonish *Treasure Island* remains more popular—proving that general audience viewers watch films, and particularly Disney films, not to be educated but entertained.

NOTES

Portions of this essay were adapted from Scott Allen Nollen, *Robert Louis Stevenson: Life, Literature and the Silver Screen* (Jefferson, NC: McFarland, 1994).

1. *Kidnapped* Disney Pressbook, p. 3.
2. Ibid., 2.
3. Leonard Maltin, *The Disney Films* (New York: Crown, 1973), 168.
4. Arthur Knight, "SR Goes to the Movies: Easter Parade," *Saturday Review*, April 9, 1960, 36.

Chapter Eight

Of Medieval Ballads and Movie Musicals

Walt Disney and the Robin Hood Legend

Shea T. Brode with Douglas Brode

The tales of Robin Hood constitute one of the most influential and celebrated hero stories of England, originating in oral tradition, running through literary manifestations, and, beginning in the early twentieth century, inhabiting cinema as well. Historically, the folklore that follows Robin dates back to the eleventh century, though his impact remains significant today, and not only in the character's country of origin. According to historian Justin Paonessa, "Robin Hood has remained one of the most infamous outlaws in . . . (world) history. His popularity has transcended national boundaries."[1] The impact of the Robin Hood phenomenon appears virtually indestructible, having lasted more than six hundred years. This appeal cracks barriers between the public at large and academics, largely owing to the ongoing image of a common man as rebel-hero, the noble outlaw, which proves equally intriguing to highbrows, middlebrows, and lowbrows, if perhaps in different forms of presentation.

As for the English, only King Arthur has remained as significant an icon. He is, of course, a classicist hero, symbolizing the status quo at its finest; Robin Hood, on the contrary, embodies a romantic ideal, protestation against the establishment at its most corrupt. Despite any differences, like Arthurian fable, contemporary Robin Hood tales must achieve a delicate balance: holding on to universal/essential elements found in the earliest versions while adjusting to the needs of a particular auteur as well as the time period during which the new version is produced. According to J. C. Holt, "The legend endured through adaptation. In each generation it acquired new twists from shifts in the composition, outlook and interests of the audience, or changes in the level of literacy, or development in the means of communication."[2] As successive civilizations long for a hero, particularly during times of social stress and cultural change, they oftentimes return to Robin. Simply put, modern takes on the character may displace one another, but the core idea of the outlaw/antihero never dies.

Not surprisingly, then, Walt Disney, one of the most important voices in twentieth-century entertainment, was drawn to this material not once but twice. Neal Gabler states in his biography that "in 1966 alone, the year of his death, 240 million people saw a Disney movie, a weekly audience of 100 million watched a Disney television show, 80 million read a Disney book, 50 million listened to Disney records, 80 million bought Disney merchandise, 150 million saw a Disney educational film, and nearly 7 million visited Disneyland."[3] Disney's immense international audience establishes him as a populist storyteller, and Robin Hood is a populist character. Walt's first take, *The Story of Robin Hood and His Merrie Men* (1952), was a live-action film, directed in England by Ken Annakin. The second was an animated feature, *Robin Hood* (1973), directed by Wolfgang Weitherman.

Both flow rhythmically through their use of music as a storytelling point of emphasis, a longtime Disney technique particularly well suited to a story that began in the medieval ballad tradition. Individually, sound and songs serve as frames while driving the plot itself. The 1950s version begins, continuously cuts to, and then concludes not with Robin but Allan-a-Dale, as actions rise and fall, one sequence segueing into another. His character transforms what might have been a generic B+ picture into a true Disney movie (think of Jiminy Cricket in the animated *Pinocchio* or Buddy Ebsen as George Russel in the live-action *Davy Crockett*), and the result is a prototypically Disney onscreen equivalent of a British folk ballad: "Come listen to me, you gallants so free, / All you that love mirth for to hear, / And I will tell of a bold outlaw, / That lived in Nottinghamshire."[4]

Here the action proper begins, as it does in versions from the centuries-old folk tradition, such as "A True Tale of Robin Hood": "Both Gentlemen, or yeomen bould, / Or whatsoever you are, / To have a stately story tould, / Attention now prepare. / It is a tale of Robbin Hood, / That I to you will tell, / Which being rightly understood, / I know will please you well."[5]

Passed along from person to person (each temporal interpreter imparting to the piece his or her own style) and community to community, whether time or place (adjusting the poem/song for its then-current audience), the versions changed slightly with the passage of time. In both Disney films, the narrative thrust is consistently highlighted by Allan's sly Disneyesque commentary. According to film historian Douglas Brode, "Allan-a Dale, so often eliminated from film versions (he does not appear in Warner Brothers' epic incarnation starring Errol Flynn, directed by Michael Curtiz), is here as played by Elton Haytes central to the story."[6] The operative word is "central," even as Jiminy Cricket (a minor figure in Collodi) comes to dominate the Disney Version: he literally becomes the center of the action (storywise and in the film's frames), a narrator who almost appears to direct what occurs onscreen, perhaps standing in for Walt himself.

Disney highlights both the playful aspect of action (likely emphasized for the family audience) of "green men" heartily joining together in the woods and, with far grimmer lyrics and musical tone, the manner in which this outlaw community operates as a group, clashing with the rawest brand of capitalism in the guise of a villainous aristocrat, Prince John, and a cynical social climber, the Sheriff. First, however, the gang must come together since, as is always true in a Disney film, this is less about any rugged individualist fighting alone but the depiction of a true community of like-minded "brothers" (and, when Maid Marian joins in, a sister, too).

One of the most memorable moments occurs with the introduction of Much, aka Midge, the Miller's son (Hal Osmond), not only bringing on board one more traditional cast member but, beyond that, cementing relationships within Robin's group. With sight and sound fused in the manner only movies can achieve, Robin (Richard Todd) searches for hidden loot in the flour bags while Allan lyrically fills us in with precisely the information we could not grasp by simply watching. In the Disney Version, Much arcs from small-scale raw capitalist to full member of the bandit community, concerned with others even at his own expense. Since Maid Marian (Joan Rice, here appealingly disguised as a pretty "boy") joins in the gleeful brawling, the sequence offers a prime example of Disney's ability to make virtually any preexisting subject matter his own, precisely as all authors and auteurs have always done, being not mere interpreters of some other true artist's work but visionaries, with a unique style perfectly suited to the chosen subject matter.

Much was one of the only named members of Robin's gang in the earliest versions. Both playful jaunting and dress-up were employed throughout those stories. In "Robin Hood and the Potter," the antihero exchanges clothes with the Potter. Likewise in "Robin Hood and Allin a Dale": "And when he came bold Robin before, / Robin askt him courteously, / 'O hast thou any money to spare / For my merry men and me?' / 'I have no money,' the young man said, / 'But five shillings and a ring.'"[7]

As in Disney's film, this ancient Allan will see the light, joining Robin to fight for the greater cause. Again, onscreen elements link the Disney Version to other Disney works of the same period: in the Darling home, for instance, the children play in dress-up before yet another English green man, Peter Pan, arrives on the scene.

One of the most iconic scenes has Robin initially encounter Little John (James Robertson Justice) on a bridge. The earliest telling of this incident in the ballads neatly sets the stage for Disney's version: "Lo! See my staff; it is lusty and tough, / Now here on the bridge we will play; / Whoever falls in, the other shall win."[8]

Long before Walt, this particular anecdote revealed what Disney would embellish: a fun, playful side of men of common stock as they naturally bond. In the film, as in the poem, they swing and parry, back and forth, each singing praises to the other: "'With all my whole heart to thy humor I yield, / I scorn in the least to give out,' / This said, they fell to't without more dispute, / And their staffs they did flourish about."[9]

Their mutual respect provides a foil for the cynical alliance between the film's villains (both "respectable" men), cynical Prince John (Hubert Gregg) and the Machiavellian Sheriff (Peter Finch). They attempt to use one another, not for a common goal but for individual gain. When villains speak, here as elsewhere in Disney, they employ nasty prose; as to the heroes, their dialogue comes close to turning into lilting song, the live-action version on the verge of becoming, like the later animated movie, a musical.

Both are filled with songs. Each features its own unique variation on "The Outlaw's Song" as a basic theme. Again, a comparison to *Davy Crockett*, appearing several years later, is in order: Like Robin and Little John or Allan, Crockett (Fess Parker) and Russell (Buddy Ebsen) are played as antiauthoritarian, standing against that film's Prince (Basil Ruysdael as general and later president Andrew Jackson) and his sheriff-like minion, Norton (William Bakewell). In that movie, like this one, righteous rebellion against stiff, conventional, arrogant, even wicked men (the removal of the Cherokee people from their land by corrupt politicians and self-interested businessmen) is carried not only by onscreen action but, in the consistent Disney manner, in song as well, driving home the anti-elitist moral.

The rebellious hero's accomplishments are always followed by "The Outlaw's Song," which, in Disney's films drawn from early ballads, offers a realistic statement of an antihero's "plight and plaint."[10] The Robin stanzas, originally sung casually at inns and taverns, were in time rendered more literary when, for more middle-class patrons, they were re-presented in a reading, often set to music. With listeners joining in, the manner of presentation mirrored the work's basic statement of a need for community among common people, enriching their singular lives by bringing the public together not only to listen but also sing in hearty group activity. Holt states: "Robin, whether real or imaginary, was a product of society where the threshold which separated lawful behavior from self-help by force of arms was indistinct and easily crossed."[11] Faith, as well as hope, is gained, back then or right now, by those who relate to the Robin Hood paradigm in times of doubt and dismay.

As performed ballads evolved into written prose and poetry, "Diversification came easily. In every generation performers and authors assessed their audience afresh and combined their own inventiveness and powers of expression with what came down to them as a literary tradition by word of mouth."[12] Precisely this aspect of the work, rather than merely the characters and plot, is what Disney set out to emphasize in 1952 and 1973. Both Disney versions not only retell the tale but serve as origination stories, making the eponymous antihero's rise to status as an alternative "prince" a significant part of our viewing experience. There are significant differences, however, in the ways the Walt and post-Walt movies develop their unique angles on this preexisting piece. In the live-action film, each segment concerns the evolution of a friendship (once more relating this to every other Disney movie, live action or animated), and also suggesting (ironically) that true chivalry is more likely to be found in the most natural and common people than aristocrats. Disney's live-action Robin is not, like Errol Flynn in the Warner film, aristocratic Lord Locksley at tale's beginning, though this common lad earns such status through hard, decent work by film's end, even as Disney's Crockett only gradually becomes "king" of the wild frontier through self-sacrificing acts of courage. In the animated version, while the first film's bonds-of-friendship theme remains significant, emphasis shifts to the power of a more individualistic hero whose inspirational qualities impact the masses, causing them to join in the good fight. The first Disney version might be perceived as expressing those essentially communal values Disney embraced while supporting Roosevelt's New Deal during the 1930s and early 1940s; the second could be conceived as reflection of Walt's Republican-style rugged individualism during the last days of his life. After all, the second film is named only for Robin Hood; the first shared his "billing" with other "Merrie Men."

In each, however, what remains consistent is the idea of a hero who cannot, will not be separated from music, a Disney device still underlining such films as *The Little Mermaid* and *The Lion King*. In the 1973 film, the initial onscreen images, as in the earlier version, feature a storybook opening to allow Disney's movie to leap up off the pages, insisting that, music aside, there's always a literary basis to such a piece. Employing anamorphic tropes, Allan-a-Dale becomes a crowing rooster. Notably, Robin and Little John have already entered outlawry as the curtain rises. Mark Pinsky notes that "Robin, a fox, and Little John, a bear, are relaxing in Sherwood Forest when they are ambushed by the Sheriff of Nottingham, another bear, who wants to hang them."[13] Though a young man/sly fox, this Robin, despite the appeal of animation for children, appears relatively mature. The earlier film hinted, despite the presence of a grown man in the role, that Robin was a teenager, fitting enough for an era in which James Dean embodied such figures in *East of Eden* (1954) and *Rebel Without a Cause* (1955). However, the teenage Robin—being a Disney character—is no rebel without a cause, rather a rebel with one. There isn't a generation gap between Rob and his father, Fitzooth (Reginald Tate), since this noble figure in no way resembles the overly authoritarian (Raymond Massey) and pathetically weak (Jim Backus) father figures in the Dean films but a rough-hewn commoner the lad can aspire to be like.[14] This is facilitated by making father and son working-class types, again in comparison to the better-known 1938 epic, "in which Robin is introduced as a knight, if one who prefers the freedom of the wood to any cramped castle."[15] Disney's initial Rob is a hero not only *for* but *of* the folk.[16]

In Disney's cartoon, Robin's gang forms as a direct result of his actions. Missing of course is the memorable friendly bridge duel. In its place, we watch them roll around and splash each other in the water. Clearly, John is here less a sidekick than an equal in heroism, a voice of reason, not unlike Odysseus to Achilles in *The Iliad*. The 1973 version also openly raises issues only suggested in 1952: "Are we good guys or bad?" John asks. Robin explains they are taking from those who are more fortunate to give to those who are less, that is, literally spreading the wealth around, as President Barack Obama would in time insist was a necessary aspect of enlightened capitalism. By omitting the killing of Robin's father and the formation of the band of merry men, this film explores the mysterious energy of a hero thrust into the position of leader without necessarily choosing this role; Disney's earlier Robin seemingly set out to create an outlaw community.

The live-action film (like the Crockett movie of its era, with bloody battles involving Indians and Mexicans) emphasizes the grimness of a fight for freedom; more in the cartoon tradition, the latter settles for allowing the antiheroes to make fools of the mostly caricatured villains through goofy, good-natured tricks (our heroes dress as women, for instance), setting this film more in the tradition of the ancient trickster-hero (true of many old ballads) than some epic figure. According to Pinsky, "Prince John is an insecure, mother-obsessed thumb-sucker, a male lion with no mane, and a crown too big for his head,"[17] as both sheriff and king are portrayed as blundering fools. In this version, Robin's defense of his assault is that the current administration is not only corrupt but also incompetent, again altering the tale in significant ways. As to tricksterism, this can directly be traced to a key ballad source, "Robin Hood and the Potter," in which the two switch clothes to fool the sheriff: "Y well prey the, good potter, / A felischepe well thow hafe? / Geffe me they clothying, and thow schalt hafe myne; / Y well go to Notynggam."[18]

Similarly, in this tale as well as in Disney's animated feature, Robin employs disguise to trick the establishment. In the 1970s, Disney's Robin and his followers become considerably more puckish than in 1952, though that aspect certainly was suggested. Pinsky reflects that "tax dodgers are in stocks and, according to the rooster acting as troubadour and narrator, the people of the town are starving to death."[19] Perhaps reflecting the *Mean Streets/Taxi Driver* sensibility of the early 1970s, this film's singing narrator conveys the notion of a truly miserable world. By story's end, however,

Robin provides a symbol of hope for the many, Disney countering the sense of hopelessness in both those concurrent Martin Scorsese movies. Disney's on-the-edge character does not, like Travis Bickle, ascertain that our ruined world is hopeless; rather, Disney's "outlaw brings another gift: hope."[20]

The action revolves around a musical hero who dances rather than walks about the distressed countryside, like all Disney protagonists making things better, though the strategies are different in Disney's two takes on this subject. In the animated version, a song of Robin's victory is neatly recycled as a ballad of failure for prince and sheriff. Ultimately, though, these are Disney films, so the ending must be absolute: victory for not only the rebel heroes but the common man, saved from evil aristocrats, attesting again to the populist theme inherent in all of this studio's projects. Our folk legend and honorable outlaw has restored order to Nottingham. In 1952, the piece ends with Allan-a-Dale, once more central, skipping off into the sunset with a Disneyesque dog by his side. In 1973, while his cartoon equivalent continues to tell the story through song, the focus remains more on Robin and Marian, the balladeer still telling the story as they ride off together.

"That's the way it really happened." Or so he explains. We know the song and the stories continue, but Disney's versions have come to an end. Still, and forever:

> Men voiced their longing for a more orderly life free from "injustice" in practical fashion, if often to little effect, through the channels of government. They also took flight in their imagination with an outlawed hero who, at one and the same time, symbolized disorder and set it all to rights.[21]

The central and consistent ideology of Robin Hood has to do with sustaining hope by believing in the common man and accepting that, at times, supposed criminality can be positive. This once-and-future outlaw (Rob Roy in the Highlands, Jesse James in the American West, etc.) means much to those who need hope but are not, during their own era, able to believe those in charge can provide that necessary element. Robin's legend (some might say myth) may be masked by historical questions, but the story's impact, as twice portrayed by Disney, never expires. Every bit as impressive: only Disney's films achieve what no others have even attempted, ascertaining that the musical ballad served as proper predecessor for musical movies.

NOTES

1. Justin Paonessa, "Robin Hood: A Myth in Flux," *Western Illinois Historical Review* 5 (Spring 2013): 66–90.

2. J. C. Holt, *Robin Hood* (repr., London: Thames and Hudson, 1993), 123.

3. Neil Gabler, *Walt Disney: The Triumph of the American Imagination* (New York: Random House, 2006), xii.

4. "Robin Hood and Allin a Dale," in *Robin Hood and Other Outlaw Tales*, ed. Stephen Knight and Thomas Ohlgren (Kalamazoo, MI: Medieval Institute Publications, 1997), http://d.lib.rochester.edu/teams/text/robin-hood-and-allin-a-dale.

5. "A True Tale of Robin Hood," in ibid., http://d.lib.rochester.edu/teams/text/true-tale-of-robin-hood.

6. Douglas Brode, *From Walt to Woodstock: How Disney Created the Counterculture* (Austin: University of Texas Press, 2004), 56.

7. "Robin Hood and Allin a Dale," in Knight and Ohlgren, *Robin Hood*.

8. "Robin Hood and Little John," in Knight and Ohlgren, *Robin Hood*, http://d.lib.rochester.edu/teams/text/robin-hood-and-little-john.

9. Ibid.

10. Holt, *Robin Hood*, 12.

11. Ibid., 12.

12. Ibid., 16.

13. Mark I. Pinsky, *The Gospel according to Disney: Faith, Trust, and Pixie Dust* (Louisville, KY: Westminster John Knox, 2004), 94.

14. Brode, *From Walt to Woodstock*, 57.

15. Ibid.

16. Ibid., 60.

17. Pinsky, *Gospel according to Disney*, 90.

18. "Robin Hood and the Potter," in Knight and Ohlgren, *Robin Hood*, http://d.lib.rochester.edu/teams/text/robin-hood-and-the-potter.

19. Pinsky, *Gospel according to Disney*, 95.

20. Ibid., 96.

21. Holt, *Robin Hood*, 12.

Chapter Nine

"Do You Believe in Fairies?"

Peter Pan, *Walt Disney, and Me*

Elizabeth Bell

> Some say we that we are different people at different periods of our lives, changing not through effort of will, which is a brave affair, but in the easy course of nature every ten years or so. . . . Perhaps we do change; except a little something in us which is no larger than a mote in the eye, and that, like it, dances in front of us beguiling us all our days.[1]

I think it odd that J. M. Barrie, author of *Peter Pan*, wrote these words in his dedication to the published play script in 1904. After all, *Pan*, at its every mention, is about a willfully permanent childhood, a deliberate standstill, an impossible stasis. Yet Barrie introduces his play with discourse of change and its inevitability.

Every ten years or so, as Barrie predicts, I have changed. Yet, and again following Barrie, a something—which is no larger than a mote in my eye—remains the same. This little something has always danced before of me, beguiling me, teasing me, steering me. I suspect that writing this will not exorcise its presence but reacknowledge its power over me. J. M. Barrie invented this "little something," Walt Disney canonized her, and my father called me Tinker Bell.

The power of that name and that image has been remarkable in my life, with equal time dedicated to living up to the name and living it down. For many years, I've denied both the nomenclature and its authority: a nickname like *Tinker* does not conjure images of scholar, teacher, mother, wife, or any of my other, later labels. On the other hand, *Tinker* enables me to make claims about Disney, Pan, and the experience of growing up female in Baby Boomer America. Teresa deLauretis maintains, "The construction of gender goes on today through the various technologies of gender (e.g., cinema) and institutional discourses (e.g., theory) with power to control the field of social meaning and thus produce, promote, and 'implant' representations of gender."[2] If so, I had two powerful teachers: Walt Disney and Tinker Bell.

As an icon in the Disney canon, Tinker Bell stands for the Disney enterprise: an animated logo, a dispenser of "Disney dust," an official greeter at the gate and screen of the Magic Kingdom. Unlike Mickey, Tink has no public relations team of handlers, makes no public appearances. Her presence at the parks is implied, a marked absence, a "mote in the eye" of those who willingly engage in Disney magic. For me, Tinker Bell is no fictive creation. She is real. And I am she.

> There was another light in the room now, a thousand times brighter than the night-lights . . . but when it came to rest for a second you saw it was a fairy, no longer than your hand, but still growing.[3]

Disney did identity work for me. Identity, never constant, never monolithic, might also be described, like story, as a tension between belief and disbelief, a willing creation and a willing suspension of self. My own complicity in and resistance to Disney identity is anecdotal of the "collective" work of growing up. For, as Barrie tells us in the first line of *Peter Pan*, "All children, except one, grow up."[4]

WHEN BABIES LAUGH AND CRY: THE BEGINNING OF FAIRIES

If *Pan* is a story of unending childhood, it is also a story about stories. In one novel version, Wendy is engaged to join Peter in Never Land to tell stories to the lost boys. "'Don't go, Peter,' she entreated, 'I know such lots of stories.'"[5] In Disney, Mr. Darling reaches the peak of his rushing-to-get-ready-bluster with: "Wendy? Story? I might have known!" For all of Wendy's promises, however, it is Peter who tells this story's first story: "You see, Wendy, when the first baby laughed for the first time, its laugh broke into a thousand pieces, and they all went skipping about, and that was the beginning of fairies."[6]

The story of the beginning of my fair name also begins with babies. "You were a *terrible* baby," my mother always began. Not unlike Wendy learning the stories she would later tell the Lost Boys, I would say to myself, "I was a *terrible* baby," working to match my mother's inflection. "Because you were so terrible, your father called you Stinker." Here, the story became my own, abbreviated, much repeated, in all introductory situations. "Stinker became Tinker," I would rush through the insufficient explanation, "and Tinker fit with Bell, and I've been called Tinker all my life."

No "Disney dust" (the company name for special effect sparkles that signal any magical act) accompany my shrug, as it frequently does in *Pan* when Tink strikes an attitude. Yet the name traveled with me like a cloud of Disney dust, and I wore it for ten years, like Pigpen in Peanuts, oblivious to its presence. "For better or for worse," writes Elizabeth Stone in *Black Sheep and Kissing Cousins: How Our Family Stories Shape Us*, "and whether we collaborate with our families or not, we are shaped by our families' notions of our identities. The image they mirror back to us exists earlier and more substantially than we ourselves do."[7] We all collaborated in my created identity. While a more contemporary audience might have Julia Roberts in mind, Stephen Spielberg's trick-of-the-screen Tinker Bell in *Hook*, Disney's Tink provided our mirror.

My mother drove me to ballet, where the mirror was floor to ceiling, two times a week, for ten years. I was never very good, but teachers called me "sprite-like." Ballet taught me to be aware of my body, to be conscious of the centers—both the delicate balance of *pointe* work and the glow of center stage. I walked into every classroom on September 1 (as) a known quantity: Tinker Bell, the good study, the ready helper, the "good girl." My teachers seemed to already know my name, something I found puzzling then. The work of figure/ground was done for me by my name. I materialized from the background of other good girls—Debbies and Jennifers and Connies—as if by Disney magic.

Every week, I was a star. On Sunday evenings, I introduced *The Wonderful World of Color*, flying across the screen, stopping only to drench the TV image in ribbons of color streaming down. "There you are!" my brothers would half tease. I took happiness for granted then. Like other eleven-year-old girls described by psychologist Carol Gilligan, "the hallmarks of the preadolescent child depict a child secure in her sense of herself, confident in the substance of her beliefs, and sure of her ability to do something of value in the world."[8] Unlike other eleven-year-old girls, I was certain that I could fly.

Postmodernism: Stories about Stories

As to Barrie, Disney*, Pan* and Tink, here is a story that "was both never written and, paradoxically, has never ceased to be written."[9] Jacqueline Rose makes that surprising statement as she attempts to trace the genesis of Peter. Barrie supposedly created the story in playful episodes with "the Five" Llewellyn Davies boys, whom he later adopted at the death of their parents. Not unlike Lewis Carroll's creation of *Alice*, the tale was born in live storytelling performances. Barrie writes in the dedication, "To the Five," "I suppose I always knew that I made Peter by rubbing the five of you violently together, as savages with two sticks produce a flame. That is all he is, the spark I got from you.[10] "

Other critics trace *Pan*'s genesis to a short story in Barrie's 1902 collection *The Little White Bird*, in which an adult male tells the story of Pan to a small boy he intends to steal. After the play was committed to paper during rehearsals and staged in 1904 under the title "Peter Pan, Or the Boy Who Would Not Grow Up," Barrie "farmed out" the writing of the novel versions to numerous authors, aimed at different age groups, illustrated by various artists. Rose's (1984) bibliography lists 45 different publications of *Peter Pan*; 22 of these *not* authored by Barrie. Of these 22, five are published by Disney. Whether live storytelling, play, novel, script, or performance, *Pan* is illustrative of the story's diaspora, the impossibility of claims to authorship, the contestation of interpretation, and slippage between genres—a thoroughly modern example of a poststructuralist view of writing; "gone is the sense of literary creation as the plenishment of any empty page" for writing "is an exchange already in progress."[11]

The Teen Years in the Mermaid Lagoon

Disney's canon centers on adolescence and the business of growing up. Feminist theorists claim this process is different for boys and girls. Gilligan maintains

> if the secrets of male adolescence revolve around the harboring of continuing attachments that cannot be represented in the logic of fairness, the secrets of the female adolescent pertain to the silencing of her own voice, a silencing enforced by the wish not to hurt others but also by the fear that, in speaking, her voice will not be heard.[12]

Mixed messages, according to Gilligan, are the hallmark of adolescent change for white, middle-class girls, "a turning point when girls' desire for relationships and for knowledge comes up against the wall of Western culture and a resistance breaks out."[13] In a culture that memorializes independence and autonomy as the epitome of maturity, girls' need for connection and relationships is seen as debilitation, not development. Moreover, the cost of connection is a high one: "these girls struggle daily with the seduction of the unattainable: to be all things to all people, to be perfect girls and model women."[14]

Disney's *Pan* taught me how to be, not a perfect girl, but Tink. I count myself lucky to have emerged from my adolescent years unscathed. As a teenager, I was one of the girls with "clear-skinned smiles," Janice Ian sings of her in her lament "Seventeen"—one of the "perfect girls" others perceived as the "unattainable." Brown and Gilligan capture such a universal tension:

> Understandably, popular girls are outwardly doted on at the same time that
> they are privately envied or despised. Other girls watch the popular girl closely
> since she has the potential to "use" or hurt people and also to elevate them in
> the eyes of adults. [15]

My own ready-made identity as Tinker, and my own efforts to live up to that
identity, became a kind of permission to be "cute" in a way that mediated
between being doted on and being despised. Not unlike puppy play or cuddly
kittens, my name linked me to a package of behaviors and attributes that
licensed mischief, laughter, and fun. In my Baby Boomer, white, middle-
class neighborhood, seventeen eleven-year-old girls filled a three-block ra-
dius. I never endured the angst of teenhood, the alienation from peers, the
disdain of adults, only the puzzled looks at others' first encounter with my
name. *Tinker* was an antibody against rejection, which Gilligan calls "the
thin dark line of not you; we—whoever 'we' are—do not want to be with
you." [16]

The politics of female adolescence is actualized in Never Land. The Lagoon is teeming with mermaids who align to drown girls like Wendy:

> It was among Wendy's lasting regrets that all the time she was on the island
> she never had a civil word from one of them. . . . [The mermaids] loved to
> bask, combing out their hair in a lazy way that quite irritated her; or she might
> even swim, on tiptoe as it were, to within a yard of them, but then they saw her
> and dived, probably splashing her with their tails, not by accident, but inten-
> tionally. [17]

Tink, however, flies above the Mermaid Lagoon—and Wendy—oblivious to
their politics.

SECOND SIGHT: THE DOUBLE-VISION OF ADOLESCENCE

> "I ran away the day I was born . . . because I heard father and mother talking of
> what I was to be when I became a man. I want always to be a little boy and to
> have fun."—Peter [18]

For writer Sallie Tisdale, America's ongoing fascination with sexuality is
marked by both inarticulation and immaturity:

> American society is adolescent; there is no other word for our restlessness and
> preachy finger-shaking. We live in a world filled with a continual proliferation
> of sexual images. . . . Still, we find it almost unbearable to talk openly about
> sex—with our friends, our lovers, our parents and children. The result is cultu-
> ral puberty: lewd, leering, intensely curious and ashamed and prudish all at
> once. [19]

For Gilligan, the politics of puberty for girls are marked not (as with boys) by lewdness and leering but by another kind of double vision, another second look—not at the idealized women (Ariel in *The Little Mermaid*, Tink in *Peter Pan*) drawn by men at the Disney Studio[20] but at the real women around them. Gilligan's theories about white middle-class adolescent girls' development center on the palpable transformation from articulate, playful, irreverent eleven-year-olds to quiet, unsure, hesitant twelve-year-olds—this occurs when girls internalize and enact cues they learn from adult women. Brown and Gilligan call this

> voice training by adults, especially adult "good women," which undermines these girls' experiences and reinforces images of female perfection by implying that "nice girls" are always calm, controlled, quiet, that they never cause a ruckus, are never noisy, bossy, or aggressive, are not anxious and do not cause trouble.[21]

Girls learn to double their vision, their own experiences running counter to authority, as they confront "two truths, two versions of a story, two voices revealing two points of view."[22] Girls in Gilligan's research wrote in their diaries "about 'building a little shield,' about 'getting afraid to say when you're mad at somebody,' about 'losing confidence in myself. I was losing track of myself, really, and losing the kind of person I was.'"[23] Tinker Bell was my "little shield," not to cloak my true "self," but my permission to "cause a ruckus" and make trouble, which as Judith Butler writes, "was . . . something one should never do precisely because that would get one in trouble." Butler continues: "Hence, I concluded that trouble is inevitable and the task, how best to make it, what best way to be in it."[24] My kind of trouble, however, involved a double vision between my own duplicity and my own willing performance of Disney's Tinker.

As I read a 1953 review of Disney's film, I was surprised at my own internalization of Tink's description:

> The show-stealer is Tinker Bell, Peter Pan's lustrously blonde playmate. . . . Through the magic of the animated cartoon, she is a bosomy little vamp, not much bigger than a dot of light, who flits about enchantingly with a silvery tinkle of bells in a sprinkle of golden pixie dust.[25]

While male spectatorship and the pleasure of watching "a bosomy little vamp" may be questionable, even at sixteen I understood this kind of doubled vision. John Berger claims that "Men watch women. Women watch themselves being looked at."[26]

What saved me from succumbing to that definition of self, an object of others' pleasurable sight, was my understanding that Tinker was thoroughly contrived, clearly a performance, a "drag show" of teenage girlhood. I could hold her and her accomplishments at arm's length, like Peter shaking Tink to dispense pixie dust.

GENDERING PETER PAN/SEXING TINKER BELL

Pan is thoroughly saturated with a confusion of sexuality and gender roles. Barrie describes Peter as "a lovely boy, clad in skeleton leaves and the juices that ooze out of trees."[27] What Barrie never makes explicit, however, is the casting of an adult woman to play him. Jacqueline Rose describes the textual Peter as "on the edge of difference between boys and girls";[28] she describes the staged Peter "as both child and woman."[29] Transvestitism in the late Victorian theater was not new; women playing boy's roles gave the audience the opportunity for licensed spectatorship—permission to look at women (the Lost Boys also were played by women) scantily clad in tights—what Michael Booth calls "a sexual, pictorial, and spectacular combination of ideal purity and handsome flesh."[30] Long after Victoria's death, the tradition of a woman playing Peter lives on. From Maude Adams in 1902, Jean Arthur in 1950, Mary Martin in 1965, to Cathy Rigby in 1993, Peter, unlike Pinocchio, never dreams of being a "real boy."

Walt Disney reversed this long tradition. His Pan, voiced by Bobby Driscoll, is a preadolescent boy and concomitantly oblivious to the constant flirting of the girls: Tinker Bell, Wendy, Princess Tiger Lily, the mermaids. It was as if Disney, so thoroughly immersed in the fantasy of an asexual boyhood, ignored any questions of Peter's sexuality. (Stephen Spielberg, often called the "son of Disney," did the same, casting Robin Williams in *Hook*.) Under Disney's direction, Never Land becomes another geographic space at Disney World, not unlike Frontierland and Tom Sawyer's (aka Pirate's) Island, where boyhood games and backyard play are memorialized.[31] John Grant describes Disney's Peter in a way that captures not that character's perpetual youth but his perpetual *boyhood*: "friendly or hostile according to whim, obeying moral rules totally divorced from those of Western culture, totally egocentric and totally uncaring about others' anguish. In short, he is very much like a . . . well, like a little boy."[32] While Disney erases all traces of sexuality, he boldly draws male privilege. Peter is very much the center of the world.

Though Disney reversed Peter's gender/sex topography, he reinvested Tinker Bell with body. Leaving the stage tradition of Tink as a spot of light, Disney latches on, like a pit bull, to Barrie's description: "It was a girl called Tinker Bell exquisitely gowned in a skeleton leaf, cut low and square, through which her figure could be seen to the best advantage. She was slightly inclined to *embonpoint*."[33] Tink's first solo appearance lands her on a hand mirror, admiring her bottom. I wonder if the Disney animators looked up "embonpoint"; they altogether captured the word in this scene. From the French *en bon point*, "in good condition."

Not all critics find this somatype pleasing. "Look at that wretched sprite with the wand and the over-sized buttocks which announces every Disney program on TV," wrote Frances Clarke Sayers, a lecturer in Library Science at UCLA. "She is a vulgar little thing, who has been too long at the sugar bowls."[34] Disney thoroughly evacuates class representation from his depiction of Tink, replacing class with ass. According to one urban legend, Disney's animators modeled her on Marilyn Monroe. John Grant adamantly insists, "This was not in fact true: she was modeled by the actress Margaret Kerry, pains being taken by the Disney publicists to point out that Ms. Kerry had a totally different personality from the pouting, spiteful, jealous Tinker Bell."[35] Still, Bob Thomas, longtime "official" Disney historiographer, confirms rather than dispels the Monroe connection: "[*Pan*] was scorned by the Barrie loyalists, particularly for its portrayal of Tinker Bell as a Marilyn Monroe kind of nymphet."[36] For Richard Schickel, Tink is "a midget (but physically well endowed) nymphet."[37] Marc Davis, who animated many of Tinker Bell's scenes and ought to know the "truth" of the legend, suggests, "She would have made a marvelous model. It'd be great if you could draw Marilyn Monroe, but she was not a consideration."[38]

While Peter's sexuality is erased, Tink's is piled on with a vengeance, linked narratively to an American icon of sexuality and vulnerability.[39] Through Marilyn, Tink invited me into a gendered sexuality that alternated between loyalty and spitefulness, indulgence and insouciance. Boys were pawns, easily moved, manipulated, and sacrificed. Barrie's narrator warns one of the Lost Boys: "Poor kind Tootles, there is danger in the air for you to-night. Take care lest an adventure is now offered you, which, if accepted, will plunge you into deepest woe. . . . Tink, who is bent on mischief this night, is looking for a tool, and she thinks you the most easily tricked of the boys. 'Ware Tinker Bell."[40]

While Monroe became iconic of the 1950s and 1960s with its "Does she or doesn't she?" coquettishness, I was a teenager of the 1960s and 1970s, when sex was both a means to get to know each other and a way to rebel against authority. Lynne Segal writes, "Political generations matter. . . . However in tune with the times we may try to be, we are all products of particular historical moments."[41] I was of the sexual generation that came of age with two divergent answers to the question, "Are you on the pill?" The first time I was asked that question, I was shocked, offended, "What kind of girl do you think . . . ?" The second time the question arose, I was quite pleased with myself and answered, "Of course." Yet the sexual bandwagon of the 1960s and 1970s was a duplicitous ride: "It's important to remember that the sexual revolution was experienced by women who were not raised to be feminists but, rather, a generation that was reared to please men."[42] Too-tles may have been "easily tricked," but he also was immensely pleased.

"TO VIVISECT A FAIRY"

Again, as to Barrie's claim that changing one's self "through effort of will is a brave affair." In the decade that marked my twenties, I attempted to change. More than that, I tried to kill Tink. I didn't drink poison as she did in Barrie's play, sacrificing herself for Peter; I didn't save Peter from Hook's bomb, as she did in Disney's film. When I started college, I merely introduced myself as Elizabeth. With that new name, I carved a new identity: a serious student, a fan of foreign films, a smoker with huge horned-rimmed glasses, a loner in a world of ideas. My new self, as far from sprite-like as I could manage, served me well; I earned my bachelor's degree in two and a half years and entered graduate school.

But my family—my parents and my brothers   never let go of that earlier identity, which leaked repeatedly into my twenties. My first roommate and I sat exhausted on our couch after a day of moving into a duplex. The phone rang. Alice picked it up, said hello, momentarily listening. Without missing a beat, she handed me the phone: "*You* must be Tinker."

She was *back!* With a vengeance. Two years later, in my new roles as wife and mother, my family, amoeba-like, surrounded and absorbed my life. I was desperately unhappy. Gilligan's web of connections, the "ideals of human relationship—the vision that self and other will be treated as of equal worth,"[43] constituted a web that caught and held me. Janice Ian again: girls with "clear-skinned smiles" soon "marry young and then retire." To my parents, my husband, my in-laws, I was still sixteen, still "Tinker"; my worth still measured by my earlier acquiescence to a performance I no longer wanted to perform. The politics of adolescence I had escaped—the angst, despair, uncertainty—visited me fifteen years late, woven anachronistically into the realities of adult life. So in my thirties I stepped into divorce, a new love, a new job—knowing full well that Tinker would not, could not, cross the line with me. Her death was a welcome one. No one clapped her back into life, answering Peter's famous plea, "Do you believe in fairies?"

In a *Times Literary Supplement Review*, J. M. Barrie's short story collection, *The Little White Bird* is described as "all Barrie-ness; whimsical, senti-mental, profound, ridiculous Barrie-ness."[44] Disney films might be described by the same adjectives—and by the same critical meltdown. Barrie and Disney invite us to set aside our critical capacities, to succumb to the pleasures of their worlds: "To analyze its merits and defects—its fun, its pathos, its character-drawing, or its sentimentality, its improbability, its lack of cohesion—would be to vivisect a fairy."[45]

Yet for me, such vivisection is imperative to make sense of my life and the image that seduced me into a self that was, by definition, incapable of growth and change. How does one treat Tinker as an independent variable? What other indices in my life—class privilege, race, the heterosexual contract—can be deemed significant? Is it possible, in academic research, to say "'look what happened to me' instead of the orthodox, generalizing goal of suggesting 'this will happen to you.'"[46]

As I searched for examples of showing and telling one's life, I came upon a chance remark by Elspeth Probyn, commenting on the difficulty of academics "trying to explicate the world metonymically from their own situation."[47] Also, I learned that I was not alone—Walkerdine writes: "Tinkerbell, (my father) called me: Tinky: the bluebell fairy, not quite of this world."[48] Our fathers named us after fairies, placing us in a kind of mythical "no man's land": no hierarchies among pixies, sprites, and elves; no work save "wondering whether to put on the smoky blue or the apple-blossom";[49] no growing up in this world. Here we could be girls without risk of repercussion. But our fathers' protection is short-lived, no matter how hard we believe.

For Walkerdine, her fairy nickname provided a place to explore class distinctions, the painful alienation of upward mobility; for me, Tinker Bell provides no metonym for explication, no place to stand for exploration. Tinker was a self—is myself—a body, an attitude, a sexuality, a way of being in the world that I performed differently every ten years: from conception to fourth grade—unconsciously; through adolescence and teenhood—willingly and self-servingly; and, as an adult, resistantly and painfully.

Now, Tinker is a critical epistemology for reviewing how Disney seized and painted Barrie's world. As Tinker, I see that in his *Pan*, Disney draws a boy as the center of the world, and all is moved at his whim. Playful heroics have no place for girls, except as admiring and peripheral audience members for Peter's bravery and conceit, his victories over authority, his exuberant self-congratulation. Girls, especially Tinker, adopt Peter's egocentrism in the "real world" at their own peril. Peter's invisible gender privilege is unveiled if a girl steps into his cocksure shoes.

Barrie and Disney created, in words and in pictures, the script for my emotional life. Collectively, we rewrite that script within the constellation of *possibilities* for growing up. But as an individual, I felt the weight of its limitations. Growing up, after all, was never one of the possibilities in Never Land. All these stories are careful negotiations and transformations of belief: if we, through sheer will, believe well enough and look hard enough, the world will be as we see it. Believing is seeing. My life as Tinker, the multiple texts of Pan, Barrie, and Disney, are constructions built on the willing suspension of disbelief—a belief that gender, class, and race, identities and relationships, sex and love, and the difficult work and play of growing up can be held in abeyance. In my forties, I find myself, like Peter, forgetting that Tink ever existed:

> "O Peter," Wendy said, shocked; but even when she explained he could not remember. "There are such a lot of them," he said. "I expect she is no more." I expect he was right. Fairies don't live long, but they are so little that a short time seems a good while to them. [50]

The comparatively short time I embraced and enacted Tinker Bell seems, now, "a good while." Unknowing colleagues describe me as wickedly funny and irreverent. I can't help but think they're believing and seeing a "mote" dancing between us. For all my murderous attempts, the *power* of story returns. And once again, this time deliberately, critically, and with no small irony, I have lovingly willed her back to life.

Tinker Bell lives!

NOTES

1. Barrie 1928, 8.
2. DeLauretis 1987, 18.
3. Barrie 1911, 29–30.
4. Barrie 1911, 1.
5. Barrie 1911, 42.
6. Barrie 1911, 36.
7. Stone 1988, 167.
8. Gilligan 1982, 30.
9. Rose 1984, 6.
10. Barrie 1928, 3.
11. Willig 1994, 88.
12. Gilligan 1982, 51.
13. Gilligan 1991, 13.
14. Brown and Gilligan 1992, 180.
15. Brown and Gilligan 1992, 101.
16. Gilligan 1991, 14.
17. Barrie 1928, 111–12.
18. Barrie 1928, 32.
19. Tisdale 1994, 14.
20. See, e.g., Bell, 1995.
21. Brown and Gilligan 1992, 61.
22. Brown and Gilligan 1992, 14.
23. Brown and Gilligan 1992, 41.
24. Butler 1990, vii.
25. "New Pictures" 1953, 78.
26. Berger 1972, 47.
27. Barrie 1911, 13.
28. Rose 1984, 28.
29. Rose 1984, 98.
30. Booth 1981, 79.
31. Gottdiener 1982.
32. Grant 1993, 241.
33. Barrie 1911, 29–30.

34. Quoted in Schickel 1968, 299.
35. Grant 1993, 241.
36. Thomas 1991, 102.
37. Schickel 1968, 197.
38. Quoted in Solomon 1989, 192.
39. DePaoli, 1994.
40. Barrie 1911, 69.
41. Segal 1994, 1.
42. Stan 1995, xxii.
43. Gilligan 1982, 63.
44. Quoted in Rose 1984, 23.
45. Quoted in Rose 1984, 23.
46. Bochner 1994, 33.
47. Probyn 1993, 10.
48. Walkerdine 1985, 68.
49. Barrie 1928, 63.
50. Barrie 1911, 231–32.

WORKS CITED

Barrie, J. M. 1911. *Peter Pan*. New York: Charles Scribner's Sons.
———. 1928. *The Plays of J.M. Barrie*. New York: Charles Scribner's Sons.
Bell, Elizabeth. 1995. "Somatexts at the Disney Shop: Constructing the Pentimentos of Women's Animated Bodies." In *From Mouse to Mermaid: The Politics of Film, Gender, and Culture*, edited by Elizabeth Bell, Linda Haas, and Laura Sells, 107–24. Bloomington: Indiana University Press.
Berger, John. 1972. *Ways of Seeing*. London: Penguin.
Bochner, Arthur P. 1994. "Perspectives on Inquiry II: Theories and Stories." In *Handbook of Interpersonal Communication*, 2nd ed., edited by Mark L. Knapp and Gerald R. Miller, 21–41. Thousand Oaks, CA: Sage.
Booth, M. R. 1981. *Victorian Spectacular Theatre, 1850–1920*. London: Routledge and Kegan Paul.
Brown, L. M., and Carol Gilligan. 1992. *Meeting at the Crossroads: Women's Psychology and Girls' Development*. Cambridge, MA: Harvard University Press.
Butler, Judith. 1990. *Gender Trouble: Feminism and the Subversion of Identity*. New York: Routledge.
deLauretis, Teresa. 1987. *Technologies of Gender: Essays on Theory, Film, and Fiction.* Bloomington: Indiana University Press.
DePaoli, G., ed. 1994. *Elvis + Marilyn: 2xImmortal*. New York: Rizzoli.
Gilligan, Carol. 1982. *In a Different Voice: Psychological Theory and Women's Development*. Cambridge, MA: Harvard University Press.
———. 1991. "Joining the Resistance: Psychology, Politics, Girls and Women." In *The Female Body: Figures, Styles, Speculations*, edited by Lawrence Goldstein, 12–47. Ann Arbor: University of Michigan Press.
Gottdiener, K. 1982. "Disneyland: A Utopian Urban Space." In *Urban Life* 11(2), 139–62.
Grant, John. 1993. *Encyclopedia of Walt Disney's Animated Characters*. New York: Hyperion.
"New Pictures." 1953. *Time*, February 2, 78.
Probyn, Elspeth. 1993. *Sexing the Self: Gendered Positions in Cultural Studies*. London: Routledge.
Rose, Jacqueline. 1984. *The Case of Peter Pan or the Impossibility of Children's Fiction.* London: Macmillan.
Schickel, Richard. 1968. *The Disney Version: The Life, Times, Art, and Commerce of Walt Disney*. New York: Simon.
Segal, Lynne. 1994. *Straight Sex: Rethinking the Politics of Pleasure*. Berkeley: University of California Press.

Solomon, Charles. 1989. *Enchanted Drawings: The History of Animation*. New York: Alfred A. Knopf.

Stan, Adele M., ed. 1995. *Debating Sexual Correctness: Pornography, Sexual Harassment, Date Rape, and the Politics of Sexual Equality*. New York: Delta.

Stone, Elizabeth. 1988. *Black Sheep and Kissing Cousins: How Our Family Stories Shape Us*. New York: Times.

Thomas, B. 1991. *Disney's Art of Animation: From Mickey Mouse to Beauty and the Beast*. New York: Hyperion.

Tisdale, Sallie. 1994. *Talk Dirty to Me: An Intimate Philosophy of Sex*. New York: Doubleday.

Walkerdine, Valerie. 1985. "Dreams from an Ordinary Childhood." In *Truth, Dare or Promise: Girls Growing Up in the Fifties*, edited by L. Heron, 63–78. London: Virago Press.

Wittig, R. 1994. *Invisible Rendezvous: Connection and Collaboration in the New Landscape of Electronic Writing*. Hanover, NH: Wesleyan University Press.

Chapter Ten

"In God's Good Time"

20,000 Leagues Under the Sea *and Cold War Culture*

Cynthia J. Miller and A. Bowdoin Van Riper

Struggling with financial problems, stung by a 1941 strike among by its artists, and awakened by wartime contracts to the possibility of live-action work, Walt Disney Studios began to experiment, in the early 1950s, with a series of costume-drama adventure stories. The films were, for the most part, based on British texts and set firmly in romanticized versions of that nation's past: *Treasure Island* (1950), *The Story of Robin Hood* (1952) and *Rob Roy* (1954). The notable exception to the pattern was Jules Verne's *20,000 Leagues under the Sea* (1954).

Verne's novel, serialized in 1869 and first issued as a book in 1870, is a scientific travelogue disguised as an adventure story and overlain with political commentary about freedom and self-determination. Disney's 1954 film adaptation, however, alters the balance between those elements in ways that are individually subtle, but cumulatively radical. In deference to its intended family audience, Disney places the adventure story firmly in the foreground, allowing state-of-the-art underwater photography to passively substitute for Verne's often-ponderous slabs of oceanographic detail. The film also sharpens and updates the novel's political message (murky to begin with, and rendered murkier by nineteenth-century editorial meddling) to fit American preoccupations of the high Cold War era. Finally, in what was considered to be a triumph of production design, it transforms Verne's day-after-tomorrow tale into visual imagery that fills the screen with the color and spectacle audiences had come to expect from the Magic Kingdom.

One among a field of cross-cultural and cross-media adaptations, the "Disney version" of Verne's novel has become a classic among live-action adventure films and a touchstone for contemporary audiences' connection to

Verne's work—one that, for many, surpasses the novel itself. However, as an artifact of a particular historical moment, Disney's *20,000 Leagues* presents not only a storyline updated for Cold War America, but a visual interpretation of Verne's literary imagery that also reflects the postwar era from which it arose—an era in which power, politics, science, and technology converged in previously unimagined ways. From the heavy ironwork and gothic-influenced interior of Nemo's submarine, the *Nautilus*, to the forceful intrusions of culture into nature, Disney's adaptation reflects the vision of a triumphant Cold War superpower, rather than that of a science fiction visionary.

TWENTIETH CENTURY VERNE

A fast-paced adventure story, Disney's adaptation attempts to bring Verne's mid-nineteenth-century tale to life and relevance for a mid-twentieth century audience. Set in 1868, the film follows the adventures of Professor Pierre M. Aronnax (Paul Lukas) and his apprentice, Conseil (Peter Lorre), as they embark on an expedition to discover the truth about reports of a sea monster attacking ships in the Pacific Ocean. Aronnax, a renowned marine biologist from the Paris Museum of Natural History, is compelled by scientific curiosity to join the team, despite reports of deadly destruction from beneath the ocean's depths. The epitome of European intellectualism and refinement, Aronnax stands in sharp contrast to his North American counterparts—particularly master harpooner Ned Land (Kirk Douglas), whose brashness and overconfidence, although created by Verne as "Canadian," is, in Disney's film, the embodiment of American postwar bravado—as he sets off in search of knowledge, rather than battle or adventure.

Just as the captain is about to abandon their unsuccessful quest and return to land, the "monster" is sighted in the distance. When the warship opens fire, their foe charges forward and rams the vessel. The short-lived skirmish ends with Aronnax, Conseil, and Ned clinging to wreckage as their ship sinks slowly into the sea. As in Verne's novel, the trio discovers the true source of their plight—the submarine *Nautilus*, designed and commanded by Captain Nemo (James Mason)—and are taken aboard, where they become both captives and guests of the visionary, but twisted, genius.

Nemo and Aronnax are kindred souls in their scientific pursuit of knowledge as a higher order goal. Recognizing the professor as his intellectual equal, Nemo proudly shows off the wonders of his submarine to the only man aboard with the capacity to truly grasp her marvels. He acknowledges that he has read and admired Aronnax' oceanic work, but admonishes that his perceptions are "limited" because the depths of the world beneath the seas have been unavailable to him. As Nemo's companion, however, those unseen wonders are within his grasp, and soon the professor's allegiance begins to shift, as his intellectual camaraderie with Nemo deepens and their mutual pursuit of knowledge overtakes all other goals. The universe of the sea—pulsing with unseen life and untold benefits—is laid open to him, and its potential seems overwhelmingly, seductively, endless.

This realignment of Aronnax' worldview underscores audiences' postwar uncertainties about the nature of science as blessing or curse. His fellow captives fear, as Jay Telotte observes, "that the professor's intellectual fascination has blinded him to Nemo's own monstrous nature,"[1] as well as overshadowing his concerns for humanity and the taken-for-granted values they presumed to share. As the pair of scientists grows closer, Ned and Conseil also form an unlikely bond, as they plan both their escape and Nemo's capture. It is here that Disney invests most of his appeals to both the Disney tradition and the American character. Ned, a forthright, rough-around-the-edges career sailor, exudes life: he drinks, dances, breaks into song, and feeds cigars to Nemo's pet seal, Esmeralda. Harboring no great respect for either science or intellect, the lively sailor destroys (and in one case swallows) the captain's carefully preserved specimens of rare ocean life, in order to put the bottles in which they are contained to practical use—carrying news of Nemo's destination across the waves—but not before drinking their alcohol-based preservative to ensure that it does not go to waste.

Infusing the story with the politics of the audience's present day, and mingling, as Brian Taves notes, oppression, totalitarianism, and science,[2] Nemo also confides to Aronnax the reason for his brutal actions—and his personal torment—relating the tale of his escape from a penal colony on the island of Rorapandi,[3] where he and his crew were once held captive, his wife and child tortured to death. Since his escape, the captain's bitterness toward humankind has deepened and festered. As a result, he has retreated into the solitary life that Aronnax observes, removed from the violence, hatred, and destruction that, for him, characterize life above the seas, seizing every opportunity to prevent the spread of human influence in the oceanic world. Nemo loses Aronnax' loyalty, however, while showing him the horrors of the island. He destroys a munitions ship setting sail off the coast, preventing the ammunition aboard from being used in yet another senseless war, but killing all those aboard without mercy. Aronnax' own sense of humanity cannot accept that a "greater good" requires the extermination of the ship's unwitting crew.

As the narrative reaches its climax, Nemo, his crew, and his "guests" reach his island base of Vulcania, where he has suggested that he will share his secrets with Arronax. Upon arriving, however, they find the island surrounded by warships—responding to the notes tossed overboard by Ned—and Nemo's plans rapidly change. As the *Nautilus* draws enemy fire, the captain steals ashore to set explosive charges that will destroy his work, preventing it from being used to promote agendas of war and domination by nations not yet ready to wisely use its power. Shot as he returns to the sub, the scientist dies along with his work as the *Nautilus* sinks to the bottom of the sea. In this, as Telotte observes, Nemo returns to the role of scientist-as-gatekeeper of dangerous knowledge,[4] further complicating his character, and allowing for no easy readings of heroism or villainy in the moral order of the film. The mushroom cloud that engulfs Vulcania is, for postwar audiences, a clear symbol of the nuclear power that complicates their own worlds.

A ROLLICKING ADVENTURE

Verne's novel, like Melville's *Moby-Dick*, is serious in tone and frequently didactic in intent: a maritime adventure story crossed with a treatise on the newborn science of oceanography. As the *Nautilus* wanders the world's oceans, Nemo acts as an expert guide to undersea geography, geology, and biology; Conseil and Ned form a (literally) captive audience; and Arronax, depending on the subject being discussed, swings between the two roles. He lectures the others (even Nemo) on the subtleties of marine life, but becomes a rapt pupil when Nemo explains the workings of the *Nautilus* or expounds on wonders that exist only in Verne's imagination.[5] "You know as well as I do, professor," Nemo says at one point, "that a man can live under water if he carries a sufficient supply of breathable air." Arronax agrees that this is so, and a three-page discourse on diving-suit technology follows, with references to real-world engineers to add verisimilitude.[6] Disney, however, chose to strip out Verne's elaborate lectures, and fill the spaces with family-friendly action and broad comedy.

The shift in tone is quickly established in the opening scenes. Both versions open with rumors of a ship-killing monster loose in the Pacific, but where Verne has Arronax recount the history of sea-monster tales, director Richard Fleischer sidelines the professor almost as soon as he is introduced, in order to place Ned Land—the character most comprehensible to Disney's middle-American audience—at center stage. Strolling the docks with a beautiful woman on each arm, Ned listens to (and loudly heckles) an old sailor's tale of his narrow escape from the sea monster. A fistfight erupts, and in short order he knocks one opponent through a nearby store window, is himself knocked face-first into a mud puddle, drags a second man down with him, and is bodily carried away (elaborately protesting his innocence) by four policemen. Ned remains the central figure in the film for most of its remaining two-hour running time, the focus of most of the action sequences and virtually all of the comic ones.

The action sequences, except for a hand-to-hand struggle with Nemo's first mate aboard the sinking *Nautilus*, mirror the opening one. They pit Ned against obviously superior forces—multiple *Nautilus* crewmen, a tribe of cannibals, a pack of giant squid—and, in doing so, underscore the defining elements of his character: pugnacity, impetuousness, and bravery that verges on foolhardiness. Ned's response to threats is manic improvisation barely restrained (if it is restrained at all) by thought or planning. The action sequences centered on him are islands of energy—of running, leaping, tumbling, and wild gestures—in an otherwise deliberate narrative. They are also, for the most part, invented or heavily embellished for the film. The flight from the cannibals, for instance, is covered in the novel by a few desultory paragraphs that climax with: "Twenty minutes later, we boarded [the ship]."[7] The film turns it into a major set-piece, with Ned and Conseil running and rowing for their lives—frantic and wide-eyed—pursued by canoes filled with dark-skinned "savages" in feathers, war-paint, and bone ornaments. When Nemo electrifies the hull of the *Nautilus* to drive cannibals away, the book notes simply that they retreated, "crazed with terror."[8] The film, however, lingers on (and invites audiences to laugh at) their humiliating defeat, yelping and gesticulating on the electrified deck before leaping into the sea.

The "man of action," a stock Verne character who acts as a foil to the contemplative "man of science," is still recognizable in the film's version of Ned.[9] The film's central tension, in fact, is between Arronax (who wants to understand Nemo) and Ned (who wants to escape from him). The film's many comic scenes, however, turn Ned into a character unlike anything in Verne's canon: a clownish figure driven by (and unable to control) his appetites. His indiscriminate desire for female companionship, suggested in his first appearance in the company of two women, is confirmed by his song "A Whale of a Tale"—a comic lament about his romantic misadventures.[10] His lust for food and drink, equally indiscriminate, leads him to savor even the alcohol from Nemo's sample jars. His greed leads him to steal gold and jewels from a captor (Nemo) willing to kill him without compunction, and to place Conseil in danger when the two hunt for sunken treasure in a shark-infested wreck.

Ned's appetites align him both with traditional stereotypes of sailors, and with other broadly drawn characters from Disney's live-action adventure films of the period: Long John Silver from *Treasure Island* (1950), Little John from *The Story of Robin Hood* (1952), and Mike Fink from *Davy Crockett and the River Pirates* (1956).[11] They also, however, serve the film's political message, which departs as sharply from that of Verne's novel as does its tone.

A DARK AND BRUTAL WORLD

The novel *20,000 Leagues under the Sea* was written at a time when the politics of Europe, and the wider European-influenced world, were in flux.

The decade prior to its publication witnessed the consolidation of Germany and Italy at the expense of smaller political entities, the establishment of direct British rule over India, and the rise of a modernizing government in Japan during the Meiji Restoration. The text reflected this upheaval, making Nemo an explicitly political figure: a nationalist freedom fighter and champion of the oppressed. The identity Verne originally planned for Nemo—a Polish aristocrat whose parents, wife, and children were slaughtered by Russian troops during the suppression of the January Uprising of 1863—was quashed by his publisher on political grounds, but the spirit behind it remained.[12] Nemo aids Greek rebels in their struggle against the Turks, and says of a pearl diver whom he rescues from a marauding shark: "That Indian, sir, is an inhabitant of an oppressed country, and I am, still and shall be, to my last breath, one of them!"[13] His attacks on Western warships are, in the novel, an act of retaliation against great powers that crush smaller ones.

Disney's *20,000 Leagues* is not apolitical, but it is *differently* political. Nemo, as played by James Mason, has European features and an English accent, but a deliberately vague national heritage. The film makes no reference to any specific country, real or fictional: Nemo speaks of his homeland only as "that hated nation," and Vulcania (the site of his secret base) is implied to be an uncharted Pacific Island. Nemo's tragic backstory is likewise denationalized: His act of rebellion against his government is not an armed uprising, but a principled refusal to share his discoveries, lest they be used for war. Nemo's imprisonment on Rorapandi and the death-by-torture of his wife and child—both inventions of the film—are framed as forms of coercion that Nemo, at great personal cost, resists.

The film thus situates Nemo firmly in the political landscape of the high Cold War, but as a dissident scientist rather than a nationalist rebel. His enmity, though focused on "that hated nation, that took everything else from me," is implicitly directed against all nations that enslave, build weapons, and make war.[14] "They're loading a full cargo of death," Nemo observes, watching the enslaved miners of Rorapandi fill a ship with nitrates and phosphates, the building blocks of explosives, "and when that ship reaches home, the world will die a little more." Told that the ship and "the evil in its hold" will never reach their destination, Arronax protests that Nemo's plan to sink it is tantamount to murder. The captain responds, again, in language that— though directed at his own country—could apply to *any* nation that uses military force for political ends: "You call that murder? Well I see murder, too, not written on those drowned faces out there, but on the faces of dead *thousands*! There are the assassins—the dealers in death—I am the avenger!"

The phrase "dealers in death" evokes the mid-1930s vilification of arms makers as "merchants of death" who engineered America's entry into World War I for their own benefit.[15] Nemo's observation that the ship loading at Rorapandi (and the ships that, later, attack Vulcania) "fly no flag" suggests that they, too, flout international law, like pirates sailing under the Jolly Roger or warships that display the "false flag" of a friendly nation even as they close with and open fire on their enemies. Arronax, who accuses Nemo himself of being such an outlaw figure, rapidly backs away from that position after learning his story. He assures Conseil that Nemo will one day judge himself far more harshly than any outsider could,[16] and berates Ned for betraying Nemo's location to his enemies. Ned's reply—"*Somebody* had to strike a blow for freedom!"—is significant, but so is Arronax' angry dismissal of it. Verne presents Ned and Nemo as kindred spirits: men who value freedom above all. Disney makes Arronax into Nemo's spiritual twin, and frames the pair of them as the story's real heroes: wise men who understand (as Ned does not) that the needs of the many must sometimes trump the desires of the individual.

Verne's *Nautilus* is driven by electricity, but Disney's is powered by an energy source that can "lift mankind from the depths of Hell into Heaven . . . or destroy it." Similar language had been used since 1945 to discuss the promise and peril of atomic energy,[17] and the final scene of the film—a mushroom cloud rising over Vulcania—removed all doubt about the nature of Nemo's discovery. Audiences, in 1954 and afterward, were thus invited to read Nemo's anxiety over the misuse of his discovery in the context of a burgeoning nuclear arms race. Atomic energy is often compared to a genie that, once released from its bottle, cannot be put back; Disney, in fact, would literalize that image in the opening sequence of the made-for-television documentary *Our Friend the Atom* (1957). The Disney adaptation of *20,000 Leagues* posits an alternate history of the nineteenth century in which (unbeknownst to the wider world) Captain Nemo released the genie, but—appalled by the behavior of his fellow men, and by the uses to which they might put it—chose to confine it again. Nemo, in choosing to destroy his life's work rather than see it used in selfish and shortsighted ways, passes judgment on the maturity of leaders and nations in his own fractious era. Arronax, in expressing his hope that mankind will become responsible enough to use Nemo's discoveries "in God's good time," invites viewers of the film to pass judgment on their own.

TRANSFORMING A *VOYAGE EXTRAORDINAIRE*

When Jules Verne wrote *20,000 Leagues under the Sea*, the startling inventions in this masterpiece impressed the world as being the limit of imagination and impossibility.
—*20,000 Leagues Under the Sea* (1916)

Disney's live-action version of *20,000 Leagues under the Sea* is, in many ways, a study in ideas about imagination and impossibility, and the ways in which those ideas are translated into images on screen. When considering the film, many critics and scholars have framed its relationship to Verne and his novel in terms of narrative fidelity, with some, such as Bill Warren, observing that the film's rendition was so effective that it supplanted the novel in public memory,[18] while others, such as Jack Moffitt, a reviewer for the *Hollywood Reporter*, argue to the contrary that "Felton's script and Disney's concept improve on Verne's original."[19] Less consideration, however, has been given to the visual language of Disney's version of Verne's story—the particular ways in which Disney engaged with the aesthetics of the narrative, and of Verne's vision, more generally—which resulted in a rendition of the tale that was specifically a product of postwar culture in the United States.

Disney's version of *20,000 Leagues* was neither the first notable US screen adaptation of Verne's novel, nor the first to connect with the zeitgeist of war. In 1916, undersea photography pioneer J. Ernest Williamson provided rare documentary footage for Stuart Paton's full-length visualization of Verne's classic adventure. With the use of a "photosphere"—an observation chamber of his own design—supplied with air via a system of deep-sea tubes,[20] Williamson filmed the wonders beneath the seas off the Bahamas. Here, the sunlight reached down to a depth of 150 feet, allowing for enhanced cinematographic possibilities, as men in diving suits, portraying Captain Nemo's crew, enacted the undersea drama. Relying heavily on the visual language of the adventure documentary for its unique appeal, the film offers nearly eighteen minutes of lingering shots of coral, sponges, reef fish, and barracuda, in support of the dramatic action. The impossible—witnessing and recording life in the depths of the ocean—was both realized and celebrated in the film. As a result, Paton's *20,000 Leagues Under the Sea* became a major popular success, enhanced by the public concern with another vision of the impossible: submarine warfare during World War I—a war the US would join in less than four months' time.[21]

Released nearly 40 years later, Disney's *20,000 Leagues* brought the studio's tried-and-true formula for visual spectacle to Verne's fantastic visions in a live action production. Considered to be one of the best examples of CinemaScope production, its scenes fill the screen with powerful images that are not only larger than life, but also larger than its contemporary moviegoing audience was accustomed to viewing. The expansive seas are overwhelming—deep, solid, and forbidding. On their surface, warships belch thick black smoke into the sky, while below, the dark iron of the *Nautilus* powers its way past fragile marine life, disrupting the gentle rhythms and flows that surround it. The vessel is a creation out of place and time—invoking both the hulking death machines of wars past and the otherworldly engines of science fictional futures—as alien beneath the waves as above. In one of the film's trademark scenes, the *Nautilus* encounters a deadly giant squid. The juxtaposition of the creature's slick, writhing tentacles against the brutal angularity of the vessel underscores the monstrosity and dislocation of Nemo's creation. Even in scenes where the crew leaves the ship and meets the natural world with less mechanical intervention, they are awkward intruders, clumsy and plodding. Technology and culture are thus consistently framed as intrusions into nature—loud, graceless, and dominating.

In contrast, other adaptations of Verne's fantastic visions, arising from different cultural and historical moments, are crafted with delicate refinement, employing visual languages that reference a subtler blend of intellect and imagination. In 1907, Georges Méliès' silent short *20,000 lieues sous les mers* blended fanciful undersea imagery, formed with sea creature cutouts patterned after Alphonse de Neuville's illustrations for Verne's novel, with follies-inspired scenes featuring ballet dancers from the Théâtre du Châtelet.[22] Here, a panorama of wonders—shipwrecks, monsters, sea nymphs, and a ballet of naiads inspired by Verne's novel—animate a fisherman's dreams of becoming a submariner. Méliès' undersea marvels dwarf and confound the fisherman with a delicate, but dangerous, otherworldly beauty. While many of the creatures inhabiting Méliès' cinematic grotto resemble those found in the original engravings published along with Verne's text, the director calls on his "paper moon" style of celestial motifs to create a fantastic rendition of Verne's undersea world.

In a similarly fantastic fashion, Czech filmmaker Karel Zeman's *Fabulous World of Jules Verne* (1958), released only four years after Disney's *20,000 Leagues*, takes a dramatically different approach to visual interpretations of work by the Father of Science Fiction.[23] According to Michaela Mertova, a historian at the National Archive in Prague, "[Zeman] was one filmmaker who was really able to capture the imagination of works by Jules Verne. In visual terms, there is no question the films continue to resonate with audiences even today."[24] The film's visuals painstakingly recreate the style of Victorian line engravings featured in the original editions of Verne's books, drawn by artists such as Édouard Riou and Léon Bennett. On the film's intricate detail, critic Pauline Kael commented that "there are more stripes, more patterns on the clothing, the décor, and on the image itself than a sane person can easily imagine."[25] Zeman utilizes a dazzling array of motion picture animation techniques—magic-lantern dissolves, stop-motion, pixilation, double-exposures, miniatures and models—to translate the technological dreams of Verne's prose for the screen and bring to life the engravings so familiar to Verne's readers.[26]

Brian Taves offers that "Disney's rendering captures the mood and atmosphere of its source . . . the feeling of Verne's narrative is powerfully rendered intact into a new medium."[27] However, it may be more to the point that Disney's rendering captures the mood and atmosphere of its *cultural* source, rather than its literary source. From an aesthetic standpoint, Disney's *20,000 Leagues* is clearly the product of a post-war, industrialized world power. Visually aggressive, it is crafted with broad strokes and little concern for subtlety. Disney's rendition of Verne's science fictional vision is heavy-handed, in line with the postwar, nuclear power worldview of the United States. Detail of the natural world, given careful emphasis in other renditions of Verne's visions is here both limited and utilitarian. The attention to visual detail is found primarily in metal structures—textures, curves, carefully welded angles, arrays of bolts and pipes—in a manner that evokes the industrial pessimism of dieselpunk, rather than the more fanciful steampunk with which Verne's work is more generally associated.[28]

CONCLUSION: NEMO IN THE NUCLEAR AGE

Disney's vision of *20,000 Leagues* has, for better or worse, eclipsed Verne's novel in many contexts. Bigger, bolder, and less nuanced, it nonetheless offers spectacle in a visual language to which audiences have become accustomed. The subtlety and sophistication found in the early renderings of Verne's story quickly gave way to the cultural politics of a new century, as did the construction of his characters. The shift from fiction in the service of science to science fiction in the service of the American character is palpable at every level of Disney's adaptation, from the exploitation of nature's unseen realms to the careful control of atomic power.

American postwar confidence permeates Disney's twentieth-century rendition of *20,000 Leagues* at every level, and is translated and given form on screen. Cold War themes of expansion, domination, and power infuse the film, while higher order goals and values such as knowledge and independence are now personalized and idiosyncratic: The tragic, politicized figure played by James Mason—not the master scientist of Verne's novel—has become our image of Nemo. Verne's passionate, freedom-seeking Ned Land, is now better recognized as Kirk Douglas' brawling, guitar-strumming comic relief. Mention of the *Nautilus* now calls forth images of the jagged-edged, rivet-studded iron monster conjured from Harper Goff's imagination in 1954, rather than the sleek, intricate visions of possibility that were given form by Verne's illustrators and painstakingly transferred to the screen by Mélies and Paton. Refashioned by time and ideology, technology, in Disney's adaptation, is dark, brooding, and heavy-laden with destructive potential—as much the offspring of Total War as humankind's reach into the future.

The irony in this triumph of the Disney adaptation over the Verne original is considerable. Verne prided himself in rooting his stories in the real (and distanced himself from H. G. Wells and other purveyors of more fantastic "scientific romances"). Even at their most fantastic, his tales of high technology and high adventure were stories enmeshed with his mid-nineteenth-century world. Disney's adaptation of *20,000 Leagues* is enmeshed in its own, very different world. Its distinctive look reflects the raw power and inhuman scale of the machines used to remake the mid-twentieth-century, and its message reflects the deep ambivalence over technology that those machines engendered—an ambivalence that resonates better with audiences than the uncomplicated celebration that pervaded Verne's work.

NOTES

1. Telotte, "Science Fiction as 'True-Life Adventure,'" 69.
2. Taves, *Hollywood Presents Jules Verne*, 59.
3. Cited in some sources as "Rura Penthe"—a spelling also associated with a penal colony in the Star Trek franchise. Here, we follow Verne scholar Brian Taves' preferred spelling.
4. Telotte, "Science Fiction as 'True-Life Adventure,'" 70.
5. On the history of oceanography in this era, see Rozwadowski, *Fathoming the Ocean.*
6. Verne, *20,000 Leagues*, 105.
7. Ibid., 153–154.
8. Ibid., 162.
9. On Verne's image of Americans as the ultimate "men of action," see Chesneaux and Chew, "Jules Verne's Image of America."
10. There is no hint that his interest is sexual, but the structure of "Whale of a Tale" echoes that of bawdy sea songs like "Bell-Bottom Trousers" and "Keeper of the Eddystone Light."
11. On these films, see West, *Disney Live-Action Productions.*
12. Miller and Waller, "Jules Verne," xv–xvi.
13. Verne, *20,000 Leagues,* 184.
14. All quotations are from *Disney's 20,000 Leagues under the Sea: Two-Disc Collector's Edition* (Burbank, CA: Walt Disney Studios Home Entertainment, 2003).
15. Coined as the title of a book by H. C. Engelbrecht and F. C. Hanighen (New York: Dodd, 1934), the phrase was popularized two years later by Senator Gerald Nye's committee investigating war profiteering.
16. Arronax and the audience know, as Conseil does not, that Nemo sacrificed his family in order to preserve his secrets.
17. Boyer, *Bomb's Early Light,* 266–275.
18. Warren, *Keep Watching the Skies,* 1:199.
19. Moffit, "[Review of] *20,000 Leagues*," 3.
20. The equipment was designed by his father, a sea captain.
21. Taves, "Pioneer Under the Sea."
22. Hammond, *Marvellous Méliès,* 145.
23. Originally titled *Vynález Akazy* (*The Deadly Invention*), the film is based on one of Verne's later novels, *Face au drapeau* (*Facing the Flag*), part of Verne's *Voyages Extraordinaries* series.
24. Velinger, "Karel Zeman."
25. Pauline Kael, *5001 Nights At the Movies* (New York; Holt, 1991), 179.
26. For more on Zeman and Verne, see Tibbetts, "'Fulminations and Fulgurators."
27. Taves, *Hollywood Presents Jules Verne,* 57.
28. While both steampunk and dieselpunk represent retrofuturism, the steampunk lifestyle and aesthetic typically exhibits a Victorian influence, while dieselpunk is more heavily influenced by the technology of the interwar years. The former is often considered more optimistic, and the latter, more pessimistic.

BIBLIOGRAPHY

Boyer, Paul. *By the Bomb's Early Light: American Thought and Culture at the Dawn of the Atomic Age*. 1985. Chapel Hill: University of North Carolina Press, 1994.

Chesneaux, Jean and Frances Chew. "Jules Verne's Image of America." *Yale French Studies* 43 (1969): 111–127.

Hammond, Paul. *Marvellous Méliès* . London: Gordon Fraser, 1974 .

Kael, Pauline. *5001 Nights At the Movies*. New York; Holt, 1991.

Miller, Walter James and Frederick Paul Waller. "Jules Verne, Man of the Twentieth Century." In Jules Verne, *20,000 Leagues under the Sea*, translated and annotated by Walter James Miller and Frederick Paul Walte, vii–xxii. Annapolis, MD: Naval Institute Press, 1993.

Moffitt, Jack. "[Review of] *20,000 Leagues Under the Sea*." *Hollywood Reporter*, December 15, 1954, 3.

Rozwadowski, Helen. *Fathoming the Ocean: The Discovery and Exploration of the Deep Sea*. Cambridge, MA: Harvard University Press, 2009.

Taves, Brian. *Hollywood Presents Jules Verne: The Father of Science Fiction on Screen*. Lexington: University Press of Kentucky, 2015.

———. "A Pioneer Under the Sea." Library of Congress. http://www.loc.gov/loc/lcib/9615/sea.html

Telotte, J. P. "Science Fiction as 'True-Life Adventure': Disney and the Case of *20,000 Leagues under the Sea*," *Film & History* 40, no. 2 (Fall 2010): 66–79.

Tibbetts, John C. "'Fulminations and Fulgurators': Jules Verne, Karel Zeman, and Steampunk Cinema." In *Steaming Into a Victorian Future: A Steampunk Anthology*, edited by Julie Anne Taddeo and Cynthia J. Miller, 125–143. Lanham, MD: Rowman and Littlefield, 2013.

Velinger, Jan. "Karel Zeman—Author of Czech Animated Films Including the Mixed-Animation Classic, 'Journey to the Beginning of Time,'" www.radio.cy/en/section/czechs/karel-zeman.

Verne, Jules. *20,000 Leagues under the Sea*. Translated and annotated by Walter James Miller and Frederick Paul Walter. Annapolis, MD: Naval Institute Press, 1993.

Warren, Bill. *Keep Watching the Skies*, Vol. 1. Jefferson, NC: McFarland, 1982.

West, John G., Jr., *The Disney Live-Action Productions*. Hawthorne and Peabody, 1994.

Chapter Eleven

Perchance to Dream

A Narrative Analysis of Disney's Sleeping Beauty

Alexis Finnerty with Douglas Brode

Much of the Walt Disney Company's (WDC) energy, resources, and creativity has been focused on reinterpreting traditional European fairy tales for contemporary American audiences. Exemplary is *Sleeping Beauty* (1959), largely based on Perrault's (1697) "The Sleeping Beauty in the Wood" and also borrowing from "Little Briar-Rose" (1812) by the Brothers Grimm and Tchaikovsky's (1890) ballet *The Sleeping Beauty*. Though not an immediate box-office hit, *Sleeping Beauty* has since emerged as one of WDC's best-known and best-loved films. [1]

One explanation for Disney's success at adapting written fairy tales into films may be the decision to keep intact the tales' basic structures. According to Carl Jung, fairy tales contain enduring story patterns and character archetypes that prove universal to people in all cultures throughout history. [2] As a result, variations on the story of a beautiful sleeping princess awoken by the kiss of a handsome prince can speak to anxieties, fantasies, and desires of people in such diverse cultures as seventeenth-century France, nineteenth-century Russia and Germany, and twentieth-century America. Given its enduring popularity, a study of this story's components, how they fit together, and why they are organized in such a way becomes necessary. Intriguing, then, is the manner in which the Disney Version of *Sleeping Beauty* corresponds to the functions of the fairy tale as enumerated by Vladimir Propp in his landmark work *Morphology of the Folktale* (1968). Propp arrived at his list of functions by analyzing more than one hundred Russian folktales; his analysis of narrative functions, as well as character types, remains widely used in today's narrative analysis. [3] Disney's plot combines Propp's structure with the classical paradigm that characterizes most American/Hollywood

105

movies, exemplifying Disney's genius at blending diverse influences in a seamless, almost magical, manner—the source of Disney's visceral impact on the mass audience of *any* decade, despite inevitable and constant social and cultural changes.

For Propp, all tales begin with an initial situation. This does not in and of itself constitute a function,[4] valuable instead for setting the stage while introducing major characters. Here, as is so often the case, Disney opens with a medium shot of a storybook. As the camera tracks toward it, *Sleeping Beauty* magically opens, and a narrator sets up the story via a voice-over.

> NARRATOR: In a faraway land, long ago, lived a king and his fair queen. Many years had they longed for a child and finally their wish was granted . . .

The initial situation, then, in a proverbial nutshell: the king and queen, desirous of a child, are finally blessed with Princess Aurora and hold a grand event celebrating her birth.

The first five of Propp's functions[5] are not yet present, though functions six and seven are superficially mentioned. However, a story does not need to contain every function in order to fit Propp's primal structure. Propp was aware that these child-oriented fictions vary in length, and that some (especially the shorter ones) imply certain functions instead of stating them outright. According to Propp, the first seven set up the tale; it is the act of villainy (function eight) that creates the narrative turning point and sets the plot in motion.[6] Due to the fast pace and short running time of *Sleeping Beauty* (seventy-five minutes), the villain is introduced early and the action begins at once, in comparison to most European fairy tales. An evil fairy, Maleficent, makes a grand entrance by conjuring a gust of wind and a flash of lightning, materializing out of an eerie green flame. This occurs after function five (delivery), the moment Maleficent discovered that she wasn't invited to Aurora's christening.

Interestingly, in Disney, when good fairy Merryweather informs Maleficent of the reason—no one wanted her there—Maleficent appears to take it in stride, lulling the characters (and the audience) into a false sense of security:

> MALEFICENT: Not wa . . . ? Oh dear, what an awkward situation. I had hoped it was merely due to some oversight. Well, in that event I'd best be on my way.

> QUEEN: And you're not offended, your excellency?

> MALEFICENT: Why no, your majesty.

This exchange corresponds to Propp's functions six (trickery) and seven (complicity). Maleficent tricks the queen. This catalystic occurrence ends the tale's "preparatory part" while allowing intriguing complications to develop.[7] The act of villainy can take many forms, here an evil spell, cast when Maleficent announces, "Before the sun sets on her sixteenth birthday, she shall prick her finger on the spindle of a spinning wheel and die." This is accompanied by visuals including a malevolent-looking spinning wheel and a sudden cut to the beautiful teenage princess, Aurora, lying still on her deathbed, visualizing Maleficent's curse, which wouldn't seem half as frightening or foreboding without the sort of spectacular imagery that defines Disney entertainment. Film is, after all, a primarily visual medium.

Necessary complication number one in the Disney Version: good fairy Merryweather commutes Maleficent's curse from death to sleep that may be broken only by "true love's kiss." The three good fairies discuss how they will hide Aurora. Flora announces they will raise the princess without magic, posing as peasants. The fairies thus fulfill the role of *donors* or *mentors*, teaching and protecting the hero while, as the form dictates, offering gifts.[8] However, they are more active in shaping the narrative's events than mentors ordinarily are, most standing back and watching as the *hero* takes control of the story. In Disney, the good fairies—a sisterhood of mature women overseeing the maturation of a growing girl—constantly meddle, ensuring (as no male character here can) that the story will end well, adding a patina of feminist thought.

This unique advice, transferring the old tale's emphasis on the lone male prince to, instead, a community of positive women, allows Disney to expand, even alter the Ur-story. After informing king and queen, these fairies smuggle the infant princess from the castle, fulfilling function eleven (departure). This scene also establishes Princess Aurora as a *victim hero*, kidnapped or transported from her home rather than deciding to leave.[9] The sequence of events that leads Aurora to prick her finger on the wheel seems inevitable within the context Disney has here created. Intriguingly, it also resembles a setup for a different but related story in which an active male, or *seeker hero*, quests (in contrast to the passive female hero) to rescue her.

Like so many tales that draw on mythic and epic elements for their sense of universality, this resumes fifteen years later. Maleficent searches for Aurora to ensure that the curse is fulfilled. To achieve this, Maleficent sends her pet raven to scout for Aurora's whereabouts. This helps establish that we are indeed watching a Disney film by connecting *Sleeping Beauty* to previous fairy tales as reimagined by this studio, echoing the raven in the wicked queen's castle in *Snow White and the Seven Dwarfs* (1937).

The villain(ess) states:

MALEFICENT: [*talking to the raven*] Circle far and wide, search for a
maid of sixteen.

This offers a classic example of function four, "the villain makes an attempt
at reconnaissance." Seemingly a violation of Propp's rule of sequence, this
proves necessary to prepare for another act of villainy that will set Aurora
into a deep sleep. Aurora's departure offers an extended case of absentation
(function one). As a result, the functions themselves are presented here in
something other than what is expected to be the "normal" order and, momentarily, Peter appears to be posited as the *only* hero. (Aurora would be a side
character, a heroine rather than female hero, the prince's prize for vanquish-
ing the evil Maleficent.) However, this fails to take into account the manner
in which Disney's narrative follows Aurora and essentially remains about *her*
until the moment she succumbs to the curse.

In Disney's female-oriented variation, Aurora (whom the fairies name
Briar Rose, after the parallel character in the Grimm brothers' version), on
the day of her sixteenth birthday, wanders into the forest. Here she meets
Prince Phillip. This is not a function, though the encounter becomes important, introducing the ideal of a romantic heterosexual romance. Aurora and
Phillip fall in love at first sight, but their love seems less a happy accident
than destiny, fated to happen as they were promised to each other at Aurora's
birth. Also, each dreamed of the other long before they met. They dance
together to the song "Once Upon a Dream." This key sequence foreshadows
the ending, suggesting that the love between Phillip and Aurora might be the
"true love" that "conquers all" and, as such, did not merely happen but was
meant to happen, had to happen, was fated to happen.

Still, Disney is far from done with the addition of destiny. The following
scene returns us to the house occupied by the three fairies, fed up with trying
to make a dress and birthday cake for Aurora in "the human way." They lock
the doors, close the windows, draw out their wands. Flora and Merryweather
argue about the color of the princess's gown, changing the dress from pink to
blue and back again, inadvertently shooting sparks that escape via the chim-
ney. The blue-versus-pink motif is characteristic of the good-natured meddling the fairies (especially Flora and Merryweather) engage in throughout.
While they remain deeply committed to sisterhood, (older) women supporting and mentoring other (younger) women, minor moments of conflict do
erupt, causing these benign Wiccans to appear relatively realistic rather than
sentimental ideals. In this case, the fairies' magic has unintended (by them)
ill effects that well serve the story line, leading directly to the horrific situation all of the positive characters have been striving to avoid. What seems a
simple moment of comedic relief draws the attention of Maleficent's crow,
who reports Aurora's location to Maleficent.

As in all well-written narratives for children and adults, this provides the necessary turning point required to keep the plot from growing stagnant. Here is the moment when the fairies inform Aurora she is indeed a princess and return her to the castle. She is devastated to learn that she's betrothed to Prince Phillip, but she doesn't know he's the same man she just met and fell in love with. This Disneyfies (that term employed in a positive sense here) this fairytale by relating it to the Disney Version of *Cinderella*, in which Disney's unique incarnation of the traditional heroine doesn't realize that the man she meets and falls in love with at the ball is the prince. Disney consistently reinvents conventional fairy-tale heroines by focusing on an enlightened modern female, interested less in marrying a rich prince than in the man she truly loves, be he prince or commoner. This recurring Disney trope appears also in such live-action films as *The Sword and the Rose* (1953) and the animated contemporary non-fairy-tale *Lady and the Tramp* (1955), as well as post-Walt features including *The Little Mermaid* (1989) and *Aladdin* (1992). Pretense to status is dismissed in Disney; honest emotions are exalted.

Now Maleficent takes advantage of Aurora's swept-away state to hypnotize her, repeating function six (trickery). Hypnotized, Aurora (function seven, complicity) follows Maleficent's evil green light to the top of the tower, where it transforms into a spinning wheel. Maleficent compels Aurora to touch the spindle with the words, "Touch the spindle. Touch it I say!" Aurora pricks her finger, falling asleep. This is a conscious repetition of function eight, "the villain causes harm or injury to a member of the family (villainy)." In earlier versions, the princess disobeyed her parents' orders not to enter that room, positing her as superficial, bratty, and self-possessed. In Disney, the princess—drawn her against her will—is, conversely, a young woman of strong values and deep integrity, another proto-feminist addition that modernizes the tale.

This plot turn owes more to classical movie structure than to Propp. Like the plot of, say, Buster Keaton's *The General* (1925), Disney's narrative follows not only a classical but also an elaborately counterbalanced pattern.[10] Revisiting key elements advances the plot while reprising what came before in an intriguingly altered way. The basic functions are reprised immediately after the midpoint, when the fairies reveal to Briar Rose her true identity. Since the decision of these essentially good characters leads inexorably to the fulfillment of the villain's curse, the good fairies share in the villain's guilt— the unintentional complicity of the well meaning—in a Hitchcockian manner by setting in motion Aurora's fate via (as in Greek tragedy) sincere attempts to avoid it.

With Aurora asleep, the narrative necessarily switches its focus to Phillip, the new *hero*. He may be termed a *seeker hero* since he willingly rides off to save the princess.[11] And, as already mentioned, an *active hero*, whereas

Aurora remained passive. Yet in Disney, far from switching to a traditional male hero story, it's the good fairies who do the most to manipulate the narrative toward a happy ending, redeeming themselves as well as achieving good for others. They put the entire castle to sleep, returning to the cottage to warn Phillip. Alas, they arrive too late; Maleficent imprisons Phillip on the Forbidden Mountain. Such blocking of what benign figures hope to achieve is essential to Disney's feature-length film, expanding on the original brief tale by providing additional elements that do not merely take up time but prove satisfying in and of themselves. Maleficent visits Phillip in the dungeon, informing him (and the audience) that he's "the destined hero of a charming fairy tale come true." This asserts that Disney did not happen on such an approach by accident but was consciously aware of such age-old classical elements.

The villain, envisioning her captive's eventual destiny (or what she naively believes it to be), says, "the gates of the dungeon part." Overwhelming a simple verbal statement with a spectacular visual, Disney fully cinematizes the literary situation by providing an indelible image of an old, decrepit Phillip riding his tired horse. This image dissolves to a medium shot of Maleficent's upper body as she says sarcastically, "to wake his love with love's first kiss, and prove that true love conquers all." This speech also foreshadows Maleficent's demise. Maleficent must be vanquished not only because she mocks the idealized love between Phillip and Aurora, but also because she scoffs at the movie's essential plot. If *Sleeping Beauty* were a parody of the fairy tale, Maleficent might be treated as a witty, sympathetic character in a postmodernist piece, as in the recent *Maleficent* (2014). But as this version is played (relatively) straight, the character that makes fun of the plot must, in a modernist work, be characterized as evil and punished accordingly.

Maleficent's vision of the couple's fate would horrifically come true were if not for, in earlier versions, the male hero's virtuosity, that is, his machismo. Not in Disney! Phillip can do nothing, achieve nothing without that sisterhood composed of three strong, smart women, who not only support Phillip but essentially get the job done for him, if humbly allowing him to receive all accolades. After Maleficent leaves, the fairies fly into Phillip's cell, magically remove his chains, and open the dungeon door, Phillip ready to rescue Aurora—thereby fulfilling function ten (beginning counteraction).

FLORA: Wait, Prince Phillip. The road to true love may be barred by still many more dangers. . . . So arm thyself with this enchanted shield of virtue and this mighty sword of truth. For these weapons of righteousness will triumph over evil.

Here, a classic *donor* figure offers a *hero* magical assistance, fulfilling function fourteen (receipt of a magical agent). Traditionally, the *donor* tests the *hero* to ensure he is worthy of magical aid before rendering assistance; Propp's functions twelve and thirteen deal with the *donor* testing the *hero* and the *hero* passing the test. However, the fairies automatically give Phillip magical assistance. His love for Aurora has already proven him a worthy *hero*, and time is of the essence if Phillip is to escape the Forbidden Mountain and cure Aurora. All the same, without them (the mature women, essentially transformed from mentors into heroes themselves, at least in the Disney Version), he (the male) is helpless.

Since this is a full-length feature (if a brief one), Phillip and the fairies can't succeed at once. Maleficent's crow sees them burst out of the dungeon and raises an alarm. Phillip fights his way out with the help of the fairies' magic; they have become a non-gender-biased community of heroes rather than the old tale's traditional ruggedly individualistic male. The fairies lead Phillip back to the castle and sleeping Aurora, fulfilling function fifteen (guidance). Maleficent shoots evil spells at Phillip, transforming herself into a dragon to block entry to the castle. Since Maleficent chases him to King Stefan's castle, this sequence can be considered an example of function twenty-one (pursuit). However, this concludes with a battle between Phillip and Maleficent, a definite example of function sixteen, "the hero and the villain join in direct combat (struggle)."

Propp's chase function trails the battle function because his structure was designed to be applicable to longer fairy tales featuring more than one villain. According to Propp, the first villain is punished only in cases where pursuit is absent. Otherwise, he is killed in battle or perishes in pursuit. [12] But Maleficent is the first and *only* villain here. Both the chase and battle fall under function sixteen (struggle) as Maleficent dies at the sequence's end. The final confrontation, according to the rules not only of fairy tales but of all good populist-oriented stories, from Gilgamesh through the Old Testament to George Lucas's *Star Wars*, must offer an inspired, original variation on the recurring ancient theme of good defeating evil. Disney makes it his own, of course. Maleficent has Phillip trapped at the top of a tall cliff, about to fall to his death. Again, the fairies have usurped Phillip's position as primary hero, so it is they who must create a positive denouement. While he lies helpless, they concentrate their magic on the sword and say, "Now sword of truth fly swift and sure, that evil die and good endure!" Taking their hint, Phillip recovers, throws the sword at Maleficent, and pierces her heart. Maleficent's demise corresponds to function eighteen, "the villain is defeated (victory)," also linking this film to Disney's canon via the similarity of this image to the witch's death in *Snow White*.

On to, then, the final resolution and expected/necessary conclusion, to satisfy the genre (fairy tale) while further qualifying this as a Disney film.

Phillip kisses Aurora; the evil spell is lifted. This fulfills function nineteen, "the initial misfortune or lack is liquidated." According to Propp, this is paired with function eight, the act of villainy: when evil creates an imbalance in a fairy tale's "world," this must be set right by the *hero*. In *Sleeping Beauty*, this villainy/restoration sequence takes the traditional form of a spell cast, then broken.

The good fairies' freezing of the castle's good inhabitants dissipates even as the spell on Aurora concludes. Phillip and Aurora descend the grand staircase, Aurora reunited with her parents. Earlier versions did not emphasize this, focusing on the romantic moment. Disney films, however, often deal with the sanctity of family, necessitating this moment. Only after mother and father embrace their daughter do Phillip and Aurora dance to "Once Upon a Dream." Although they aren't literally married, the scene heavily implies they will be soon. So the ending corresponds to function thirty-one (wedding). Functions twenty through thirty, which only apply to longer tales with multiple villains, are omitted.

Although Propp's structure is useful for examining fairy tales' narrative structure and organization, it cannot be used to draw conclusions about any one story's impact on an audience. Like Jung's conception of the collective unconscious, Propp's structure tends to universalize fairy tales while failing to take the specific social context of each retelling into account. [13] Proppian analyses, then, are most useful when combined with criticism that does consider this, such as Hippolyte Taine's sociopsychic approach. [14] A combination of a Proppian and sociopsychic analysis might consider the ways the expressions of function eight (villainy) and function thirty-one (marriage) in Disney's *Sleeping Beauty* address social anxieties about gender roles, love, and marriage in America in the 1950s. Less than three years following the film's release, Betty Friedan's *The Feminine Mystique* would introduce American women to mainstream feminist thought and the need to emancipate oneself emotionally, intellectually, and spiritually. Simultaneously, Hugh Hefner and *Playboy* suggested that a woman's "emancipation" might begin with physical/sexual freedom. The competing women's magazines *Ms.* and *Cosmopolitan* would, during the 1970s, continue this debate, the latter sharing Hefner's vision with women, the former arguing that sexual liberation in no way presaged mental, social, economic, or cultural freedom. The understandable confusion of many American women, considering the emerging choices to be negotiated, and Aurora's own obvious confusion (even as to her identity/name), might be seen as representing the tip of this oncoming social/ cultural/personal iceberg. Still, Disney's film, however temporal such an interpretation may be, continues to successfully play today—suggesting that, however effective in 1959 as a topical retelling of the Sleeping Beauty myth, the Disney Version also caught the very core of this essentially universal story.

APPENDIX

Propp's thirty-one functions, taken from *Morphology of Folktales*:

1. One of the members of a family absents himself from home (absentation)
2. An interdiction is addressed to the hero (interdiction) *
3. The interdiction is violated (violation)*
4. The villain makes an attempt at reconnaissance (reconnaissance)**
5. The villain receives information about his victim (delivery)**
6. The villain attempts to deceive his victim in order to take possession of him or his belongings including direct application of magical means (trickery)
7. The victim submits to deception and therefore unwittingly helps his enemy (complicity)
8. The villain causes harm or injury to a member of the family (villainy)*** [8a. Member of family lacks/desires to have something (usually in cases with no overt villain)]
9. Misfortune or lack is made known, the hero is approached with a request or command, he is allowed to go or he is dispatched (mediation, the connective incident)
10. The seeker agrees to or decides upon counteraction (beginning counteraction)
11. The hero leaves home (departure)
12. The hero is tested, interrogated, attacked, etc., which prepares the way for his receiving a magical agent or helper (the first function of the donor)
13. The hero reacts to the actions of the future donor (the hero's reaction)
14. The hero acquires the use of a magical agent (provision, receipt of a magical agent)
15. The hero is transferred, delivered, or led to the whereabouts of an object of search (guidance)
16. The hero and the villain join in direct combat (struggle)
17. The hero is branded (branding, marking)
18. The villain is defeated (victory)
19. The initial misfortune or lack is liquidated***
20. The hero returns (return)
21. The hero is pursued (pursuit, chase)
22. Rescue of the hero from pursuit (rescue)
23. The hero, unrecognized, arrives home or in another country (unrecognized, arrival)
24. A false hero presents unfounded claims (unfounded claims)
25. A difficult task is proposed to the hero (difficult task)

26. The task is resolved (solution)
27. The hero is recognized (recognition)
28. The false hero or villain is exposed (exposure)
29. The hero is given a new appearance (transfiguration)
30. The villain is punished (punishment)
31. The hero is married and ascends the throne (wedding)

Asterisks indicate paired functions. The two functions with one asterisk (*) are paired with each other, the two functions with two asterisks (**) are a separate pair, and the two functions with three asterisks (***) are a third pair. Paired functions follow cause-and-effect logic (e.g., information is sought and received), although the first of the two may be implied rather than stated outright.

NOTES

1. Box Office Mojo, "Sleeping Beauty."
2. Giannetti, *Understanding Movies*, 364.
3. Propp, *Morphology of the Folktale*, xi.
4. A function is similar to a plot point; it is a marked event in a story.
5. A complete list of Propp's thirty-one functions can be found in the Appendix to this essay.
6. Propp, *Morphology of the Folktale*, 31.
7. Ibid.
8. Vogler, *Writer's Journey*.
9. Propp, *Morphology of the Folktale*, 36.
10. Giannetti, *Understanding Movies*, 344.
11. Propp, *Morphology of the Folktale*, 36.
12. Ibid., 56.
13. Giannetti, *Understanding Movies*, 364.
14. Ibid., 359.

BIBLIOGRAPHY

Box Office Mojo. "Sleeping Beauty." 2012. Retrieved from http://www.boxofficemojo.com/movies/?page=main&id=sleepingbeauty.htm.
The General. Produced by B. Keaton and J. Schenck and directed by B. Keaton and C. Bruckman. United Artists, 1926.
Giannetti, L. D. *Understanding Movies*. 12th ed. Boston: Allyn & Bacon, 2011.
Grimm, J., and W. Grimm. "Little Brier-Rose." In *Kinder- und Hausmärchen* 1, no. 50 (1812): 225–29.
Penner, E. *Sleeping Beauty*. Script. 1959. Retrieved from http://www.fpx.de/fp/Disney/Scripts/SleepingBeauty/sb.html.
Perrault, C. *Les Contes des Fées en Prose et en verse*. 1697; rep. Lyon: Louis Perrin, 1865. Retrieved from https://books.google.ca/books?id=TTIJAAAAQAAJ&pg=PP11&redir_esc=y#v=onepage&q&f=false.
Propp, V. *Morphology of the Folktale*. 2nd ed. Austin: University of Texas Press, 1968.

Sleeping Beauty. Produced by W. Disney and directed by C. Geronimi, L. Clark, E. Larson, and W. Reitherman. Walt Disney Productions, 1959.

Tchaikovsky, P. *The Sleeping Beauty*. Ballet. 1890. Retrieved from http://classicalmusic.about.com/od/balletsynopses/a/sleepingbeauty.htm.

Vogler, C. *The Writer's Journey: Mythic Structure for Writers.* 3rd ed. Studio City, CA: Michael Wiese Productions, 2007.

Chapter Twelve

"It's a Jungle Book out There, Kid!"

Walt Disney and the American 1960s

Greg Metcalf

Walt Disney has long been praised and vilified for the worldview presented in his films.[1] Whether hailed as a defender of traditional American values or demeaned as a cultural strip miner who turned complex children's literary classics into simple-minded pabulum, the Walt Disney Company (WDC) produced a widely consumed vision of how things are and how they ought to be. *The Jungle Book* (1967) is uniquely suited for an analysis of Disney's processes. The last film Disney actively participated in creating, it features a bare-bones plot, any entertainment value carried by what WDC called "strong characterizations."[2] During the precise three-year period during which *The Jungle Book* was produced, America experienced radical social and cultural changes. Such real-life issues significantly impacted the film's temporal content. Specifically, Disney's version of Rudyard Kipling's 1894 novel was reimagined so as to present caricatures of then-current issues Disney perceived as threats to *his* America; rock and roll, the drug culture, as well as the rights movements of blacks, women and homosexuals. As a result, the movie communicates, if only by implication, Disney's proposed solutions to problems facing American youth, doing so in the guise of mere escapist entertainment.

I

"The Rock Culture signaled the appearance of a radically different youth culture in the late-1960s, one that saw alienation as a way of life. . . . The scenario shifted from the innocuous non-adult world of *Beach Blanket Bingo* and Beatlemania to the anti-adult sphere of Sergeant Pepper and Haight-Ashbury. Rock

Culture became a collective voice that made sense of revolution. People embraced its reality, values, and alternative vision to the prescribed way of life by articulating, reflecting, and reinforcing the social flux of the period."—George Plasketes[3]

While Disney rarely stated his political beliefs explicitly, he was at this point in his life a Goldwater/Reagan conservative and viewed his own values as Protestant, middle class, and midwestern. The late 1960s could not have been a comforting era. First, there was the issue of civil rights and related racial protests and violence. This struck close to home, since *Dumbo* and *Song of the South* were increasingly criticized for their unsympathetic or racist portrayal of black Americans. Though denying that the charges had any validity, Disney temporarily pulled both films from public exhibition.[4] In 1965, the Watts riots caused more than $200 million of damage. The man who had once declared himself "the King of Los Angeles"[5] could hardly have been blind to such an event in his own backyard. Likewise, the women's liberation movement began in earnest, while a rising counterculture promoted homosexual rights and drug experimentation. Rock and roll music artistically supported such revolution. Such occurrences were not only supplanting Disney and his conservative political friends in the pages of popular magazines but also reshaping the entertainment business as Walt knew it.

In 1967, the year Disney released *The Jungle Book*, the most prominent Academy Award–winning films were *In the Heat of the Night* and *Guess Who's Coming to Dinner*, movies in which black Americans demanded equality with whites, as well as *The Graduate* and *Bonnie and Clyde*, each criticizing traditional values while positively presenting alternate lifestyles. The New York Drama Critics Awards went to the theatrical versions of *Cabaret* (homosexuality uncondemned) and *Your Own Thing* (a hippie theme).

II

You can work it out by Fractions or by simple Rule of Three,
But the way of Tweedle-dum is not the way of Tweedle-dee.
You can twist it, you can turn it, you can plait it till you drop,
But the way of Pilly-Winky's not the way of Winkie-Pop!
—Kipling, *The Jungle Book*

Kipling wrote *The Jungle Book* seventy-three years before Disney transformed it into one of his most successful animated films. The original contains three stories focused on Mowgli, an Indian baby raised by wolves after Shere Khan, a crippled tiger, attacks his human family. Mowgli learns the law of the jungle in his ten or eleven years living as a wolf, then is forced back into the man-village by several wolves hostile to his humanity. Later, while herding cattle for the village, Mowgli catches his arch enemy, Shere Khan the tiger, unawares, killing him with the help of his wolf-brothers. Owing to Mowgli's unique abilities and the jealousy of the village leaders, Mowgli is cast out of the man-village as a witch, virtually a young man without a country.

In another tale of Mowgli's youth, while a student of Baloo the Bear, revered teacher of the law of the jungle, the wolf-boy is kidnapped by leaderless monkeys, eager to have him teach them how to weave huts so they might gain the respect of other jungle creatures. Kaa, the boa constrictor, helps Baloo and Bagheera, the panther, rescue Mowgli. A story in *The Second Jungle Book* recounts Mowgli's compelling the greatest of jungle creatures, Hathi the elephant, to destroy the man-village and drive all humans away.

In Disney's version, Mowgli is found in a basket in a wrecked boat on a riverbank by Bagheera. He recognizes that a man-cub should not be left untended and takes Mowgli to be raised by wolves. Ten years later, Shere Khan, who hates all men, comes to that part of the jungle, so Bagheera insists on taking Mowgli to the man-village where the boy will be safe. Along the way, Mowgli, encounters a series of animals who try to hinder or hurt him. Finally, he scares off Shere Khan with lightning-spawned fire. While there is no longer a reason for Mowgli to leave, love strikes. Mowgli willingly follows a little girl into the man-village while his animal friends return to the jungle.

As is common in a Disney adaptation, character complexities are removed. Kaa, pure evil in Disney, was in Kipling a self-serving snake who saves Mowgli but also feasts on monkeys in a manner repulsive to other jungle creatures. While the resulting simplification does make the characters less multidimensional, this also renders any remaining or added character traits and symbolic qualities more easily discernable.

III

"In the early stages, the story was all about the panther and the troubles he had getting the young boy Mowgli back to the man-village. Each of the animals they met along the way reflected a different philosophy."—Frank Thomas and Ollie Johnston[6]

Disney's Mowgli is a boy who, though nominally Indian, shows every sign of being a modern American Caucasian. Except for a deeper tan and a pudgier nose, he could be Wart, the young King Arthur in Disney's *The Sword in the Stone* (1961), or an updated Pinochio, sans shellac. Mowgli speaks unaccented American English, while the animals he encounters each display distinctive accents. Also—and so obvious that it is easily overlooked—Mowgli has somehow acquired a loincloth during his years in the jungle, setting him apart from the other naked jungle residents. Mowgli's generic American boyhood is further established in his relationship with the wolf family. While his wolf parents disappear from the scene shortly after they accept him, his litter brothers magically remain little puppies—they have been drawn as dogs, not wolves—while Mowgli ages ten years. When it comes time for him to leave, they climb all over Mowgli and lick him in a manner that calls to mind a then-famous Pepsi commercial (later Bagheera tugs Mowgli by his loincloth, repeating the iconic Coppertone advertising image of a puppy pulling at a tanned baby's diaper). These are the only animals unable to speak. Unlike Kipling's wolves, these are not Mowgli's brothers but his pets.

As in the case of Disney's 1940 *Pinochio*, Mowgli's story has become the interrupted journey of a disobedient child. In Pinochio's case, he's truant from school. Mowgli won't go "home" (to the man-village). Each boy remains insistent on ignoring the wishes of those who know what's best for him. Therefore, each gets into trouble. Where Pinochio had only a conscientious cricket at his side, Mowgli is gifted with two exemplary mentors. His first foster parent is Bagheera. Though protector of Mowgli throughout the movie, Bagheera never appears completely comfortable with his role as guardian, as Kipling's panther indeed did. In Disney, Bagheera more resembles a stern parent who wants whatever is best for the child, even though Mowgli can't understand his concern. Sebastian Cabot, the maternal butler Mr. French in television's *Family Affair*, appropriately provides Bagheera'a voice.

Possessing no "real" parents, Mowgli is free to adopt some wherever he finds them. After rejecting Bagheera's tough love and good intentions, he finds a fun and permissive father in the person of "Papa Bear" Baloo, a slob with a knack for living effortlessly. He can defend himself in a fight while basically remaining a softie. Disney's Baloo appears slow on the uptake, a notable shift from Kipling, where the bright bear teaches Mowgli and is as dour a character as Disney's Bagheera. Disney's Baloo is a liberal in child rearing, as much a pal as a parent, and a social liberal. He likes the monkeys' jazz music and hip speech and, much to Bagheera's frustration, sees nothing wrong with marrying out of his species.

The film also presents a negative example of the too-stern parent in the form of Colonel Hathi, leader of the Dawn Patrol, father of Mowgli's nameless elephant doppelganger. An old-fashioned rigid parent, Hathi views family as a military operation, swatting his wife's rump when she fails to pass inspection. Hathi is so wrapped up in organizational rituals that he forgets his son completely and shows no concern over a lost child, dismissing Mowgli's disappearance as "fortunes of war and all that" until his wife intervenes.

The film, then, defines by example for its audience good parents and bad parents at the extreme—according to Disney, that is. Hathi has confused his family and his business. In Bagheera and Baloo, we perceive the contrast between the stern if mindful conservative parent, misunderstood by the child, and the permissive liberal parent, willing to let the child do as he wishes. Disney's view of which approach is best is clearly conveyed; Baloo's permissiveness allows Mowgli to be captured by monkeys. Bagheera must once again intercede to save the boy. Eventually, Baloo also realizes the wisdom of Bagheera and agrees to follow suit. Stern parenthood, as compared to overly rigid or too permissive, triumphs.

IV

BAGHEERA: Shere Khan hates man and he's not going to allow you to grow up to become a man . . . just another hunter with a gun.

MOWGLI: We'll have to explain to him that I'd never do a thing like that.

BAGHEERA: Nonsense. No one explains anything to Shere Khan.

—Walt Disney's *The Jungle Book*

Similarly, Disney robs the tiger of his unique motivation. Kipling's Shere Khan pursues Mowgli because the boy is a potential meal and an insult to Shere Khan's stature in the jungle. Disney's Shere Khan hunts Mowgli simply because he hates all men. Shere Khan never mentions eating him. It may not stretch too far to suggest that this was also Disney's worldview; there are hostile, irrational forces out there that only want to destroy what is good. If pressed, Disney probably would have identified those forces as communism, the Soviet Union, or the union movement in America—perhaps all three in combination, aligned against him personally. However we interpret this malignant force, it speaks through Kaa and exists in harmony with the vultures, whom it thanks for delaying its victim. These alignments become evident in subtler threats to Mowgli.

V

"How can you talk to a guy like that? Next thing you know, he's got you hypnotized, and you're standing on a corner in Hollywood, dressed like one of the Pointer Sisters."—Friend warning Jodie Foster's character in *Foxes*

Kaa is the first bad influence to appear. He drops down upon Mowgli immediately after the boy insists he doesn't need Bagheera's protection and doesn't want to go to the man-village. Kaa is a snake with a whiny voice that resembles a Truman Capote impression and a speech impediment that causes him to stress "esssssessss" in a lisping manner.[7] Kaa also has a whimpering laugh and a habit of lasciviously licking his mouth while gazing at his intended victim. Kaa hypnotizes Mowgli, lulling him into a false sense of security with sensual promises as he wraps his body around the child. Here is as sexualized a character as can be found in Walt's sanitized world. Kaa's speech habits and seduction of the innocent conform to the 1960s caricature of a child-molesting homosexual who drags the defenseless into a world of sensual debasement. Kaa's line while seducing Mowgli is also a typical attribute of the child molester. He sings that he is Mowgli's only true friend and will fix things so that Mowgli will never have to leave the jungle if he only trusts Kaa. This aspect of Kaa's character is revealed in a scene between Shere Khan and Kaa that resembles Sidney Greenstreet's attentions to Peter Lorre in *The Maltese Falcon*. There Greenstreet plays an aristocratic and slightly sadistic villain (note Shere Khan scratching the inside of one of Kaa's nostrils with his claw), ever so politely trying to extract information about the location of the prize from the fidgety Lorre, playing Joe Cairo, a turncoat of questionable, perhaps multiple, sexual preferences. The message is that little boys should be cautious of whom they talk to and trust—especially if the people in question "flounce," as the animators put it, when they move.[8]

VI

"There has been considerable controversy over the Black Crow sequence in recent years, most of it unjustified. The crows are undeniably black, but they are black characters, not black stereotypes. There is no denigrating dialogue, or Uncle Tomism in this scene, and if offense is to be taken in hearing blacks call each other "brother," then the viewer is merely being sensitive to accuracy."—Leonard Maltin on *Dumbo*[9]

In light of ghetto riots that occurred during the film's production period, the monkeys constitute the most interesting of the film's conservative social commentaries. They steal Mowgli from Baloo, then cruelly pummel the bear, ridiculing him, dragging Mowgli off to meet their leader, King Louie. In the grand Disney tradition, the monkeys are stereotyped caricatures—Leonard Maltin's opinion not withstanding—of black Americans, except for a few "hippie fellow swingers" who come complete with enlarged sideburns. Beyond having "black" accents, they dance to jazz music, talk in hipster slang, and sing scat. They also have prominent lips, a point stressed by Baloo, who wears two coconut halves to exaggerate his lips when he disguises himself as one of them. The monkeys are drawn in the manner of early cartoon stereotyping of African Americans.

King Louie—a name Disney added in a clear reference to Louis Armstrong—presides over a kingdom that is a slum in "the man-village ruins." He is assisted by a right-hand monkey with a white shock of swept-back hair and a tail swept out like the traditional image of a plantation houseboy in tails. This sidekick also plays trumpet solos on his lips in the same way as done by one crow in *Dumbo*. By juxtaposing Mowgli with these monkeys-as-blacks, Mowgli is more clearly defined as white. Having established the situation, then, as Disney's generic American white boy seduced into the slums by black hipsters, Disney projects two more personal insights into the nature of the 1960s black experience. First, King Louie forces bananas into Mowgli's mouth where they resemble oversized cigars or marijuana joints. These bananas have the same effect on Mowgli as his hypnotism by Kaa. Mowgli grows glassy-eyed, developing an enormous dumb grin. Recalling stories prevalent in the 1960s about banana-skin smoking, it would appear King Louie is getting the boy stoned. Shortly, Mowgli (and his grin) are up and dancing around with the monkeys.

Why was Disney's Mowgli kidnapped? King Louie explains that he has gone as far as he can as a monkey—that is to say, as black. Now he wants to be a man, white. He sings, "I want to be a man, man-cub / And stroll right into town / And be just like the other men / I'm tired of monkeying around / I want to be like you / Oh yes it's true / I want to walk like you / Talk like you do / You see it's true / An ape like me / Can learn to be human, too."

Mowgli is supposed to accomplish this transformation by giving Louie fire—notably different from the hut-building in Kipling and an interesting demand in the context of the Molotov cocktails of the even more radical late 1960s. When Mowgli explains that he doesn't know how to make fire—in effect, that the monkey is not going to be able to pass as a man—Louie becomes casually violent and begins to bounce Mowgli around by his hair. This proves significant because the monkeys are the only creatures gratuitously cruel to Mowgli and his foster parents. Baloo and Bagheera, of course, arrive to save Mowgli, sneaking in on the monkeys while absorbed in jazz-and-banana-inspired revelry. In the process of trying to hang on to Mowgli, the monkeys successfully destroy what is left of the ruins, their home. Given that blacks rioting in Watts destroyed large sections of their communities at the same time *Jungle Book* was in production, the parallels seem obvious. Thus, a Disney explanation of black discontent in the late 1960s is offered to Americans; the film argues that blacks want to be white and become destructive after learning they cannot.

VI

DIZZY: Hold it lads, look what's coming our way.

ZIGGY: Come on, lads, Come on! Let's have some fun with this little fella, this little blokey. . . .

BUZZIE: Aw, just look at him. Why the poor fellow. You know, he must be down on his luck.

DIZZY: Yeah, or he wouldn't be in our neighborhood.

—Vultures discussing Mowgli in Disney's *The Jungle Book*

After this incident, once again escaping Kaa, Mowgli arrives in the middle of a burned-out, desolate landscape spotted with pools of fetid water and a dead tree upon which four vultures perch. Bored and looking for cheap thrills while waiting for something to die, they recognize Mowgli's dire situation, falsely offering friendship. Their motives initially appear fairly innocent. But as they sing "That's What Friends Are For," they are revealed as creatures who prey on those less fortunate, predators that consume the defenseless. When Shere Khan shows up, they run over each other trying to escape while Khan thanks them for detaining his victim. The vultures hang around, ready to pick Mowgli's bones when Shere Khan is done. They are foul-weather friends. Opportunists.

And they represent the Beatles.

There are four vultures; three sport Beatle haircuts and talk with Liverpudlian accents. Dizzy has a voice that might well be John Lennon's as he tells the "lads" to check out Mowgli. The three sing—Mowgli is recruited as their fourth—although, in deference to Disney's hostility to rock and roll, the group performs a barbershop quartet.

The one that does not sing, Buzzie, is obviously older than the others. Buzzie has the Cockney accent of an earlier generation of British entertainers and is balding. Buzzie sympathizes with Mowgli, convincing the others to help the boy after Baloo is seemingly killed. It is Buzzie who tells Mowgli how to scare away Shere Khan with fire. The three Beatles—or "hippies," as one of the animators characterized them—are willing to profit by Mowgli's misfortune until shown the light by their elder. They are not beyond hope. They help Mowgli and, therefore, are superior to those black monkeys.

By their age and by the company they keep ye shall know them.

Interestingly, while these vulture-hippies are depicted as redeemable, they choose, in the end, to remain in squalor rather than fly over to the beautiful sunny jungle clearing only a few feet away. They end where they began, mimicking the classic indecision routine from 1955's *Marty* as they unproductively try to decide what to do for cheap thrills. Although they retain the possibility for positive action, these are the rock culture members that Plasketes noted; they choose to remain alienated and prefer to live under a cloud rather than moving into light.

VIII

BAGHEERA: Baloo, you can't adopt Mowgli as your son.

BALOO: Why not?

BAGHEERA: How can I put this? Birds of a feather should flock together.

—Walt Disney's *The Jungle Book*

To ascertain that Bagheera was right, Mowgli is given the choice at film's end to remain with his buddy-parent, Baloo, or enter the man-village. Mowgli willingly chooses the latter, a detail insisted upon by Walt during the scripting process. Mowgli's return is facilitated by the presence of a coquettish girl with the big doe eyes of a 1960s painting by Margaret Keane. The unnamed female's success in enticing Mowgli confirms two more staples of Disney's vision. As Ariel Dorfman and Armand Mattelart have noted, a female's only power in Disney's comic books derives from flirtation.[10] With minor alterations, this holds true for the movies as well. The girl drops her water jug; Baloo observes, "She did that on purpose!" The suddenly smitten Mowgli refills it and follows her back to the village.

Lest we think Mowgli is heading for anything but a middle-class (albeit deeply suburban) existence, the girl lures him with a song that tells Mowgli exactly what lies in store:

> Father's hunting in the forest
> Mother's cooking in the home
> I must go to fetch the water
> Till the day that I am grown
> Then I will have a handsome husband
> And a daughter of my own
> Then I'll send her to fetch the water
> I'll be cooking in the home
> My own home
> My own home.[11]

Lest we've missed the point, Baloo and Bagheera spell it out: "He's hooked." "It was bound to happen." "He's where he belongs . . . and we should get back to where we belong."

IX

"It is just as it should be, Baloo. [Bagheera said] Our Mowgli is safe in the man-village at last. He has found his true home."—*The Jungle Book*, Little Golden Book[12]

"'Man Pack and Wolf Pack have cast me out,' said Mowgli. 'Now I hunt alone in the jungle.'"—Rudyard Kipling's *The Jungle Book*

The message communicated to the viewer of Disney's *The Jungle Book* is notably different from that communicated to Kipling's reader. After the experiences of Kipling's Mowgli in the world of man and the world of the jungle, the boy finds himself unable to fit into either society. Kipling's unsettling theme, that Mowgli belongs nowhere and is destined to be an outsider wherever he goes, is turned on its head by Disney. Walt's version repeats the message of many WDC films: Everyone has a place to belong. Know your place and stay there. Even Disney's jungle bum gets the point, as Walt's silly Baloo (not Kipling's wise Baloo) explicitly states: "He's where he belongs . . . and we should get back to where we belong."

Of all the key Disney themes, knowing your place is most prominently phrased. Likewise, it's the message that most easily transcends the time period during which the film was made. This basic theme is one of traditional American values that many of Disney's films insist on. These old-fashioned values are further reinforced through a condemnation of bad characters who veer from such a traditionalist tenet. The monkeys are wrong because they want to leave their lot in life and become white. The vultures and Kaa interfere with Mowgli's return to his place. Even Baloo, the liberal who loves Mowgli, comes to see that a boy requires a traditional upbringing and that the boundaries exist for a reason. Disney's world of conservative values triumphs, even in the late 1960s, confirming Pete Seeger's axiom, "If you don't know by now, little lady, I'll tell you: lullabies are propaganda."[13]

Walt Disney's *The Jungle Book* presents a didactic, if metaphorical, vision that defends the values Walt believed crucial by attacking changes he viewed as disturbing. Kipling's stories of a boy who fell between cultures—a vision that might have been extremely relevant to the American public, youth in particular, at this time of changing values—was turned into an affirmation that the right thing to do was not "drop out" but know and accept your place rather than attempt to change the world around you. But the movie doesn't stop at a simple restatement of by then bygone axioms. Those who advocated change in the late 1960s are presented in distorted caricatures of the youth movement, blacks, and other "seducers of the innocent," their values portrayed as self-serving, self-hating, or just plain ridiculous.

NOTES

1. This essay was originally published as "'It's a Jungle Book out There, Kid': The Sixties in Walt Disney's *The Jungle Book*" *Studies in Popular Culture* 14, no. 1 (1991): 85–97.

2. Thomas and Johnston, *Disney Animation*, 27.

3. Plasketes, "From Woodstock Nation to Pepsi Generation," 8.

4. Maltin, *Disney Films*, 78.

5. Schickel, *Disney Version*, 364.

6. Thomas and Johnston, *Disney Animation*, 407.

7. These traits, which might be dismissed as "snakiness," are absent when this snake reappears as Sir Hiss in the 1973 Disney film *Robin Hood*.

8. Thomas and Johnston, *Disney Animation*, 426.

9. Maltin, *Disney Films*, 52. Maltin overlooks a few lines, like "Why don't you boys get back where you belong?" directed at the crows by Dumbo's protector, Timothy the Mouse.

10. Dorfman and Mattelart, *How to Read Donald Duck*, 64.

11. This same theme, without lyrics, occurs at two other points in the film: when Mowgli is accepted into the domestic bliss of the wolf family and, in a minor key, when Baloo must tell Mowgli that he should go to the man-village. This foreshadowing provides emphasis the third time we encounter it and also hear the lyrics.

12. Walt Disney Productions, *Jungle Book*, 23.

13. Pete Seeger, while performing at the Takoma Park Folk Festival, Takoma, Maryland, September 8, 1985.

WORKS CITED

Dorfman, Ariel, and Armand Mattelart. *How to Read Donald Duck: Imperialist Ideology in the Disney Comic*. New York: International General, 1975.

Maltin, Leonard. *The Disney Films.* New York: Bonanza, 1973.

Plasketes, George. "From Woodstock Nation to Pepsi Generation." Unpublished manuscript, Bowling Green University, Department of Communications, 1984.

Schickel, Richard. *The Disney Version.* New York: Simon and Schuster, 1968.

Thomas, Frank, and Ollie Johnston. *Disney Animation: The Illusion of Life.* New York: Abbeville Press, 1981.

Walt Disney Productions. *The Jungle Book.* New York: Golden Press, 1967.

Chapter Thirteen

"Higitus! Figitus!"

Of Merlin and Disney Magic

Susan Aronstein

In July 2015, WDC announced that *The Sword in the Stone* would join *Beauty and the Beast*, *Aladdin*, *Mulan*, *Dumbo*, and *The Jungle Book* in the lineup for proposed live-action remediations. This was met with tepid enthusiasm at best, generating more interest in the chosen screenwriter than a new version. *Vulture*'s headline captured the tone of popular response: "*Game of Thrones*' Bryan Cogman Will Try to Pull a *Sword in the Stone* Remake out of the Rock of Obscurity."[1] While *Vulture*'s response may have been harsh, *The Sword in the Stone* is—despite the continuing popularity of the Arthurian legend and the T. H. White novel (1938) upon which the animated film was based—one of Disney's least beloved, least well-known animated features. Its rerelease history is sparse: only two theatrical (1972 and 1983), four VHS (1986, 1991, 1994, and 2001), and three DVD (2001, 2008, and 2013 [Blu-ray]) releases in the United States.[2] Merchandising was minimal: some Colorforms, book and record tie-ins, an occasional playset or puppet, a handful of trading pins and commemorative figurines. Apart from "The Sword in the Stone Ceremony," which ran in Fantasyland from 1983 to 2006, the film has remained oddly absent from Disney Parks, a rarity for properties that function to invoke memories—and inspire consumption—of the canon. On the day that the studio announced a remake, the only relic of the original in Disneyland was a roped-off replica—the stranded, abandoned sword-in-anvil in front of King Arthur's Carousel, which, oddly, is decorated with murals drawn from *Sleeping Beauty*! Shops offered no trading pins, no stuffed animals or action figures, swords or shields. Merlin and Wart did not appear in parades or shows.[3]

The film, which has its charming moments, was well received by original audiences and critics. Nor has it been forgotten in academia, providing fodder for discussions of the Americanization (and Disneyfication) of the Arthurian legend.[4] If obscure, Merlin, through a metonymical drift that begins with *The Sword in the Stone*'s transformation of the fabled character into an avatar for Walt himself and Disney magic in general—"a whiz bang wizard of whimsy" and marvelous educator—remains pervasive in WDC's mythos. As a metonymy, a sign or substitution, Merlin has been detached from his Arthurian context, recontextualized within the Disney uber-imagination as a signifier of its ability to realize "visions fantastic" and a magical world.[5] Fascinatingly, then, Merlin is both nowhere and everywhere in the Disney cosmos.

MERLIN AS PROFESSOR: RAISING THE DISNEY CHILD

In the film, Merlin makes his first appearance as an educator, in possession of a bag of magic tricks, sent to prepare young Arthur to assume his destined role. So perceived, Merlin is hardly T. H. White's portrait of a fifth-century sorcerer, rather the reification of Disney's post–World War II rebranding of itself as a leader in education in the wake of a postwar shift in American child rearing. As discussed by Nicholas Sammond in his study *Babes in Tomorrowland*, after the war, "child-rearing [became] an issue of national infrastructural planning . . . equated with building airports and the construction of the interstate highway system," and America turned its attention to providing children with "an inoculation against communism," ensuring they would become "cold war tool[s]" to protect a bright national and global future.[6] Experts abandoned the previously regimented management system, based on strict schedules and measurement of social, intellectual, and physical progress designed to produce a carefully charted/documented standardized child, an approach that had been in place since the early years of the twentieth century. In the wake of Hitler's Germany and ramping up of the Cold War, Americans feared that people who were regimented in childhood would become easy targets for totalitarian regimes. To counteract these fears, doctors, educators, and parents "reimagined the child as a higher-order animal that needed to be encouraged to grow in harmony with its aptitudes."[7] Children, experts argued, were individuals, in possession of unique gifts and talents. Kids, through guided play and imagination, would develop "in [their] own way" and become leaders to whom the nation could confidently entrust "the fate of the planet."[8]

This shift in philosophies and practices plays out in two Disney productions. The first is a short, part of the studio's war effort: *Education for Death: The Making of a Nazi* (1943), which traces the education of little Hans as the state transforms him from a sweet, blond, Disneyesque boy into a killing machine. This begins in kindergarten with "the fairy tales of the new order"—a "distortion" of *Sleeping Beauty* in which Hitler stands for the Prince, the princess for Germany, the wicked witch for Democracy. The induction of Hans includes a group of children performing the Nazi salute.[9] As Hans's schooling continues, he learns to draw the "correct" moral from natural history lessons: not "poor rabbit" when the rabbit is eaten by a wolf, but "the world belongs to the strong and the brutal. The rabbit is a coward and deserves to die." Hans's education, the narrator intones, succeeds; he becomes one of a sea of boys "marching and heiling, heiling and marching." So "grim years of regimentation have done their work." Hans has "no seed of laughter, hope, tolerance or mercy." Meanwhile, the marching bodies multiply, in an animated instance of fascist aesthetic that could have been rotoscoped from a Leni Riefenstahl documentary. Their faces become masked and mechanized until, finally, their bodies mutate to crosses, a mass of graves. The short concludes: "an education for death."

Three years after its release, Disney explored the sudden shift in American child-rearing policies in a film better known, and vilified, for its problematic depiction of race. *Song of the South* is a family drama centered on the conflict between regimentation and imagination, discipline and play, rules and stories.[10] The film ends with a celebration of tale-telling, play, and imagination—the family reconciled, Johnny, Uncle Remus, and friends skipping off into a utopia that recalls the time long ago when "the critters were closer to the folk, and the folk were closer to the critters, and things were better all around." Such a reclamation is realized in the "live" world of the film's final moment through animation combined with live action.

Song of the South enshrines the power of stories and the imagination. In "Mickey as Professor," an op-ed written for *Public Opinion Quarterly* during its filming, Disney argued that his studio was uniquely positioned to extend its gifts to education, continuing the pedagogical project it started during World War II, when Disney partnered with the Canadian and American governments to produce films on subjects ranging from paying taxes to military manuals.[11] Disney staked out the studio's claim to "edutainment" (a term he coined in 1948), based on skills honed in previous productions: animation, capable of revealing "what is hidden to the camera, or even the most penetrating ray," with "story values" capable of arranging the material so "that clarity and interest are never lost, character sharply defined, and narration kept balanced at the point . . . where intelligibility and completeness meet."[12] Disney edutainment, Walt claimed, would hold "a higher degree of attention and retention" than textbooks while providing "the closest approximation to actual experience and practice."[13]

Following publication of "Mickey as Professor," Disney Studios ramped up its pedagogical production. In the years leading up to *The Sword in the*

Stone, Disney established a firm footing in our educational system. The studio, bolstered by animation to "reassure and explain," soon "developed a voice of scientific authority" that promised "Nature" and "common sense" would provide answers to issues ranging from "the vanishing prairie" to the common cold.[14] Uncle Walt became Professor Walt (presaging, of course, Professor Merlin), who, through the magic of film, could make learning fun, the most complex scientific concepts clear to the average American.

One of the earliest entries in Disney's pedagogical canon was 1948's *Seal Island*, the inaugural film in the True Life Adventure series. As Sammond notes, these documentaries, with their anthropomorphized explorations of family dynamics and child development, naturalize American family structures and notions of childhood, inscribing the suburban nuclear family— complete with nosy neighbors, coquettish wives, nervous mothers, clueless fathers, and adventurous children—on the natural world.[15] Each True Life Adventure includes extended scenes of courtship, homemaking, and family life. One favorite stock scene features the boys-will-be-boys trope: they wander off on adventures, bite off more than they can chew, indulge in play and roughhousing. But, as the narrator asserts, play is actually nature's school, an essential part of growing up and finding one's place in the natural order.

While True Life Adventures anthropomorphized and naturalized post–World War II American child-rearing philosophies, *The Mickey Mouse Club* (1955–1959) implemented these, as the show "encouraged [the child] to grow in harmony with its aptitudes."[16] The variety series centered around creative play—singing and dancing, dramatized serials and skits, and informational shorts, all aimed at allowing viewers, in the words of the club's roll-call song, to "develop faithfully" those "talents given you and me." Even as the play school of the True Life Adventures ensured young polar bears and cougars would grow up to find their place in the natural order, so the Disney school that was *The Mickey Mouse Club* ensured that its (American) viewers would become, as the news segment promised, "the leaders of the twenty-first century."

THE KING ARTHUR OF LEGEND FOR YOU, THE LEADERS OF TOMORROW

Disney's 1963 version of *The Sword in the Stone* owes more to this postwar confluence of educational films, nature documentaries, and *The Mickey Mouse Club* than to T. H. White or the Arthurian legend.[17] The film's ambiguous relationship to its source material (Disney only reluctantly green-lighted the project following the success of Lerner and Loewe's *Camelot*) is oddly signaled in its initial montage, which employs the studio's ongoing technique of beginning with an opening book. However, unlike earlier Disney animated features (such as *Snow White*, *Pinocchio*, and *Sleeping Beauty*) that move seamlessly from the static book illustrations to Disney animations, *The Sword in the Stone* stylistically distances itself from the tale of "when England was young." For as the book opens, and pages turn, the illustrations remain flat, bound by text, some pages filled with dense manuscript writing, lacking illustrations. Camera movement is limited to panning from page to page; the only spark of animation occurs when the sword appears in the stone. The accompanying song of a time "when knights were brave and bold" lacks Disney vim and verve, sounding archaic, its rhymes awkward. Then (unlike any other Disney film that opens with a book) the screen fades to black, indicating a complete break from what has gone before. The scene rematerializes with the film's first animation—a hawk pursuing a squirrel— as the narrator concludes, "This was a dark age . . . and men lived in fear of one another, for the strong preyed upon the weak." This is precisely true of ancient Arthurian myth, also of the White novel—but not of the film to follow.

With the studio's trademark multiplane camera panning through layers of forest, the imagery focuses on Merlin drawing water as the story proper begins. "Dark Age indeed," the wizard laments, "age of inconvenience. No plumbing. No electricity. No nothing. Everything one big medieval mess." An opening shot in "the Disney animated film vocabulary" invariably identifies the story's primary character. Here that is Merlin, not Wart, only introduced later, after Merlin has misidentified Kay as his future pupil. The advertising and reception confirms that this "Whiz Bang Wizard of Wizardry," who educates the "leader of tomorrow," preparing Wart to lead the world out of its medieval mess, is the true star.[18] As such, *The Sword in the Stone* is more concerned with the pedagogical than the Arthurian, as Merlin becomes a metonymy for Walt and the studio's educational philosophy and techniques.

Not surprisingly, then, the wizard provides a modern, Disney-style education, one that allows Wart to "find a direction" and "prepare for the future"— and most importantly, helps him channel his natural aptitudes, "real spark," "spirit," and "throw[ing] himself into everything he does," into the right channels. Also, the wizard helps Wart "develop faithfully," like a good Mouseketeer, "the talents given to you and me." Merlin offers Wart the new educational method, departing both from that of Sir Ector, with his tight schedule and demerits, or Archimedes, employing books and blackboards. Disney's reimagined Merlin possesses Disney magic, used, as he informs Ector, "mainly for educational purposes." He, like Disney, is prepared to use "magic, every trick in the book" to catch Wart's attention and prepare him for his future.

Merlin's Disney schoolroom transforms White's seminars in political philosophy into a series of True Life Adventure sequences interspersed with some science and health instruction. Merlin's magic as aided by Wart's imagination transforms the boy into a fish, a squirrel, and a bird. Each lessons begins, as do Disney's pedagogical films, with the voice of scientific authority, here provided by Merlin. He explains basic principles: wildlife biology (the location and function of the caudal fin, the mechanics of the bird's wing), physics (for every to, there is a fro), gravity ("the phenomenon that any two bodies, if free to move, will be accelerated towards each other"). The sequence then segues into a predator-and-prey flight narrative (also a standard building block of the True Life Adventures). These animated sequences strongly resemble the anthropomorphized scenes found in Disney's nature documentaries, which resolves happily when the prey deploys the lesson of "brains over brawn." Finally, each lesson also contains a moral, an ideological takeaway to develop character as well as the brain: "Set your sights, upon the heights, don't be a mediocrity"; "That love business is a powerful thing—greater than gravity"; "knowledge and wisdom is the real power."

As Wart learns these lessons, the books in *The Sword in the Stone*, as Gossedge argues, remain largely unread.[19] Instead, the film provides an animated/narrative example of Disney's argument in "Mickey [Disney] as Professor," wherein textbooks become supplemental and secondary to the magic of film. While in terms of books and Merlin's formidable list of subjects, Wart's lessons may seem, in Gossedge's words, "content free," they are in line with lessons offered in the studio's documentary and health films—lessons appropriate to an energetic young boy with spark and spirit.[20] In them, Merlin employs every trick available in the Disney repertoire, from the calm voice of scientific authority, capable of explaining complex concepts to the layperson, through analogy and illustration, to the magic of animation.

These lessons dominate *The Sword in the Stone*'s seventy-five minutes. Only fifteen relate directly to Arthurian legend, all of these perfunctory. Even the triumphant conclusion, in which Wart draws forth the sword, proving himself the "rightwise born king of England," feels tacked on and anticlimactic, somehow separate from the film's true interests/ambitions. In White, Wart's lessons in the animal world directly provide him with the knowledge to become king. In the Disney Version, there is no apparent connection between Wart's lessons in science and natural history and the ruling of a country. Indeed, the young king, hiding on his throne, recognizes this himself: "I don't know anything about ruling a country." However, through years of watching Disney's educational films, the audience assumes that, with more time in Merlin's magical Disney schoolroom, Wart—like American children brought up in the real-world equivalent of that schoolroom—will mature to take his proper place as leader of tomorrow.

THE SORCERER'S HAT: MERLIN, MICKEY, AND MAGIC

The Sword in the Stone is very much a product of its time, an animated fantasy locating Disney's pedagogical policies in the medieval past, equating Disney and Merlin as ideal educators for a future generation. As such, *The Sword in the Stone*, Gossedge observes, is one of the few Disney versions that has failed to replace its source material in cultural memory.[21] However, the film does succeed in erasing the Arthurian through the metonymical drift that detaches Merlin from his Camelot context by inserting him into the chain of metonymies that stand in for an idealized Walt and Disney magic. This process began pre–*Sword in the Stone* with "The Sorcerer's Apprentice" segment of *Fantasia* (1940). The blue robes and pointed blue wizard's hat (later transferred to Merlin) of Yen Sid (a clear metonymy for Disney) mark his magical powers—the power of animation, the power to bring the stuff of dreams and visions to life. The hat becomes a metonymy for that power, bestowing it on Mickey, "starring" as the sorcerer's apprentice.[22] In *Fantasia*, this "bright young lad's" foray into animation—"practicing some of the boss's best magic tricks before learning how to control them"—ends badly. His dream of conducting the stars, waves, and clouds becomes a nightmare of out-of-control brooms and flooding that concludes with Mickey meekly returning the hat to Yen Sid and resuming his dull labor.

This 1940s version of the tale seemingly argues for a Disney/corporate control over the magic. It is tempting to read this segment in the context of the labor disputes between Walt and his animators, culminating in the 1941 strike. WDC, beginning with the nighttime Park extravaganza *Fantasmic!* (1992 in Disneyland, 1998 in Walt Disney World, 2011 in Tokyo Disney), has remediated and repurposed "The Sorcerer's Apprentice" to enshrine Mickey's overambitious servant as a multivalent metonymy for Disney (both man and company), magic, and imagination. Mickey now assumes Merlin's role. However, instead of an avatar for the use of Disney magic in the education of the next generation (the leaders of tomorrow), Mickey serves as an agent of anamnesis by evoking "magical memories of Disney," memories provided by the astounding imagination of Walt/Mickey. The show begins as the stretch of Frontierland on the banks of the Rivers of America is plunged into darkness. The narrator announces:

> Tonight your friend and host, Mickey Mouse, uses his vivid imagination to create magical imagery for all to enjoy. Nothing is more wonderful than the imagination . . . but, beware, nothing is more powerful . . . for it can also expand your greatest fears into an overwhelming nightmare. Are the powers of Mickey's imagination strong enough and bright enough to defeat the evil forces that invade Mickey's dreams?[23]

Music swells, lights and sets rise up out of darkness. A spotlight snaps on to reveal Mickey conjuring fireworks from the sky and a dancing fountain from the river. The waters form a screen for clips of Disney animation that flow from Mickey's imagination, beginning with "The Sorcerer's Apprentice," now accompanied by real water and light effects. This repurposed version collapses Mickey and Yen Sid; Mickey has emerged as the sole sorcerer. His vision resolves into the flowers and butterflies that Yen Sid conjured at the beginning of the *Fantasia* segment. The show's theme song plays: "Seek within your mind and you will find in your imagination / Mysteries and magic, visions fantasic / Leading to strange and wonderful dreams." Drawn from Mickey's imagination, animation becomes real. Figures and boats appear, and water, light, animation, a collage of film melodies. Dancers merge to provide the viewers with a technological spectacle full of Disney memories: *Jungle Book*, *Dumbo*, *Pinocchio*, *Peter Pan*, and princesses ("tales of enchantment, beauty and romance, happily-ever-afters"). Maleficent introduces conflict, and the *Sleeping Beauty* dragon to slay, declaring, "Now I will turn that little mouse's imagination into a nightmare fantasmic. Imagine this!" Of course, Mickey's imagination *is* "strong enough and bright enough to defeat the evil forces," conjuring pixie dust and Tinkerbell. The Mark Twain steamboat appears, chock-full of Disney characters celebrating Mickey's triumph. Mickey reappears in full sorcerer's regalia, including that iconic hat, to conduct water and lights in the finale. The show ends with him asserting, "Some imagination, huh?"

In *Fantasmic!* and "The Sorcerer's Apprentice," Merlin is present only through the metonym of the hat, symbolizing the magical powers of animation and imagination. However, Disney's July 2010 live-action film *The Sorcerer's Apprentice* ("suggested by the animated short") makes explicit the connection between Merlin and Yen Sid while echoing the pedagogical concerns of *The Sword in the Stone* in a considerably more Arthurian tale as to tone, if lacking either Arthur or a sword.[24] That film features Merlin and three apprentices, also a promised child heir to Merlin's powers, the Prime Merlinian, who will be identified by the dragon ring and save the world.

The film that follows is clichéd and silly. However, like *Fantasmic!*, *The Sorcerer's Apprentice* encapsulates a significant shift in WDC's pedagogical mission and corporate identity. Its modern-day plot features young David, a twenty-first-century Wart in full-possession of Disney imagination. He creates impromptu animation of King Kong and attacking planes to line up with the background of the (real) Empire State Building on the "cell" of the school-bus window. Fate and the dragon ring identify David as the Prime Merlinian, but the powers of evil thwart Balthazar and traumatize David. If Wart is the product of Merlin's Disney pedagogy, the older David (ten years later) is signaled in the shot of this grown-up. A plain digital clock has replaced the Buzz Lightyear clock of his childhood. This adult David is the sorry product of a world without Disney. *The Sword in the Stone*'s Merlin appears, using magic to teach Wart science, providing the education that will prove he's not a "nobody . . . lucky to be Kay's squire." Balthazar shows David that there is a magical world beyond science, teaching him to "clear your mind, believe." Only when David learns to see the magic (to produce a spectacle of light and sound out of the Tesla coils, on which he was "so fixated with [their] technical aspect, [he] almost failed to see something beautiful") and believe in it can he save the world by using science, magic, and imagination to defeat Morgana in a light-show spectacle worthy of a Disneyland finale.

The final shot dwells on the ultimate metonymy for Disney magic: Yen Sid's, Mickey's, Merlin's pointed blue hat. This connection between Mickey, magic, and imagination has been solidified in two recent versions of "The Sorcerer's Apprentice": the video game *Epic Mickey* (2010) and the Disneyland show *Mickey and the Magical Map* (2013). Both begin with Yen Sid's voice extoling his latest magical creation, with the ability to reify imagination, to provide dreamers with an embodied experience of "the Disney real." In *Epic Mickey*, this realm takes the form of "a world for things that have been forgotten"; in *Mickey and the Magical Map*, "it [is] a map, unlike any other, with power to transport dreamers to any place imaginable."[25] Both game and show adapt "The Sorcerer's Apprentice" to extol the power of imagination, animation, and Disney magic. In both, Mickey, as the sorcerer's apprentice, must learn to trust the power of the imagination; to heal the Wasteland at the end of the game and discover the secret of the map in the show. If Merlin educates the Wart in science and nature, Yen Sid teaches Mickey (and audiences) to "let the voice of inspiration be [their] guide." "If we all believe in the world of dreams and imagination . . . there's no way to know where the spark will take us."

"The possibilities," Yen Sid concludes, "are endless." Yet these endless possibilities are *Disney* possibilities. The map that "will never be completed, not as long as there is imagination in the world," is Disney's map—realized in the corporation's films, shows, games, cruise lines, and theme parks—all made possible through Disney magic. The symbol is Merlin's hat, which detaches Merlin from the Arthurian and appropriates him for the Disney legend. And this is why the Sword in the Stone, alone in the parks, is a stranded object removed from the context that would give it meaning within the Disney mythos. Merlin as a metonymy for Disney, however, thrives within his new context; his hat is multiplied, replicated, and is for sale—on pins, on figurines, in snow globes, as earrings and key chains, as a hat (with or without Mickey ears), everywhere.

It remains to be seen how this Merlin—this Disney Mickey Merlin—will be recontextualized in the forthcoming Disney version of *The Sword in the Stone*. Perhaps, if Cogman succeeds in his quest to draw the film from its "rock of obscurity," Arthur will come to Disneyland, the now-generic swords and shields will sport his image, and figurines, costumes, and playsets will fill the shelves. Perhaps even the half-forgotten stone in front of King Arthur's Carousel will finally find a place on the Disney map.

NOTES

1. Nate Jones, "*Game of Thrones*' Bryan Cogman Will Try to Pull a *Sword in the Stone* Remake out of the Rock of Obscurity," *Vulture*, July 23, 2015, http://www.vulture.com/2015/07/sword-in-the-stone-remake.html.

2. As opposed, for instance, to *Cinderella*, which has received five theatrical rereleases, four VHS, two LaserDisc, two DVD, and two Blu-ray.

3. These observations were made on a July 19, 2015, visit to Disneyland.

4. I have discussed the film in "Twice Knightly: Democratizing the Middle Ages for Middle Class America," *Studies in Medievalism* 6 (1994): 213–31 (co-authored with Nancy Coiner), and *Hollywood Knights: Arthurian Cinema and the Politics of Nostalgia* (New York: Palgrave Macmillan, 2005). Other discussions include Raymond Thompson, "The Ironic Tradition in Four Arthurian Films," in *Cinema Arthuriana: Twenty Essays*, rev. ed., ed. Kevin J. Harty (Jefferson, NC: McFarland, 2010), 110–17; Alice Grellner, "Two Films That Sparkle: *The Sword in the Stone* and *Camelot*," in Harty, *Cinema Arthuriana*, 118–26; Pamela Morgan, "One Brief Shining Moment: Camelot in Washington D.C.," *Studies in Medievalism* 6 (1994): 185–211; and Rob Gossedge, "*The Sword in the Stone*: American Translatio and Disney's Antimedievalism," in *The Disney Middle Ages: A Fairy Tale and Fantasy Past*, ed. Tison Pugh and Susan Aronstein (New York: Palgrave Macmillan, 2012), 113–21.

5. *Fantasmic!*, live-action show, Disneyland, Anaheim, CA, July 18, 2015.

6. Nicholas Sammond, *Babes in Tomorrowland: Walt Disney and the Making of the American Child, 1930–1960* (North Carolina: Duke University Press, 2005), 251, 209. Other factors that led to this rebranding include the studio's complicated financial situation that lent attraction to the idea of extending its product line to films that could be completed quickly and cheaply and the positive response to the educational and training films that had been Disney's contribution to the war effort.

7. Ibid., 252.

8. Ibid.

9. *Education for Death: The Making of a Nazi*, directed by Clyde Geronimi (uncredited) (Buena Vista, CA: Disney Studios, 1943).

10. *Song of the South*, directed by Wilfrid Jackson and Harve Foster (Buena Vista, CA: Disney Studios, 1946).

11. Walt Disney, "Mickey as Professor," *Public Opinion Quarterly* 9 (1945): 119–25.

12. Ibid., 120.

13. Ibid., 122, 123.

14. A. Bowdoin Van Riper, "Introduction," in *Learning from Mickey, Donald, and Walt: Essays on Disney's Edutainment Films*, ed. A. Bowdoin Van Riper (Jefferson, NC: McFarland, 2011).

15. Sammond, *Babes in Tomorrowland*, 227.

16. Ibid., 252.

17. *The Sword in the Stone*, directed by Wolfgang Reitherman (Buena Vista, CA: Disney Studios, 1963).

18. Gossedge also notes the film's focus on Merlin ("*Sword in the Stone*," 122).

19. Ibid., 125.

20. Ibid.

21. Ibid., 115.

22. For a thorough discussion of "The Sorcerer's Apprentice" and its adaptations, see Erin Felicia Labbie, "'The Sorcerer's Apprentice': Animation and Alchemy in Disney's Medievalism," in Pugh and Aronstein, *Disney Middle Ages*, 97–14.

23. *Fantasmic!*, live-action show, Disneyland, Anaheim, CA, July 18, 2015.

24. *The Sorcerer's Apprentice*, directed by Jon Turteltaub (Buena Vista, CA: Disney Studios, 2010).

25. *Mickey and the Magic Map*, live-action show, Disneyland, Anaheim, CA, July 18, 2015; *Epic Mickey*, designed by Warren Spector (Glendale, CA: Disney Games, 2010).

Chapter Fourteen

"This Is Not the Mary Poppins I Know!"

P. L. Travers Goes to Hollywood

David S. Silverman and Olga Silverman

For a receiver to shift back and forth between *Mary Poppins*, the book (1934), and *Walt Disney's Mary Poppins*, the film (1964), can easily lead to a disconcerting disconnect. British author Neil Gaiman experienced just such a problem when he read P. L. Travers's novel *after* watching the Disney film: "The book I read was utterly wrong—it was not the Mary Poppins I remembered—and utterly, entirely right."[1] His words echo the experience of those who read *Mary Poppins* first and then catch the movie—except the latter receivers are left with the sense that it's the movie that got it all wrong.

This essay examines the dichotomy not only through an academic lens but also from a dual perspective, allowing for autoethnographical exploration. When my wife and co-author, Olga, and I were invited to write about Marry Poppins, our own immediate disconnect between Disney's movie and the books by Travers (1899–1996) (of which there are eight, appearing over a fifty-four-year period until 1988) swiftly became the subject of heated conversations. Olga grew up reading the Poppins canon (translated into Russian) as a child in Latvia. She did not have an opportunity to see the movie until after she had immigrated to the United States as an adult. When Olga finally did see it, her reaction was one of irritation and confusion. In an identical (if completely reversed) reaction to Gaiman's experience, Olga felt the film is "utterly wrong," yet so right at the same time.

Contrarily, I was raised solely on the Disney product, never exposed to the Travers books until Olga bought them for our daughter. Before finally experiencing them in a familial situation, I had tried to understand what was "so wrong" with the Academy Award–winning classic that has hijacked the hearts of several generations of people around the world. So I repeatedly asked questions: "Does Mary Poppins ride up the bannister in the book?" "Does she speak to animals? Does she have tea party in the air?"

"Yes, yes, and yes," came the answers.

"Then what's wrong?"

"It is not the Mary Poppins I know!"

We continued to try to understand each other, until it occurred to Olga that the difference does not so much exist in the actions of Mary Poppins as it does in the overall aura of Disney's film—the philosophy of individual characters and Disney's personal/artistic vision as expressed through their interactions. After innumerous viewings, rereading the book series, researching academic writing about the adaptation, and fighting over the interpretation of every sequence, as well as debating every song Disney's craftspersons created and included, we finally reached a modicum of common ground. At last, we can watch *Mary Poppins* in peace while popping popcorn and singing along to "A Spoonful of Sugar" instead of squabbling.

After sifting through the differences between the books and the movie, Olga noted that *Mary Poppins*, as text, is a body of work containing no one specific villain strong enough to carry the entire scenario. The plot of every book proves anticlimactic: each consists of a selection of interactions between Mary and the children and ends, intriguingly, not (as is normally the case) when conflicts are resolved, but because the universe calls for Mary Poppins to leave her current setting. The whole notion of Mary's magic is illusive; the children in her care are uncertain if anything actually happened. Such unconventional scenarios are not easy to adapt from text to screen even today; by Hollywood standards of the 1950s and 1960s, they were deemed unfilmable,[2] an assessment I agreed with. My personal attitude: "Perhaps someone could turn them into a television series." Our conclusion? Disney set out to create his own version of Mary Poppins, one with a concise and clear plot, a simplified and resolvable conflict, and pleasantly memorable musical numbers.

MARY POPPINS, THE TEXT

First, *Mary Poppins* is not a singular novel, but a series of eight by P. L. Travers.[3] These are connected by the interaction of a set of common characters—Mary, the nanny, and the Banks family: Mr. and Mrs. Banks and their *four* children (and a fifth on the way).[4] Each of the first three books begins with Poppins's appearance and ends with her sudden departure. The fourth, *Mary Poppins in the Park*, is a collection of nanny and children's adventures while Mary stays with the family; however, it is unclear during which of her visits the tales told here take place.[5]

The Beginning and the End Are Accidental

The first novel opens with Poppins's initial arrival. She discovers that Mr. Banks is a grumpy, overworked man who can barely provide for his family. Similarly, Mrs. Banks is an overwhelmed mother. The kids are kids, lively and curious, exhausted by the ever-changing caretakers. At the point of Poppins's first departure, the family is calmed and relaxed, including even the ever-bickering and useless servants. Clearly, Poppins arrives because they need her. In a way, we might claim Mrs. Banks conjures Mary up by writing letters to the newspapers. The text does not reveal if these were actually ever mailed; also, it is not clear how Poppins influences the climate of the house other than taking the burden of child care away from their mother.

Travers skillfully shifts the third-person narrative in such a way that we view all the adventures through Jane and Michael Banks's eyes. Afterward, no tangible evidence exists to prove to them or us as readers that Mary's magic did indeed occur. Scarce objects that link the children's imagination to their reality, such as Poppins's snakeskin belt,[6] can be explained as mere coincidences or, perhaps, inspiration drawn from their childhood fantasies. Simply, it is perhaps impossible to create that same level of ambiguity, and do so successfully, in a medium such as film, where adventures either happen or do not. This is particularly true of a Hollywood film of the mid-1960s, long before surreal experimentation entered into the mainstream product. More so with a family film, expected to speak directly, and clearly, to children of all ages, as the saying goes.

Genre identification of Travers's books is also ambiguous. Filled with magic and adventure, they do not fit the profile for fairy tales, nor can they be neatly included in an alternative realm of children's literature dubbed "magical realism." The nature of Mary's magic is never fully explained to the reader or her fellow adventurers, the Banks children. Poppins herself is neither fairy nor sorceress, she does not possess any magically empowered objects, such as a magic wand or a crystal ball. Moreover, at every opportunity, she refuses to acknowledge the presence of magic in her own actions. Things just happen, and that's that. The children's adventures are assigned to the expansion of their understanding of the world, the everyday magic of reality. The movie simplifies and grounds these experiences by attributing them utterly to Poppins's supernatural abilities.

No Explicit Conflict

Poppins scholar Giorgia Grilli wittily points out that ever since the Disney Version first appeared, Mary has become a recognizable image within our culture, identifiable not only by visual accessories such as her hat, umbrella, and carpet bag, but also her "defining characteristics: the ability to solve all problems and sooth all worries."[7] Poppins does not "fix" anything in what might be thought of as an ambiguous manner. Truthfully, there is nothing she can fix, since she can neither help Mr. Banks earn more money nor replace the incompetent help. Nevertheless, her mere presence brings spiritual peace to the Banks household. When Travers's Mary "comes back" to visit in the volume of that title, the Banks family calms down. Mr. Banks, who was livid in the morning about his servant giving him one black shoe and one brown, changes his mind, telling his wife: "The mixture was much admired in the Office. I shall always wear them that way in the future." This exemplary incident reveals that Poppins doesn't alter reality, instead magically revealing an alternative (and by implication magical) way of perceiving and dealing with daily life.[8]

That Poppins does not "fix" the Banks is stated clearly in the narrative. The second book, *Mary Poppins Comes Back*, opens with Mrs. Banks' lamentations that everything has gone wrong since Mary left. By her departure at the sequel's conclusion, Poppins takes a "return ticket," hinting that she will need to return again. Indeed, she comes back again in the third entry, *Mary Poppins Opens the Door*. This time, it's made clear her departure will be final. Still, she does not actually resolve any explicit conflicts, nor does she solve any problems.

No Explicit Villain

Every good story requires a villain. Such characters scare and repulse us, make us root for the protagonist, and, when finally defeated, fill us with a sense of accomplishment and righteousness. This is not the case with Travers's books. The first features no antagonist whatsoever. While the major conflict, as stated earlier, is Mr. Banks's dissatisfaction with life, Poppins does not correct or influence his comings and goings in any direct way. There is no confrontation between the nanny and Mr. Banks, as seen in the film; there is no life-changing experience that their remarkable visitor offers him. Mr. Banks becomes happier because his wife becomes happier and because the kids are more effectively cared for.

Overall, the primary focus of the texts is on the children's experiences with the unknown, which have little to do with the well-being of the household. All of the adults' problems appear secondary and unimportant; the only thing that matters is the children's ethical and intellectual growth.[9] From this perspective, Poppins has nothing—and most certainly, no one—to fight with her.

When she returns in *Mary Poppins Comes Back*, the eponymous hero is challenged with one tangible villain, Miss Andrew. The third book, though, returns to the approach of the original; Travers does not provide any villain or antagonist. The fourth installment doesn't even have a comprehensive plot per se, existing only as an ensemble of adventures that may have taken place at any time within the context of the first three. In Travers's books, the unfolding series of Poppins's interactions with the children are channeled toward the demonstration of the simple nonmaterial joy that comes from being together, giving instead of taking, and the like. Throughout the series, Poppins continues to expose Jane and Michael to the miracles of life— talking, joking, and wise animals; constellations shopping for Christmas presents; dancing cows. Travers's narrative insists that the experience—task, even—of human growth is not only miraculous but important enough to comprise an adventure on its own terms. On the other hand, to be successful, a "family movie" (whether weak, mediocre, or brilliant, as this Disney film certainly is) requires a villain to allow the audience what they most want, a rooting interest. For this purpose, Disney introduces the mean-spirited bank owner Mr. Dawes, a stern taskmaster with a skewed set of values, to constantly oppose our protagonist, Mr. Banks, who if nothing else clearly "means well."

MARY POPPINS, THE FILM

The story of how Walt Disney pursued Travers in obtaining the film rights to her books, the lasting aftermath, and the dichotomy of text verses film[10] served as the basis for WDC's 2013 release *Saving Mr. Banks*.[11] The story begins in 1944, when Walt's daughter Diane was overheard laughing at the text. She and her mother asked Walt if he could make it into a movie.[12] He sent his brother Roy to meet Travers as early as 1945, to no avail, since Roy and Walt made animated films and she was adamant that *Mary Poppins* not be presented as a feature-length cartoon.[13]

In the ensuing years, Travers—while continuing to reject Disney—also turned down offers from no less than the esteemed theater artists Rodgers and Hammerstein and Hollywood's renowned producer of posh projects Samuel Goldwyn. As Disney's songwriter Robert B. Sherman would later reflect, this "was just plain weird considering how minor a writer she actually was."[14] Meanwhile, during the late 1940s, Disney evolved beyond his initial identity as a creator only of high-quality cartoons by branching first into documentaries[15] and then into live-action films.[16] By the time Travers seriously entered into negotiations with Disney, only four of her books had been published and sales had already languished (a fifth, *Mary Poppins from A to Z*, would be published during production). By 1959, her financial situation worsened; her only steady income was from a lodger at Travers's home. Disney's offer of $100,000 for the film rights, plus 5 percent of the producer's gross,[17] was too solid and desperately needed to pass up at this point in her life, personal apprehension aside.[18]

Disney sent two emissaries, William B. "Bill" Dover, his executive story editor, and a Mr. Swan,[19] to visit Travers in London. According to the contract, Travers was to provide a story treatment, with a guarantee that she would be consulted on casting and artistic issues. Notably, Travers would have final script approval in exchange for granting full cinematic rights to her stories.[20] The deal did not, however, give her sole film treatment rights— Disney had already set Bill Walsh and Don Da Gradi to work on developing a film treatment in 1959.[21] Also, Disney inadvertently asked the Sherman brothers to do the same in 1961 when he handed them a copy of the book.[22] He didn't like their results—despite Sherman's claim that it was the first "script treatment for *Mary Poppins* that possessed a single, linear storyline."[23] Yet what would remain from the Sherman treatment would change the course of the eventual film and impact subsequent meetings with the formidable Ms. Travers.

According to Sherman, Travers had set *Mary Poppins* firmly in the London of the 1930s and the Great Depression. He and his brother Richard felt this far too drab for the musical they envisioned. This, not surprisingly, led to heady arguments between Travers and Disney and, more recently, for the authors of this article. Olga insisted that as this had been the era Travers had originally intended, it ought to have been maintained, the author's intent for the piece respected. I argued that Sherman had been right since this would not be Travers's book on film but a Disney motion picture derived from her novel, therefore insisting on Disneyfication in order to satisfy Walt's ongoing/loyal audience. This particular argument has, to date, not been resolved between the two of us.

As for the Shermans, their idea—a musical in the tradition of the grand old English music hall—required a shift from the 1930s to 1910, the last year of King Edward's reign. This is established early through Mr. Banks's song "The Life I Lead." In the two weeks before their initial pitch to Walt, the Shermans completed several potential songs, including "Supercalifragilisticexpialidocious," which in their minds would provide the story's children (and the general audience) with a magical word that wouldn't disappear without a trace as Travers's elusive brand of magic does in the books. Another song written in those two weeks was "Tuppence a Bag" (or "Feed the Birds"), which immediately became Walt's favorite.[24]

Travers Signs On

By June 1960, Travers had entered into a six-year "service agreement" with Disney, protecting her copyrights before and during the arrangement while requiring her to produce a version of a potential treatment within sixty days. Needless to say, personal problems complicated matters. Her adopted son Camillus began to suffer from alcoholism and other odd behavior, ultimately resulting in a six-month prison sentence.[25] Silence prevailed. Disney finally contacted Travers by telegram that December to let her know the project was on, suggesting she visit the West Coast that spring, all expenses paid.[26]

The visit, in late March of 1961, was not an easy experience for any of the parties involved. According to Sherman, Walt met with Travers, then took off for a two-week vacation; however, Lawson, Travers's biographer, notes that she "did not turn away during their long talks in Burbank that April."[27] Regardless of which account ought to be considered most accurate, one thing is for certain—much of Travers's time was spent in the studio. Her treatment had called for using no less than seventeen stories from three of her novels, while Walt's scriptwriters had selected three strong dramatic scenes from the first book and four lesser ones from the first and second.[28] The Disney team also insisted upon collapsing various male characters in the books into Bert—a creation from the 1961 script treatment—to simplify while adding more cohesion.[29]

Disney Creates a Villain

The scenario united these seven scenes by a common conflict derived from Travers's text: the children's father is aloof, stern, too much concerned with material well-being. As a result, he doesn't find happiness in his family life. Along with "fixing" other issues with this "unfilmable" book, Disney sensed the need to create a villain for a clear, easy-to-grasp conflict. This, as Olga mentioned, would be Mr. Dawes, the bank president,[30] whose death leads to the catharsis of the plot and the resolution. The entire piece ends when this conflict is resolved, allowing Mary to leave the family, now united.

Travers initially objected but in the end relented to the Hollywood machine that required "a storyline of black-and-white sentiments," not a family at the center of "gentle short stories."[31] The Sherman brothers took note after note on Travers's objections—including that there should be no red in the film because there was no red in London.[32] Travers also insisted that the film be set in the Edwardian era, that there could be no hint of romantic love between Bert and Mary,[33] and that the cast be made up of English actors. Walt ultimately accepted the latter two, with the notable exceptions of American actors Dick Van Dyke and Ed Wynn.[34]

Over the next two years, the scriptwriters worked their Disney magic. By February 1963, Walt sent Travers the latest script and his ideas for the cast; Travers's reply consisted of fourteen pages.[35] As she had final script approval, Travers wanted her objections to be known. But Walt had cleverly retained "final cut";[36] in the end, most of her objections were ignored, including what she considered to be many American forms of speech, the opulence of the Banks's home, and the entire "outing" to the Bank of England.[37] Film production proceeded as Walt (perhaps aware of his own ill health; death would claim him less than two years later) envisioned his "magnum opus."[38] After the premiere[39] in Los Angeles on August 27, 1964, Dick Van Dyke recalls the now-infamous story of her objection to Disney over the inclusion of animated sequences: "Walt was unfazed. 'Sorry,' he said. 'But the ship has already sailed.'"[40]

And, indeed, sailed onward. Various sources note that *Poppins* reached number one at the box office as 1964's most popular film, netting well over forty-five million dollars then and more than one hundred million in the ensuing years. While a clear accounting of Travers's lifetime earnings is unknown, by the time of her death she was a multimillionaire[41]—the bulk of her money coming from her uneasy relationship with Walter Elias Disney.

MARY POPPINS SAVES YET ANOTHER FAMILY

In the end, *Mary Poppins* (the book series) and *Walt Disney's Mary Poppins* (the film) should be viewed as examples of separate art forms. While the former inspired the latter, two strikingly different artists, with different goals and different audiences in mind, created these works. The books of P. L. Travers are timeless, deeply philosophical, and focused on interaction and process rather than on action and results. *Walt Disney's Mary Poppins* remains a jewel of cinematographic entertainment: beautiful, colorful, musical, dynamic, and memorable. Once we, the authors of this article, stopped looking for a movie matrix in the books, or seeking a mirror image of the books in the film, we resolved a comprehension conflict unavoidably ignited by the comparison of the two media. Our daughter tucks a volume of *Mary Poppins* into a bookshelf tightly packed with P. L. Travers's books, then pulls out Disney's DVD and pops it into a player; now we can peacefully enjoy both of these outstanding creations.

NOTES

1. Neil Gaiman, preface to Lawson, *Mary Poppins, She Wrote*, xiii.
2. Sherman, *Moose*, 362.
3. Complete list of Mary Poppins books by P. L. Travers: *Mary Poppins* (London: Gerald Howe, 1934); *Mary Poppins Comes Back* (London: L. Dickson & Thompson, 1935); *Mary*

Poppins Opens the Door (London: Peter Davies, 1943); *Mary Poppins in the Park* (London: Peter Davies, 1952); *Mary Poppins from A to Z* (London: Collins, 1963); *Mary Poppins in the Kitchen* (New York: Harcourt Brace Jovanovich, 1975); *Mary Poppins in Cherry Tree Lane* (London: Collins, 1982); *Mary Poppins and the House Next Door* (London: Collins, 1988).

4. One of the first excisions by the Disney team was to eliminate the infant twins from the story.

5. At the time when P. L. Travers and Walt Disney started their cooperation, only the first three books were in print; the fourth was written and published in 1963.

6. Travers, *Mary Poppins*, 178.

7. Grilli, *Myth, Symbol and Meaning*, 1.

8. Travers, *Mary Poppins Comes Back*, 29.

9. Algeo, "Theosophy, Fantasy, and Mary Poppins," 19.

10. From the beginning of cinema, there has been a race by various studios to produce film versions of popular texts. Some texts, such as *Gone with the Wind*, came to the big screen quite quickly after their press runs; other texts, such as *Catcher in the Rye*, have never been made.

11. Ironically, the movie was produced by Walt Disney Pictures due to intellectual property rights that would have made any production impossible without their permission.

12. Lawson, *Mary Poppins, She Wrote*, 246; Sherman, *Moose*, 363; Van Dyke, *My Lucky Life*, 112.

13. Lawson, *Mary Poppins, She Wrote*, 248.

14. Sherman, *Moose*, 371.

15. Beginning with 1948's True-Life Adventure *Seal Island*.

16. Beginning with *Treasure Island* in 1950, Disney produced several film adaptations of classic novels and historical figures.

17. According to Lawson, the producer's gross as defined was the distribution receipts after print costs, distributors' costs, and advertising costs (*Mary Poppins, She Wrote*, 243).

18. Ibid., 247.

19. Outside of the Lawson text, or articles that cite Lawson, the authors can find no other source as to who "Mr. Swan" is, or even what his first name was.

20. Lawson, *Mary Poppins, She Wrote*, 243.

21. Ibid., 247.

22. According to Sherman, the brothers had never heard of Mary Poppins.

23. Sherman, *Moose*, 364.

24. Ibid., 363–64.

25. Lawson, *Mary Poppins, She Wrote*, 248.

26. Ibid., 249; Sherman, *Moose*, 372.

27. Sherman, *Moose*, 372; Lawson, *Mary Poppins, She Wrote*, 250.

28. Lawson, *Mary Poppins, She Wrote*, 251.

29. Sherman, *Moose*, 378.

30. Lawson, *Mary Poppins, She Wrote*, 253.

31. Ibid., 253.

32. Sherman, *Moose*, 373.

33. Lawson, *Mary Poppins, She Wrote*, 255.

34. Ibid., 263–64; Sherman, *Moose*, 385.

35. Lawson, *Mary Poppins, She Wrote*, 264.

36. Sherman, *Moose*, 374.

37. According to Travers, "outing" is an Americanism (Lawson, *Mary Poppins, She Wrote*, 265–66). However, most sources pin this term to Middle English of the fourteenth century.

38. Sherman, *Moose*, 376.

39. Travers is listed, in small print, as "Consultant" and "Based on the Stories by P. L. Travers" in the film.

40. Van Dyke, *My Lucky Life*, 119.

41. Lawson, *Mary Poppins, She Wrote*, 360.

BIBLIOGRAPHY

Algeo, John. "Theosophy, Fantasy, and Mary Poppins." *Theosophy Forward* 11 (December 2013).

Bergsten, Staffen. *Mary Poppins and Myth*. Stockholm: Almqvist & Wiksell International, 1978.

Flanagan, Caitlin. "Becoming Mary Poppins: P. L. Travers, Walt Disney, and the Making of a Myth." *New Yorker*, December 19, 2005. www.newyorker.com/magazine/2005/12/19/becoming-mary-poppins.

Grilli, Giorgia. *Myth, Symbol and Meaning in Mary Poppins*. Translated by Jennifer Varney. New York: Routledge, 2007.

Henderson, Amy. "How Did P. L. Travers, the Prickly Author of Mary Poppins, Really Fare against Walt Disney?" Smithsonian.com, December 20, 2013. http://www.smithsonianmag.com/smithsonian-institution/how-did-pl-travers-the-prickly-author-of-mary-poppins-really-fare-against-walt-disney-180949052/?no-ist.

Kunz, Julia. *Intertextuality and Psychology in P.L. Travers's Mary Poppins Books*. Edited by Elmar Schenkel and Alexandra Lembert-Heidenreich. Approaches to Literary Phantasy 7. Frankfurt am Main: Peter Lang, 2014.

Lawson, Valerie. *Mary Poppins, She Wrote: The Life of P. L. Travers*. New York: Simon & Schuster, 1999.

Sherman, Robert B. *Moose*. Bloomington, IN: AuthorHouse UK, 2013.

Travers, P. L. *Mary Poppins*. Boston: Houghton Mifflin Harcourt, 1997.

———. *Mary Poppins Comes Back*. New York: Harcourt Brace Jovanovich, 1976.

———. *Mary Poppins Opens the Door*. New York: Harcourt Brace Jovanovich, 1976.

Van Dyke, Dick. *My Lucky Life in and out of Show Business: A Memoir*. New York: Crown Archetype, 2011.

Chapter Fifteen

The Wonderful Worlds of Dickens and Disney

Animated Adaptations of Oliver Twist *and*
A Christmas Carol

Shari Hodges Holt

As architects of personal empires, nineteenth-century author Charles Dickens and twentieth-century entertainer/entrepreneur Walt Disney offer rich material for comparative media studies. Their strikingly similar methods of negotiating the boundaries between high and low culture suggest that if Disney was the "Last Mogul" to achieve almost exclusive control over an entertainment empire,[1] Dickens was the first. From childhoods scarred by financial misfortune and family unhappiness, each turned to popular fairy tales for compensatory utopian visions while engaging in obsessive, sometimes ruthless business practices to achieve commercial success. Both attained unprecedented fame in their respective fields by experimenting with new communications technologies (from serial fiction and public readings to animated films and television). As the best-selling novelist of his age and first to amass a fortune through advertising and celebrity,[2] Dickens, like Disney, astutely marketed his work as morally wholesome family entertainment (casting himself in the narrative role of the "kind-hearted bachelor uncle" for readers[3] as "Uncle Walt" did for television viewers), creating a virtual universe of characters that inundate the popular consciousness. Like Disney's "Wonderful World," Dickens's literary land posthumously expanded into a pastiche of commodities—stage, television, and film adaptations (including those produced by Disney); merchandising spin-offs; even a "Dickens World" theme park.

But the most obvious intersection of the Dickens and Disney industries is film. Here is the primary medium through which Disney built his corporation and through which Dickens (as the author whose works are most frequently adapted)[4] maintains cultural relevance. Animated film adaptations of *Oliver Twist* and *A Christmas Carol—Oliver & Company* (1988), *Mickey's Christmas Carol* (1983), and *Disney's A Christmas Carol* (2009)—exhibit the same combination of sentimentalism and social conscience, craftsmanship and crass commercialism, as Dickens's originals, demonstrating the ideological paradoxes inherent in these popular artists, sparking similar dissension in academic criticism. While Douglas Brode has traced the foundations of progressive cultural movements to messages of youthful rebellion, tolerance, and social inclusivity present in Disney films,[5] most academic studies of WDC accuse it of propagating dominant racist, sexist, and classist values in support of its capitalist agenda.[6] Similarly, while Dickens considered himself a political radical denouncing abuses of industrial capitalism, critical consensus tends to fault him for evincing a comfortable bourgeois paternalism that perpetuated the social inequities he supposedly critiqued.

In particular, *Oliver Twist* (1837) and *A Christmas Carol* (1843) have elicited more criticism than Dickens's later works for the kind of ideological simplicity and conservatism often attributed to Disney. However, their adaptation as Disney films reveals elements of a more mature and progressive social vision.

CLASSIC DISNEY: *MICKEY'S CHRISTMAS CAROL*

From its inception to modern reincarnations, *A Christmas Carol* has garnered criticism for its perceived political inconsistencies. Despite the indictment of Victorian materialism inherent in Scrooge, the sentimental transformation of this greedy miser into the philanthropic capitalist has been interpreted as a naïve endorsement of patronage between the classes that does little to address the systemic sources of poverty.[7] Conceived in response to the unprecedented poverty of the "Hungry Forties," Dickens's story was conceived as a "sledge hammer" political piece,[8] awakening middle-class audiences to the working-class crisis, but morphed into a money-making endeavor. Although Dickens designed the novella's first edition as an expensive Christmas commodity (complete with gilt pages and hand-colored illustrations), he lost revenue by selling this luxury item at reduced cost to reach the broadest audience.[9] However, as the inaugural piece of what would become Dickens's lucrative Christmas franchise and the basis for reading tours that would guarantee his fortune, the novella more than recouped its financial losses and remained the premiere commodity of the Dickens industry following his death.

Such altruistic consumerism marks Disney's first animated adaptation of Dickens's classic. Produced in 1983, when neoconservative materialism dominated both American and British politics, *Mickey's Christmas Carol* unites the most marketable features of the Disney and Dickens industries.[10] WDC brought back Mickey Mouse for his first film appearance since 1952, animating him in classic Disney hand-drawn style, despite the then-recent emergence of computer animation technologies. From its commencement, the project capitalized on sentimental nostalgia for Walt's own products.[11]

The film's wistful title sequence unites communal spirit with commodity fetishism as the credits appear over sepia-tinted images of venerated Disney characters depicted in the style of Victorian etchings, carolers intoning the joy of "Sharing a season of good cheer / With the ones we hold so dear."[12] Led by Scrooge McDuck in the central role, with Donald as his nephew, Goofy as Jacob Marley, and Mickey and Minnie Mouse as the Cratchits, the film is populated with major and minor Disney characters, delighting fans with beloved "stars" cast in new (if familiar) roles. The first cinematic *Carol* to target a child audience and inspire spin-off merchandise,[13] WDC's film exploits popular characters that had long been family commodities, positioning itself within an already established Disney market.

The target audience and truncated length also result in the sanitizing effect so many Disney critics decry. Although some effective visual touches approximate Dickens's psychological symbolism (the image of Scrooge on the snowy streets recalls the frost metaphors in Dickens's opening description), the psychological depth that distinguishes many live-action versions (particularly Alastair Sim's titular performance in the 1951 *Scrooge*) is gone. Significantly, Scrooge's visit with the Ghost of Christmas Past to his lonely childhood is eliminated to focus on Fezziwig's ball (providing another opportunity to incorporate even more Disney characters) and Scrooge's romance with Belle (Daisy Duck).

The novella's more subversive political elements are likewise discarded. Scrooge's merciless Malthusian comments about consigning the poor to prisons and workhouses are markedly absent. The terrifying child phantoms of Ignorance and Want that the Ghost of Christmas Present displays as an omen of working-class revolution are replaced by sentimental images of Christmas consumption. The Ghost of Christmas Present (played by Willie the Giant, appropriately suggestive of plentitude) appears to Scrooge surrounded by a massive Christmas feast, assuring the miser that all these goodies come "from the heart." At the Cratchit family "feast," meager material goods are supplemented by the wealth of family love. When Scrooge inquires about Tiny Tim's future, Christmas Present refrains from repeating Scrooge's vicious assessment of the "surplus population" (one of those "sledge hammer" moments in Dickens's original), replying merely that an empty chair will reside in Tim's place "if these shadows remain unchanged," leaving Scrooge's responsibility for Tim's death indirectly expressed.

Instead of brutal utilitarian economics, Disney's ongoing intemperate version of the American work ethic here motivates Scrooge McDuck, preventing him from striking the appropriate balance between personal gain and communal responsibility.[14] When Scrooge objects to giving Bob Cratchit a holiday because "Christmas is just another workday," Bob replies, "It's a time for giving and being with one's family," offering *the family* (always a key Disney concern) as the site to reconcile the apparent conflict of spiritual and material values. The contrasting mise-en-scène of Scrooge's countinghouse and the Cratchits' home initially highlights this opposition between family and commerce (a plaque declaring "Time Is Money" looms behind Scrooge McDuck's famous stacks of coins, while "Bless Our Home" adorns the wall above the Cratchit hearth). But the film undermines this neat dichotomy by continuously maneuvering Scrooge and Bob between both worlds. Disney's Cratchit does domestic duty for Scrooge, carrying home his laundry in bags visually analogous to McDuck's characteristic money bags. While Dickens's Scrooge is shamed into anonymously sending a Christmas goose to the family after witnessing their poverty, Disney's film visualizes Scrooge's remorseful generosity in a conclusion that unites commodity consumption with family communion. Instead of waiting to confront Bob at the countinghouse the next day, Scrooge bursts into the Cratchit home distributing goodies from a bag of toys indistinguishable from his bags of gold and laundry. Declaring that he will give Bob a raise and promotion, Scrooge snuggles the Cratchit children beneath the plaque "Home Sweet Home," Mickey and Minnie gazing on contentedly. As the camera tracks backward, framing the little community within a Christmas wreath, the image assumes the sepia tones of the film's opening tableaux, carolers reprising the introductory song.

This conclusion highlights the conservative nostalgia of Dickens's narrative by eliding its potentially revolutionary discourse to present a sentimental union of consumer capitalism and family values. Harry Stone sees such formulaic denouements, in which benevolent fairy godfathers "use the magic wand of money to transform, reverse, and save," as indicating Dickens's failure to integrate fairy-tale elements with political commentary in his early works.[15] However, the assimilation of Scrooge McDuck into Mickey Mouse's family dramatizes one of the more subversive characteristics of Dickens's domestic ideology. The novella notes that Scrooge became a "second father" to Tiny Tim,[16] an example of what Holly Furneaux deems the "queering" of the conservative domestic ideal through the integration of such "bachelor dads" into families.[17] This combination of conservative fairy-god-father and progressive bachelor-dad indicates the propensity of the Dickens and Disney industries to hover between subverting and supporting the status quo, a tendency that would become more marked as later Disney productions attempt to adapt Dickens to evolving cultural attitudes.

MULTICULTURAL DISNEY: *OLIVER & COMPANY*

If *Mickey's Christmas Carol* evokes nostalgia for Disney traditions, *Oliver & Company* (1988) appears more progressive in technique and content. Marking Disney's return to feature-length animated musicals, the film showcases a "non-integrated pop score" designed less to advance the narrative than highlight the talents of celebrity singers such as Billy Joel and Bette Midler. The film's financial success would prompt Disney to adopt the more coherent "book musical" format, resulting in features such as *The Little Mermaid* and *Beauty and the Beast* that reclaimed the studio's preeminence in animation and led Disney to the Broadway stage.[18] The first Disney animated feature with its own computer graphics department, *Oliver* combines traditionally hand-drawn characters with computer-generated cityscapes,[19] melding the classic Disney style with a gritty urban realism that captures the hyperrealism of Dickens's London descriptions. The film incorporates contemporary trends toward multiculturalism through the diverse canine breeds of Fagin's gang, voiced by a multiethnic cast.

Opening shots introduce the film as a transitional piece in the Disney canon by shifting the audience's perspective from earlier medieval fairy tales to the new urban fable. "Once Upon a Time in New York City" cues to the familiar Disney logo of Cinderella's palace, which dissolves into the urban palaces of Manhattan, as skyscrapers soar into a golden sunrise. This song's lyrics indicate the city's fairy-tale potential: "It's always once upon a time / In New York City. / It's a big old, bad old, tough old town, it's true. / But beginnings are contagious there. / They're always setting stages there; / They're always turning pages there for you."[20] Colorful street-level shots depict Oliver and his siblings, presented to passing pedestrians in a box labeled "kitties need good home." When night falls, the setting becomes Dickens's Gothic city, as Oliver is washed away by a thunderstorm into a labyrinth of mean streets. Subjective shots accentuate his terror while fleeing speeding vehicles and murderous strays. But the musical track encourages Oliver: "don't be scared. . . . Keep your dream alive. / Dreaming is still how the strong survive, / Once upon a time in New York City." Celebrating the innocent orphan's ability to "keep the dream alive" in a nightmarish world, this sequence dramatizes Dickens's abandoned child as victim and potential vanquisher of the dehumanized urban world.

The second montage more explicitly proclaims the individual's magical capacity to master the threatening urban environment. As in Dickens, the first urban character to befriend orphan Oliver is streetwise thief Dodger, here a wise-cracking mutt voiced by Billy Joel. After showing the epony-mous hero how to steal hot dogs from a vendor, Dodger launches into the central ballad, "Why Should I Worry?," demonstrating his mastery of the city by maneuvering through varied urban perils with impeccable panache. Computer technology animates the backgrounds, transforming the city into "another character in the picture."[21] As inanimate objects spring to life, Dodger dances across moving cars and construction equipment, singing his confidence: "Why should I worry? / Why should I care? / I may not have a dime / But I've got street savoir faire!" He crowns his demonstration by inspiring packs of domesticated dogs to jump their leashes and strut in defi-ance down the street, literally stopping traffic. The sequence impressively approximates the famous animism of Dickensian London, in which "the animation of inanimate objects suggests both the quaint gaiety of a forbidden life and an aggressiveness that has got out of control."[22]

Dodger's parade through the city embodies another feature of Dickens's urban aesthetic: the persona of the accomplished flaneur. Inspired by long city walks that provided Dickens with suitable material, the perspective of the able urban rambler engaged and detached Dickens's audience from his spectacles. This enabled "key ideological fantasies for his readers and for Dickens himself about their privileged position in England's commercial economy and, more importantly, their insulation from that economy's de-structive effects on the lower classes and on themselves."[23] In the mutt who "may not have a dime" but masters all environments "from the Bowery to St. Marks," Disney replicates class paradoxes in Dickens's text, identifying the ostensible "underdog" with the privileged perspective of the middle-class audiences to whom Dickens and Disney each marketed their narratives.

According to Natchee Blu Barnd, Dodger's confident perambulations sig-nify "heterosexual White maleness," of which one key privilege is "geo-graphic freedom."[24] She argues that while other canines reflect various eth-nicities, the leads Oliver and Dodger are coded as white through voice cast-ing and musical choices, particularly the adoption of Billy Joel's soft-rock style for the central anthem at a time when hip-hop was challenging the racial inequities of the urban experience.[25] The film's racial politics grow more problematic when Oliver meets others in Fagin's gang. Although, as Douglas Brode notes, the film celebrates urban diversity through assorted canine breeds,[26] their representation relies on racial stereotypes. Barnd particularly objects to Tito (voiced by Chicano comedian Cheech Marin), the "fast-talk-ing, violence-prone, sexually predatory, and criminally inclined Chihuahua" whose attributes "are all predetermined by dominant representations of Lati-nos."[27]

Although the Disney production may normalize white male dominance through Dodger and Oliver while negatively racializing characters such as Tito, positions of white privilege are interrogated through the film's human characters. Disney's Fagin (voiced by Dom DeLuise) is an impoverished human with no apparent ethnic or religious affiliation. To eliminate Dickens's anti-Semitic connotations, Disney sanitizes and humanizes Fagin, positioning itself within a revisionist tradition dating back to Lionel Bart's musical *Oliver!*[28] In both Dickens and Disney, Fagin provides makeshift shelter, sustenance, and community for his gang. But Dickens's Fagin uses domesticity to exploit gang members, whereas Disney's Fagin constructs a truly loving family, as illustrated in a key scene after Oliver's arrival. Kitten and canines beg a bedtime story. In an image reminiscent of a typical Victorian family by the hearth, the animals congregate around Fagin as he reads from a storybook about the adventures of Sparky the dog and Bumper the rabbit, romping through an idyllic setting that recalls Disney's pastoral fantasies (particularly *Bambi*, through the allusion to the rabbit Thumper) and the country paradise to which Oliver retreats at the end of Dickens's novel. Dickens reserves this paradise for the middle classes, eliminating his criminals through murder, execution, and transportation, while magically restoring Oliver to a lost bourgeois inheritance, allowing him to escape the city with his adopted family. The Disney Version offers a more radical alternative by extending a loving family dynamic to those still marked by poverty and crime.

The film most explicitly acknowledges the inadequacies of white privilege through Jenny Foxworth, who substitutes for Oliver's prosperous patrons. The transformation of the novel's privileged characters into a vulnerable female child, whose disenfranchisement is palpable despite her Fifth Avenue address, complicates the Disney adaptation's treatment of class and race. In Dickens, Mr. Brownlow and the Maylies aid Oliver out of charity; in Disney, wealthy Jenny adopts the homeless kitten out of her own emotional lacking. As her parents travel abroad, she lives in a lonely Manhattan townhouse with the company only of butler Winston and show dog Georgette, a pet valued as property rather than for companionship. Visual parallels between Jenny's opulent home and Sykes's criminal enterprise, the wealthy mobster to whom Fagin owes money, suggest the emotional impoverishment of a world defined by material affluence. The dark recesses of the limousine from which Sykes conducts business resemble the cavernous interior of Jenny's limousine, where she sits alone, reading a letter in which her jet-setting parents inform her they will not be returning for her birthday. High-angled long shots of the friendless child in her empty townhouse echo shots of Sykes's vast shipping warehouse where he plots murder for material gain. While Dickens draws clear distinctions between the peaceful/prosperous homes of Oliver's adopted family and the squalid, dangerous dens of the criminals, the film makes unsettling connections between home and business, licit and illicit wealth, to imply that material prosperity does not guarantee family stability.

In the novel, Oliver achieves stability with his bourgeois friends, who form "a little society, whose condition approached as nearly to one of perfect happiness as can ever be known in this changing world."[29] Although this constitutes a family of choice rather than kinship, it remains a conservative ideal owing to its exclusivity. Paupers and criminals, whose sufferings dominate the novel, are effectively forgotten in a celebration of bourgeois plenty. In comparison, the film returns to Fagin's gang for a more inclusive family structure. After rescuing Oliver and Jenny from kidnapper Sykes, Fagin and his canines celebrate Jenny's birthday at her townhouse. In the absence of Jenny's parents, Fagin and Winston bond as "bachelor dads" while the dogs share birthday gifts with the delighted child. A battered doll, a hubcap, and a broken tennis racket, items scavenged or stolen, are transformed into tokens of friendship with intense emotional subtexts. Leaving Oliver with Jenny as their uptown representative, the gang promises future visits, departing amid a joyous reprise of "Why Should I Worry?," transformed into an ensemble piece. Although this retains some of the original's political weaknesses (the economic inequities remain), admission of the poor and crime-ridden into the family ideal presents a striking departure from Dickens. The closing vision of an extended family composed of characters representing diverse races and classes is significantly more progressive than the family structures envisioned by Dickens's Victorian novel or the neoconservative milieu of 1980s America. *Oliver & Company* deserves recognition as an important step toward WDC acknowledging multicultural values.

VIRTUAL DISNEY: *DISNEY'S A CHRISTMAS CAROL*

While *Mickey's Christmas Carol* presents a primarily conservative view of Dickens's world and *Oliver & Company* gestures toward a more inclusive social vision, the immersive animation style of *Disney's A Christmas Carol* (2009), combining 3-D and motion-capture technologies, utilizes the novella's combination of spectacle and spectrality, offering a more subversive social statement. Joss Marsh has examined how Dickens's text deliberately incorporates features of Victorian visual technologies (particularly the magic lantern), a precursor of the cinema. Like magic lantern projectionists, who were "showmen-educators" enlightening Victorian audiences through visual spectacle,[30] the specters that Dickens conjures present a lesson in social responsibility through magical visions in which they immerse the protagonist. The technologically enhanced virtual world of *Disney's A Christmas Carol* visualizes this potential for ideological transformation through spectatorship, as Scrooge is converted from miser to philanthropist "after watching virtual morality plays about his own conduct."[31]

While questions of authorship are evoked by the title *Disney's A Christmas Carol*, the film is clearly a collaborative enterprise of studio, filmmaker, and novelist. Director Robert Zemeckis's script adheres closely to Dickens's narrative; his hybrid animation technique, which digitally records live actors to thereafter be animated in computer-generated environments, approximates Dickens's distinctive blend of fantasy and realism. The result is a stunning simulacrum of Dickensian London, at the heart of which stands Scrooge and his Christmas specters, all portrayed by actor Jim Carrey. This casting choice suggests the ghosts are Scrooge's psychological projections. Liberated from restraints of makeup, costume, and set design by virtual imagery, Carrey illustrates the true emotive power of Dickens's hyperreal world. The 3-D technology literalizes the novella's symbolism as viewers experience Scrooge's spiritual frigidity through the almost palpable snow of virtual London or share his psychological disorientation as he passes through walls and over rooftops in a spectacular journey reminiscent of Disney theme park rides or Epcot's multisensory experiences. The film brings Dickens's spectral visions into the new literacy of video games and virtual reality, through which contemporary audiences routinely construct and consume narratives.

The opening sequence introduces this new literacy through a series of symbolic objects. The first shot acknowledges the source text with an image of a book, embossed with the title "*A Christmas Carol* by Charles Dickens," lying on a table next to a writer's quill, inkwell, and lighted candle.[32] In the background, a window reveals a busy Victorian street decorated for Christmas. Shortly, a close-up of the novella's first sentence, "Marley was dead," dissolves into an engraved illustration of Marley's corpse, slowly assuming a 3-D quality as viewers discover themselves in the undertaker's shop with Scrooge, who is haggling over his dead partner's funeral expenses. Snatching coins from the dead man's eyes in an act of greedy defiance, Scrooge traverses the frigid streets to his countinghouse. There he exhibits his equally frigid attitude toward humanity by denouncing the holiday to his nephew Fred, his clerk, and visiting philanthropists. As Big Ben looms through the countinghouse window (an anachronistic but symbolically impressive image), Scrooge snaps shut his pocket watch while uttering a final complaint about giving Cratchit the day off. This sequence invites the viewer to enter the text as a window into Scrooge's spiritual dilemma, which will become the viewer's own through this "virtual experience." While clocks and coins indicate that Scrooge's greed is an attempt to stave off death by hording time and money, windows and candles (which repeatedly appear throughout the subsequent supernatural visions) represent the enlightening potential spectatorship holds for Scrooge and the audience. The Ghost of Christmas Past appears as a lighted candle, literalizing Dickens's light imagery; the Ghost of Christmas Yet to Come morphs out of Scrooge's own shadow in a terrifying representation of the darkness he carries within, anxious to be personified if he fails to see the significance of the supernatural tableaux.

This symbolic connection of spectacle and spectrality proves most power-ful in the visitation of the Ghost of Christmas Present. As in Dickens, the ghost first appears as a youthful, vigorous Father Christmas, sitting atop a pile of plenty and carrying a blazing cornucopia. Then, images of abundance are counteracted by surrounding clocks that chime repeatedly as the spirit warns Scrooge of their limited time on earth. Sparks from the specter's torch dissolve the floor, creating a window to the world through which Scrooge witnesses visions of poverty. The ghost's social critique becomes most vivid when he presents the phantoms of Ignorance and Want, represented (as in Dickens's original) as bestial pauper children lurking beneath the ghost's robe, the dark antithesis of Christmas plenty. As Scrooge stands in the im-prisoning frame of Big Ben's shadow, phantoms emerge from the ghost's gown while the clock tolls midnight, signifying the end of Christmas Present's life on earth. Horrified by the spectral children, Scrooge asks if they have no refuge. Laughing maniacally, Christmas Present decays to a skeleton while the children rapidly age into adults, replying with Scrooge's own Malthusian refrain, "Are there no prisons? Are there no workhouses?," as they mature into the twin horrors of Victorian poverty, the pickpocket and the prostitute, one ending up behind prions bars, the other in an asylum. At the stroke of midnight, Christmas Present's skeletal remains disintegrate be-neath Scrooge's shadow, mutating into the Ghost of Christmas Yet to Come, who visualizes future consequences of Scrooge's (and humanity's) present failure of spiritual vision. This stunning sequence recovers the novella's Gothic horror from the sentimental approach that has dominated so many adaptations (after all, the novella is subtitled *A Ghost Story of Christmas*) and approximates the "sledge hammer" effect Dickens desired.

By retaining the novella's rage against the horrors of nineteenth-century utilitarian economics, Zemeckis's film proved particularly relevant for audi-ences reeling from the first major financial crisis of the twenty-first century, 2008's Great Recession. Critics such as Richard Corliss claimed the film reenvisioned Dickens's Victorian tale as "a fable for this time, . . . when Wall Street money lenders, Scrooges in Armani suits, are multiplying their stash and breeding Ignorance and Want in the surplus population."[33] The film tapped into the rising tide of indignation against income inequality that would develop into anarchist political movements including Occupy Wall Street. Importantly, though, neither the novella nor the film advocates the overthrow of consumer culture.

Instead, both offer a vision of benevolent capitalism as panacea to eco-nomic suffering. Unlike adaptations that conclude with an interpolated scene in which Scrooge visits the Cratchit family on Christmas day, Zemeckis's script (like the novella) depicts Scrooge meeting Bob at the countinghouse.

After raising Bob's salary, Scrooge brings the charity of Christmas into the business by offering to discuss Bob's "affairs" (both economic and familial) over a steaming bowl of punch. Elated at his employer's transformation, Bob, departing, glances back through the countinghouse window to enjoy the spectacle of Scrooge gleefully singing Christmas carols. Turning to the camera, Bob shatters the fourth wall (already rendered nebulous by the film's 3-D effects) to address the spectators. As he recites the novella's final passage, recounting Scrooge's transformation into Tiny Tim's "second father" and "as good a friend, as good a master, and as good a man, as the good old city knew,"[34] a glowing image of Scrooge carrying Tiny Tim appears behind him. In a final spectacle of benevolent capitalism, the newly charitable businessman and formerly disabled child unite, traversing a shop-lined street whose windows are ablaze with light, as Tiny Tim invokes God's blessings on the community. The film reverts to its frame device as figures freeze into an engraved illustration and the camera tracks backward, exiting Dickens's text, now a closed book on the table beside the lighted candle, the inkwell, and a newly inked quill. This concluding image posits the film's spectators as coauthors of the text as well as narrative participants who through the immersive spectacle of Scrooge's story have shared his transformation. Whereas the concluding tableau of *Mickey's Christmas Carol* allows the audience a comfortable retreat into consumerist nostalgia, *Disney's A Christmas Carol* evokes active engagement in the narrative's transformative powers for the broader community. The film, like the novella, posits spiritual transformation as possible within the consumerist system, sharing Dickens's vision of culture as "a money-making business that also facilitates community cohesion."[35] Immersing the audience in visions of social horror and disenfranchisement as well as consumer sentiment and community, the film replicates the novella's urgent appeal to make existing social structures more inclusive, dramatizing the more progressive features of Dickens's reformatory discourse.

By connecting the most pervasive entertainment empires of the last two centuries, Disney's animated versions of Dickens's world effectively illustrate the ongoing tug-of-war between progressive and reactionary social forces, demonstrating the power of media to disseminate ideology that simultaneously reinforces and challenges cultural norms. While the terms "Dickensian" and "Disneyfication" are frequently associated with reductive/reactionary worldviews, careful examination of the intersection between these kingdoms indicates that the cultural work they perform may be more complex than acknowledged. As their presence extends into the twenty-first century, the Dickens and Disney industries continue to provide an instructive window into the ideological conflicts of living, evolving cultures.

NOTES

1. Richard Schickel, *The Disney Version: The Life, Times, Art and Commerce of Walt Disney*, 3rd ed. (Chicago: Elephant Paperbacks, 1997), 29.

2. For a thorough assessment of Dickens's media career, see Juliet John, *Dickens and Mass Culture* (Oxford: Oxford University Press, 2010).

3. Michael Slater, quoted in James Chapman, "God Bless Us, Every One: Movie Adaptations of *A Christmas Carol*," in *Christmas at the Movies: Images of Christmas in American, British, and European Cinema*, ed. Mark Connelly (London: I. B. Tauris, 2000), 10.

4. John, *Dickens and Mass Culture*, 187.

5. Douglas Brode, *From Walt to Woodstock: How Disney Created the Counterculture* (Austin: University of Texas Press, 2004) and *Multiculturalism and the Mouse: Race and Sex in Disney Entertainment* (Austin: University of Texas Press, 2005).

6. For a noteworthy critical collection from this perspective, see Elizabeth Bell, Lynda Haas, and Laura Sells, eds., *From Mouse to Mermaid: The Politics of Film, Gender, and Culture* (Bloomington: Indiana University Press, 1995).

7. For a recent example, see Joseph W. Childers, "So, This Is Christmas," in *Contemporary Dickens*, ed. Eileen Gillooly and Deirdre David, 113–30 (Columbus: Ohio State University Press, 2009).

8. Charles Dickens, quoted in Michael Slater, *Charles Dickens: A Life Defined by Writing* (New Haven, CT: Yale University Press, 2009), 220.

9. Slater, *Charles Dickens*, 219–20.

10. Paul Davis complains that *Mickey's Christmas Carol* "reduced [Dickens's narrative] . . . to a commercial property" and "removed the conflict between rich and poor," reflecting the neoconservative political climate surrounding "the great Christmas Carol controversy of 1983." Ronald Regan's presidential advisor Edwin Meese, who had been labeled a "Scrooge" for claiming that allegations of hungry children in America were a myth, defended Scrooge as a supply-side hero whose free-market policies ultimately benefited his employee and his society (Paul Davis, *The Life and Times of Ebenezer Scrooge* [New Haven, CT: Yale University Press, 1990], 220–21). *Mickey's Christmas Carol* was likewise framed by two live-action versions of *Twist* and *Carol* that adapted Dickens's narratives from a more radical stance. Directed by Clive Donner as British/American coproductions and released in 1982 and 1984, their subtext critiqued Regan's and Thatcher's neoconservative principles. Scrooge becomes a ruthless businessman forced to recognize the poverty caused by his laissez-faire business practices (Chapman, "God Bless Us," 28).

11. Thomas Leitch, *Film Adaptation and Its Discontents: From Gone with the Wind to the Passion of the Christ* (Baltimore: Johns Hopkins University Press, 2007), 88–89.

12. *Mickey's Christmas Carol*, directed by Burny Mattinson (1983; Walt Disney Home Entertainment, 2013), DVD.

13. Chapman, "God Bless Us," 31.

14. Scrooge McDuck, who originated in Disney comics, was famously interpreted as an icon of American cultural imperialism and consumerism by Ariel Dorfman and Armand Mattelart in *How to Read Donald Duck: Imperialist Ideology in the Disney Comic* (New York: International General, 1971).

15. Harry Stone, *Dickens and the Invisible World: Fairy Tales, Fantasy, and Novel-Making* (Bloomington: Indiana University Press, 1979), 73.

16. Charles Dickens, *A Christmas Carol and Other Writings* (New York: Penguin, 2003), 116.

17. Holly Furneaux, *Queer Dickens: Erotics, Families, Masculinities* (Oxford: Oxford University Press, 2009), 7.

18. Marc Napolitano, "Disneyfying Dickens: *Oliver & Company* and *The Muppet Christmas Carol* as Dickensian Musicals," *Studies in Popular Culture* 32, no. 1 (2009): 84.

19. "The Making of *Oliver & Company*" (1988; Walt Disney Home Entertainment, 2009), DVD.

20. *Oliver & Company*, directed by George Scribner (1988; Walt Disney Home Entertainment, 2009), DVD.

21. George Scribner, quoted in "The Making of *Oliver & Company.*"

22. Dorothy Van Ghent, "The Dickens World: A View from Todgers's," *Sewanee Review* 58, no. 3 (1950): 419.

23. Amanpal Garcha, *From Sketch to Novel: The Development of Victorian Fiction* (Cambridge: Cambridge University Press, 2009), 139.

24. Natchee Blu Barnd, "White Man's Best Friend: Race and Privilege in *Oliver and Company,*" in *Diversity in Disney Films: Critical Essays on Race, Ethnicity, Gender, Sexuality, and Disability,* ed. Johnston Cheu (Jefferson, NC: McFarland, 2013), 79.

25. Ibid., 78.

26. Brode, *Multiculturalism and the Mouse,* 3.

27. Barnd, "White Man's Best Friend," 75.

28. Sharon Aronofsky Weltman, "'Can a Fellow Be a Villain All His Life?': *Oliver!,* Fagin, and Performing Jewishness," *Nineteenth-Century Contexts* 33, no. 4 (September 2011): 376. This revisionist tradition developed in reaction to the character's anti-Semitic qualities in David Lean's 1948 film. Disney studios similarly sanitized the character in a 1997 live-action television movie starring Richard Dreyfuss.

29. Charles Dickens, *Oliver Twist* (New York: Penguin, 2003), 451.

30. Joss Marsh, "Dickensian 'Dissolving Views': The Magic Lantern, Visual Story-Telling, and the Victorian Technological Imagination," *Comparative Critical Studies* 6, no. 3 (October 2009): 335.

31. John, *Dickens and Mass Culture,* 191.

32. *Disney's A Christmas Carol,* directed by Robert Zemeckis (2009; Walt Disney Home Entertainment, 2010), DVD.

33. Richard Corliss, "Spirited Away," *Time,* November 16, 2009, 61.

34. Dickens, *Carol,* 116.

35. John, *Dickens and Mass Culture,* 55.

Chapter Sixteen

The Tao at Pooh Corner

Disney's Portrayal of a Very Philosophical Bear

Anne Collins Smith and Owen M. Smith

According to the International Licensing Industry Merchandisers' Association, Disney's *Winnie the Pooh* franchise is the third-highest revenue-producing entertainment franchise in the world. Only the Disney Princess and *Star Wars* franchises (both also owned by Disney) rank higher.[1] Estimates of the annual income generated for Disney by *Pooh* range from two[2] to six billion dollars.[3] Clearly, Winnie the Pooh has done well for Disney. However, another question must be raised: has Disney done well by Winnie the Pooh?

A. A. Milne's children's books about Christopher Robin and his friends consist of four slim volumes: two books of poetry, *When We Were Very Young* (1924) and *Now We Are Six* (1927), and two books of prose, *Winnie-the-Pooh* (1926) and *The House at Pooh Corner* (1928). These have long captured the imagination of children; one charming aspect of the prose stories is the way the author draws the audience into the narrative by directly addressing both the reader and the characters in the stories. Christopher Robin, Pooh, and Piglet all interrupt the storytelling to ensure the stories are told "very sweetly," puzzling details are explained, and sufficient attention is paid to them.[4] Milne's style is characterized by a distinctive self-deprecating form of humor, as he defers to the characters, even asking—and taking— Owl's advice.[5] The author also addresses the reader directly, again in a self-deprecating way. Sometimes, this is done to acknowledge his responsibilities, as when he announces it's time "to get on with the book."[6] In other instances, this device is employed to explain that he doesn't know any more about a given topic than the reader does.[7]

In the latter part of the twentieth century, Benjamin Hoff used *Winnie-the-Pooh* as a springboard for a surprising and successful project: the explanation of the ancient Chinese philosophy of Taoism through Winnie-the-Pooh and the explanation of Winnie-the-Pooh through the ancient Chinese philosophy of Taoism.[8] In *The Tao of Pooh* (1983) and *The Te of Piglet* (1993), Hoff employed Milne's books together with excerpts from Taoist literature and his own original vignettes featuring characters from the Pooh universe to explore traditional Taoist principles and insights. By so doing, he added a new dimension to Milne's works—not only do the books provide entertainment for children but also education to adults. Indeed, John Tyerman Williams credits Hoff's books, along with Frederick C. Crews's *The Pooh Perplex*, with introducing the world to the understanding of *Winnie-the-Pooh* as "no mere children's classic,"[9] but rather a treasure trove of rewarding philosophical insights. Like the original author, Hoff allows the characters to interrupt his exposition with their own questions and concerns. He also addresses the reader directly rather than proclaiming wisdom from on high. Further, he evinces a form of self-deprecatory humor that comports well with both the original style of Milne's books and the Taoist worldview he advocates.

THE DISNEY FEATURETTES

The first Disney adaption was *Winnie the Pooh and the Honey Tree* (1966); its success led to the production of *Winnie the Pooh and the Blustery Day* (1968) and *Winnie the Pooh and Tigger Too* (1974). WDC then commissioned brief transitional scenes and compiled these featurettes into a full-length film, released as *The Many Adventures of Winnie the Pooh* (1977). Disney later adapted additional material from Milne's works into a fourth featurette, *Winnie the Pooh and a Day for Eeyore* (1983).

These works adhere closely to the originals, preserving the narrative tropes first encountered in Milne's stories. In particular, the featurettes present their narrative content as stories from a storybook; the words of the narration are frequently visible as the text of the storybook. Individual vignettes begin and end on freeze frames that serve as equivalents to the book's illustrations. This self-referential feature is extended in an innovative way in *Winnie the Pooh and Tigger Too*, when Milne's original account of Tigger's rescue from a tall tree is modified to give the narrator an active role, tilting the storybook so Tigger can slide along the edge of the text to the ground.[10] The featurettes depart from Milne's text in three principal ways: organization of material, substitution of new song lyrics, and introduction of a new major character. [11] Lest the audience mistake Gopher as a feature of the original Pooh canon, he repeatedly mentions that he's "not in the book." [12] The type of animal chosen for inclusion in the featurettes provides a clue to his significance. As a tunneling animal, gophers routinely engage in construction projects. Also, he has a distinct propensity for using explosives. Gopher thus brings a familiarity with technology that ushers the featurettes into a world more recognizable to its modern audience.

The final Disney featurette was accompanied by the appearance of a television series on the Disney Channel, *Welcome to Pooh Corner* (1983–1986). In contrast to the featurettes, this featured costumed actors and puppets. The direct heir to the featurettes was another television series, *The New Adventures of Winnie the Pooh* (1988–1991). Episodes in this series were animated, initially featuring many of the same voice actors as in the four featurettes. Since the stories in *The New Adventures of Winnie the Pooh* consist almost entirely of newly written material, [13] this series affords us the opportunity to assess Disney's own contribution to the Pooh canon. The question is: Are the new stories consistent with the principles so elegantly extracted from the original stories by Hoff? And do they provide additional illustrations of Taoist values so that these philosophic concepts can be understood and embraced by a new audience of children and adults?

THE NEW ADVENTURES OF WINNIE THE POOH

The New Adventures of Winnie the Pooh ran for four years (1988–1991), beginning on the Disney Channel and later moving to ABC. [14] The series comprises fifty episodes, some consisting of a single story, others made up of two shorter stories, for a total of eighty-two stories. [15]

This incarnation features all the main characters in Milne's originals as well as the noncanonical Gopher. Indeed, he becomes one of the central characters, appearing in forty-three stories, more than Eeyore (thirty-seven), Christopher Robin (twenty-seven), Owl (twenty-five), Kanga (eight), or Roo (eleven). Unlike the featurettes, individual episodes aren't presented as chapters in a storybook. Rather, several are framed as vehicles for the characters themselves to tell stories. As other characters disagree with a story's direction, the narrative within stories changes, often dramatically, as in "The Monster Frankenpooh" (28-2), "Three Little Piglets" (30-2), and "Piglet's Poohetry" (50-1). This approach also draws attention to the art and action of storytelling. Introducing alternate narrative elements reminds the viewer that a story, like the Tao itself, is "filled with infinite possibilities." [16] With reflection, viewers will recognize that all the stories, even those that do not display these narrative tropes, were constructed by storytellers, perhaps not only for entertainment but also to stimulate reflection and discussion.

As to whether the series reflects Taoist themes, a simple affirmative or negative answer cannot be given. Many stories do not address Taoist themes. Some instead express a particularly disturbing message identified by Hoff as unhealthy and contrary to Taoism. Most, however, are admirable vehicles for exploring Taoism and illustrate a wide variety of this philosophy's elements.

First, stories that are neutral with respect to Taoism fall into two categories: stories that parody popular culture icons and others that seek to teach object lessons to children. Among the former are "Tigger, Private Ear" (21-2), based on Sherlock Holmes; "The Masked Offender" (14-1), spoofing Zorro; and "The Good, the Bad, and the Tigger" (46), a marvelous pastiche of spaghetti Westerns. Parents would especially appreciate "Cleanliness Is Next to Impossible" (6), regarding the value of having a clean bedroom; "Babysitter Blues" (9), about obeying babysitters; and "Pooh Day Afternoon" (45), an alarming yet hilarious lesson about the proper care of pets. [17]

From a Taoist perspective, however, a number of stories are marred by a recurring element that conflicts with the overall positive tone. In these, a character undergoes an experience that leads him to believe himself unworthy of his companions' friendship. Hoff would characterize this theme as a version of the Eeyore Within,[18] a sense of low self-esteem reflected in an aura of worthlessness in the eyes of others. This condition manifests itself in the Eeyore Effect, magnifying inner fears and doubts of an individual, leading to a state of despair and hopelessness that has a negative impact on everyone. In the *New Adventures*, the most common response is an attempt to withdraw from the group, even to the extent of leaving the Hundred Acre Wood. In the pilot story, "Pooh Oughta Be in Pictures" (1), Piglet is frightened by a scary movie and, feeling that his friends should not associate with a coward, withdraws into his house. In "Prize Piglet" (37-1), Piglet is confronted by his limitations, in this case his inability to run fast. He decides to leave in search of "someplace where the unexceptional won't be expected to excel beyond expectations."[19] Even Christopher Robin is afflicted when he breaks a family heirloom and seeks to avoid his mother's wrath by running away in "Home Is Where the Home Is" (47).[20] Occasionally, characters reveal their insecurity in ways other than by withdrawing, as in "Balloonatics" (3-2). Here, the main characters withhold the truth about a broken balloon from Christopher, fearing that if he learns the truth, "he'll never speak to us again!"[21]

In some stories, afflicted by the Eeyore Effect, a character's sense of worthlessness is never refuted and may even be reinforced. In "Pooh Oughta Be in Pictures," Piglet returns to the community after rescuing Pooh from an apparently real danger. However, rather than acknowledge that Piglet is worthwhile, even when he cannot overcome fear, the narrative suggests he is only worthy of friendship when he acts outside his normal pattern of behavior. Similarly, Piglet decides to rejoin the community in "Prize Piglet" only when it turns out he has won a footrace, although his victory was achieved not by his own fleetness but by the misfortune of his competitors in falling victim to the perils of a bog. Once again, his welcome back is portrayed as a result solely of an exceptional performance. Even in the case of the conspiracy of silence about the broken balloon in "Balloonatics," we learn that the balloon was not popped, only deflated; since it had never truly been damaged, the ensemble never truly escapes their insecurity about Christopher's reaction to their transgression.

Some stories, however, do confront the Eeyore Within and affirm the intrinsic value of characters. In "Home Is Where the Home Is," Christopher cannot escape the love of his companions: the core ensemble attempts to build a new home for him (with predictably disastrous results), Pooh accompanies him on his exile, and Eeyore brings him an umbrella to shield Christopher from a thunderstorm. From Eeyore, Christopher learns that making mistakes is an inevitable part of life and "there's no runnin' away from 'em."[22] This story concludes with a rejection of the Eeyore Within. However, the repeated tendency of the characters in the *New Adventures* to fall prey to their own inner doubts and fears, and to take drastic action in response, remains disturbing.

TO TE OR NOT TO TE

Hoff's practical exposition of Taoism focuses especially on one aspect of the *Tao*—the Inner Nature of each individual thing. According to Taoism, each being is a unique individual with its own distinct nature; this in turn bestows upon that individual a specific set of abilities and limitations, collectively known as *Te*. The secret to happiness in Taoism is simple: one must acknowledge and respect the *Te* that flows from one's own Inner Nature as well as the *Te* that flows from the Inner Nature of all other things. A characteristic example is "Donkey for a Day" (2-2). Eeyore's friends infer from his gloomy demeanor that he is unhappy and take turns trying to cheer him up. Pooh, Owl, Rabbit, and Tigger all make the same unfortunate assumption: "The activity I find most enjoyable will make Eeyore happy as well." Eeyore, however, does not particularly enjoy eating honey, flying, gardening, or bouncing; he naturally concludes that his friends have colluded in "Make Eeyore Miserable Day."[23] The flaw behind the characters' reasoning is clear from a Taoist perspective. Any attempt by one character to impose his own Inner Nature on Eeyore must inevitably result in misery, not happiness. The central message is communicated by a frustrated Piglet. Eventually, he realizes that, instead of imposing his idea of happiness on Eeyore, he must simply listen to Eeyore, discovering Eeyore is not unhappy at all. A gloomy disposition is simply part of his Inner Nature; the best way to make Eeyore happy is to let Eeyore be Eeyore. A similar project may be witnessed in the story "Stripes" (8-1), in which Rabbit, Pooh, and Piglet attempt to provide a new identify for a temporarily stripeless Tigger, with predictably disastrous results.

Since respect for each thing's Inner Nature is essential for happiness, Taoists place a high value on an accurate understanding of Things as They Are. As Hoff points out, when we disregard this, we instead fabricate a false reality; attempting to operate within it, we inevitably fail to achieve our goals while creating problems that would never have arisen otherwise.[24] We can also be overwhelmed by fear.[25] It is all too easy to focus instead on Things as We Fear They Might Be; multiple storylines feature a character drastically misinterpreting an experience, becomimg afraid, and implementing an elaborate but unsuccessful plan to alleviate a situation that does not, in fact, exist. All but the youngest children in the audience are sufficiently experienced to recognize such an episode's central error in reasoning and are able to enjoy the ensuing antics without succumbing to fear or concern.

A striking first-season example occurs in "Owl Feathers" (18-2). The ensemble happens across a pile of feathers from a damaged pillow, erroneously assuming they've fallen from Owl. Fearing he will never fly again, they seek to provide him with a number of alternate modes, none successful, only to learn the feathers do not really belong to him. So too, in the second season's surreal "Pooh Moon" (32-1), Pooh and Piglet believe they've been transported to the moon during a nighttime camping trip; they subsequently interpret the creatures they encounter as moon monsters; in reality, they are only their friends and companions. "Invasion of the Pooh Snatcher" (41-2) features a comic mix-up in which Pooh and Tigger each mistakenly fear that the other has been kidnapped by a Jaguar, though neither is in danger. In "Grown, but Not Forgotten" (44), the animals fear that Christopher will mature and forget them; these fears become exaggerated to the point where they imagine him as an adult already, when many years of his childhood still remain.

Another way of creating a false reality is focusing on Things as We Think They Should Be.[26] The character who most frequently commits this error is Rabbit. In "Tigger Is the Mother of Invention" (40-1), Rabbit bemoans nature's inherent untidiness: "I wish snow would fall more neatly and not drop all over everywhere."[27] In the story "Party Poohper" (22-1), Rabbit throws a party for all his relations. He enlists the help of his friends to prepare, but they keep running afoul of his central maxim: "Happiness is making a schedule and keeping to it."[28] When he explains that "the key to giving a perfect party is an airtight schedule,"[29] Tigger protests that Rabbit's plan doesn't sound like any fun. In response, Rabbit expostulates, "This is a party! Who said anything about fun?"[30] Rabbit's elaborate plans to throw the perfect party are, of course, doomed to fail, but when Rabbit realizes his relations are enjoying themselves nonetheless, he stops worrying that things are not exactly as he thinks they should be, instead learning to appreciate Things as They Are by tearing up his impractical schedule, realizing that "you can have fun whenever you want."[31]

One recurring source of mirth is the penchant of certain characters to devise and implement complicated plans in response to potential problems. These plans almost invariably end in catastrophe, problems they are meant to address resolving themselves. Virtually every story can serve as an illustration of the Taoist principle of *Wu Wei*, usually translated as "effortless action" or "noninterfering action"—a person must learn to work with Things as They Are and allow things to happen naturally.[32] Any attempt to impose one's will on others and force them to act in a manner contrary to their Inner Natures is doomed to fail.

An elegant example may be found in the series' second story, "Friend, in Deed" (2-1).[33] Pooh is concerned that his close friend Rabbit has become alienated by Pooh's constant visits to borrow honey. Pooh's friends concoct increasingly elaborate plans to help him get honey from a honey tree, but they all fail. A final, grandiose scheme accidentally carries Pooh atop a cascade of water through the honey tree, and Pooh fills his pot by the simple expedient of scooping honey from the walls as he passes by.

An interesting variation occurs in the story "Fast Friends" (31-2).[34] Disturbed by Pooh's habitual lateness, companions attempt to find ways to speed up Pooh. While plans involving strict schedules (Rabbit), traveling in straight lines (Piglet), and racing stripes (Tigger) fail, Gopher's plan involves a high-tech contraption that succeeds in making Pooh travel at a high rate of speed. However, Pooh is now unable to interact with the others. To deal with this complication, the companions implement a series of plans to slow Pooh back down, all of which predictably fail. Then they attempt to speed up themselves, working at a frenetic pace until they wear themselves out. Finally, Pooh loses his momentum and returns to his normal slow pace. The ensemble abandons their efforts to interfere in Pooh's Inner Nature, accepting him as he is. As Tigger observes, "Not being on time is right on time for a Pooh Bear."[35]

The antics of Gopher admirably illuminate the Taoist principle of *Wu Wei*. While the others generally content themselves with simple hand tools, Gopher embodies the modern fascination with technology. In "Shovel, Shovel, Toil and Trouble" (48-1), Gopher orders a "power shovel," using his new tool to improve his friends' lives. As might be expected, they are not pleased by his disastrous efforts. Gopher eventually realizes he has exceeded the bounds of propriety. Apparently, gophers possess an innate desire to interfere with nature. In "Easy Come, Easy Gopher" (41-1), Gopher's attempt to complete the "ultimate tunnel" envisioned by his grandpappy wreaks havoc on the Hundred Acre Wood. Then his efforts to fulfill his grandpappy's lifelong dream of building an aboveground underground city in "To Dream the Impossible Scheme" (49-2) not only fail but endanger the special plant Rabbit is carefully nurturing. Disasters such as these result from attempts to impose one's will on nature, fueling the Taoist suspicion of technology. Despite his destructive activity, Gopher is always welcomed as a friend by the canonical characters. This depiction of patient tolerance and acceptance, so characteristically Taoist in nature,[36] may be the ultimate legacy of Disney's desire to put its own stamp on the Pooh universe.

For Hoff, Taoism is a "Way of Transformation" by which we can become the happy, successful people we desire to be.[37] A fundamental strategy for achieving this involves reenvisioning aspects of our lives that we find troublesome or harmful, transforming them into opportunities for growth and empowerment.[38] In "How Much Is That Rabbit in the Window?" (10),[39] Rabbit runs away from the Wood because he feels unappreciated; he is picked up by a kindly junk dealer who places on him a tag reading "SPE-CIAL," offering Rabbit for sale at his secondhand shop. Various stuffed animals are jealous of Rabbit's tag and take it from him by force. At story's end, Christopher Robin convinces the shopkeeper that he values Rabbit and is permitted to purchase him. With the dramatic tension resolved, Rabbit might well have departed with a triumphant look at his former rivals. Instead, he tells them that they too will be special to someone someday, affirming their value, ending the episode on a note of hope for everyone.

Another application involves a character's reassessment of a figure traditionally considered an enemy. In "The Great Honey Pot Robbery" (7),[40] the characters encounter Stan the Woozle and Heff the Heffalump, who want to steal everyone's honey. Pooh resolves the dramatic confrontation by offering to share his honey with the erstwhile thieves; after all, honey can't be stolen if it's given freely. Similarly, in "There's No Camp Like Home" (3-1),[41] Pooh, Piglet, and Tigger are terrified of a Heffalump family whose members are equally terrified of them. When Piglet and Junior Heffalump become lost, however, the adversaries must overcome their fear and join forces; resolution of the dramatic tension is possible only when the two groups reassess and revise their views of one another.

Finally, this strategy appears in stories in which a character mistreats one of his friends. Surprisingly, the character who most frequently commits this lapse of judgment is Rabbit, ordinarily mature and responsible. In both "Tigger's Shoes" (20-2)[42] and "Rabbit Marks the Spot" (24-1),[43] Rabbit plays pranks so his friends will not interrupt him while gardening. In the former, Rabbit provides Tigger with special shoes to help him bounce; unbeknownst to Tigger, the shoes are weighted down with rocks so that bouncing will be more rather than less difficult. In the latter, when his friends pretend to be pirates, Rabbit concocts a treasure map, leading them on a merry chase to a chest filled with ordinary rocks rather than valuables. In each case, Rabbit eventually repents of his cruel joke and tries to redeem himself by confessing. To his surprise, other characters choose not to view Rabbit's actions negatively, focusing instead on their unintended benefits. After all, by strengthening Tigger's muscles, the weighted shoes did indeed help him bounce, while the rocks in the treasure chest admirably met the pirates' desire for doorstops, nutcrackers, and the like. Rabbit can only marvel at such gratitude as the audience, privy to his culpability, realizes the happy resolution of stories' dramatic tension is due solely to the positive attitude of Rabbit's intended victims.

Such behavior is given a comical twist in "Rabbit Takes a Holiday" (36-1).[44] Here Rabbit finds himself in the unusual position of having completed all his work. Seizing this opportunity to visit his extended family, he entrusts his house and garden to the care of Pooh, Piglet, Tigger, and Gopher. Upon arriving home, Rabbit encounters a scene of devastation. Rather than blaming his friends for their well-intentioned but disastrous actions, Rabbit rejoices that he now has work to do. Perhaps as a result of observing the choices of his friends in earlier episodes, Rabbit has transformed himself from a personality afflicted by forces outside his control into one with the power to invest his experiences with meaning and value.

CONCLUSION

Benjamin Hoff made great strides in using Milne's Winnie-the-Pooh stories as a vehicle for illustrating Taoist principles. These are approaching their centennial, however, and their usefulness may very well be waning. The animated Disney featurettes bring a few of these to life, though their illustration of Taoist principles is limited by their small number. However, the *New Adventures* offers a much wider range of stories that convey the central Taoist principles. Taoism is best taught through stories, and many of the stories in this series can proudly take their place among other classics of Taoist literature.

NOTES

1. Marc Graser, "With Star Wars and Princesses, Disney Now Has Six of the Top 10 Licensed Franchises," *Variety*, June 2013, http://variety.com/2013/biz/news/disney-star-wars-princesses-licensing-1200498040.

2. Patrick M. Sheridan, "'Frozen' Joins Disney's Top Franchises," CNN.com, May 13, 2014, http://money.cnn.com/gallery/news/companies/2014/05/13/frozen-disney-franchises/index.html.

3. Louise Rosen, "Don't Pooh-Pooh the Pooh Bear," *Forbes*, March 2000, 186.

4. See, for example, A. A. Milne, *Winnie-the-Pooh* (New York: Dutton Children's Books, 1926), "Introduction," 3–5.

5. A. A. Milne, *The House at Pooh Corner* (New York: Dutton Children's Books, 1928), "Contradiction."

6. Milne, *Winnie-the-Pooh*, "Introduction."

7. For example, after Christopher Robin's somewhat baffling explanation of Pooh's unusual name: "'Ah, yes, now I [understand],' I said quickly; and I hope you do too, because it is all the explanation you are going to get" (Milne, *Winnie-the-Pooh*, 4).

8. Benjamin Hoff, *The Tao of Pooh* (New York: Penguin Books, 1983), xii.

9. John Tyerman Williams, *Pooh and the Philosophers: In Which It Is Shown That All of Western Philosophy Is Merely a Preamble to* Winnie-the-Pooh (New York: Dutton Books, 1996), 1–2.

10. *Winnie the Pooh and Tigger Too*, directed by John Lounsbery (1974; Burbank, CA: Walt Disney Studios Home Entertainment, 2013), DVD.

11. Minor changes include the setting of the stories in the "Hundred Acre Wood" rather than "The Forest," as well as the reimagination of Rabbit as a far less realistic animal than the one pictured in the original illustrations by Shephard.

12. *Winnie the Pooh and the Honey Tree*, directed by Wolfgang Reitherman (1966; Burbank, CA: Walt Disney Studios Home Entertainment, 2013), DVD. To be precise, the description "not in the book" is spoken three times by Gopher and once by Pooh.

13. The exceptions are "Eeyore's Tail Tale," which is loosely based on chapter 4 of *Winnie-the-Pooh*, and "The Old Switcheroo," which is loosely based on chapter 7 of *Winnie-the-Pooh*.

14. The first season was the longest at twenty-two episodes, split between the Disney Channel (thirteen episodes) and ABC (nine episodes); all subsequent seasons appeared on ABC and were ten episodes in length.

15. To designate individual stories, we provide episode number and story, e.g., 5 (episode 5, sole story), 24-1 (episode 24, first story), and 49-2 (episode 49, second story).

16. Stephen Mitchell, trans., *Tao Te Ching* (New York: HarperPerennial, 1992), poem 4.

17. The attentive reader will have noted by now that a number of the story titles are intended primarily to amuse the parents.

18. Benjamin Hoff, *The Te of Piglet* (New York: Penguin Books, 1993), 54–56.

19. "Prize Piglet," *The New Adventures of Winnie the Pooh*, ABC (Burbank, CA: November 18, 1989).

20. "Home Is Where the Home Is," *The New Adventures of Winnie the Pooh*, ABC (Burbank, CA: October 5, 1991).

21. "Balloonatics," *The New Adventures of Winnie the Pooh*, Disney Channel (Burbank, CA: January 31, 1988).

22. "Home Is Where the Home Is."

23. "Donkey for a Day," *The New Adventures of Winnie the Pooh*, Disney Channel (Burbank, CA: January 24, 1988).

24. Hoff, *The Te of Piglet*, 107–9.

25. Ibid., 171.

26. Ibid., 158–60.

27. "Tigger Is the Mother of Invention," *The New Adventures of Winnie the Pooh*, ABC (Burbank, CA: October 27, 1990).

28. "Party Poohper," *The New Adventures of Winnie the Pooh*, ABC (Burbank, CA: March 4, 1989).

29. Ibid.

30. Ibid.

31. Ibid.

32. Hoff, *Tao of Pooh*, 66–70, 77–80.

33. "Friend, in Deed," *The New Adventures of Winnie the Pooh*, Disney Channel (Burbank, CA: January 24, 1988).

34. "Fast Friends," *The New Adventures of Winnie the Pooh*, ABC (Burbank, CA: November 18, 1989).

35. Ibid.

36. See Mitchell, *Tao Te Ching*, poem 5: "The Tao doesn't take sides; it gives birth to both good and evil. The Master doesn't take sides; she welcomes both saints and sinners."

37. Hoff, *The Te of Piglet*, 231.

38. Ibid., 234–35; see also Hoff, *The Tao of Pooh*, 128 and 134–35.

39. "How Much Is That Rabbit in the Window?," *The New Adventures of Winnie the Pooh*, Disney Channel (Burbank, CA: March 20, 1988).

40. "The Great Honey Pot Robbery," *The New Adventures of Winnie the Pooh*, Disney Channel (Burbank, CA: February 28, 1988).

41. "There's No Camp Like Home," *The New Adventures of Winnie the Pooh*, Disney Channel (Burbank, CA: January 31, 1988).

42. "Tigger's Shoes," *The New Adventures of Winnie the Pooh*, ABC (Burbank, CA: February 4, 1989).

43. "Rabbit Marks the Spot," *The New Adventures of Winnie the Pooh*, ABC (Burbank, CA: September 16, 1989).

44. "Rabbit Takes a Holiday," *The New Adventures of Winnie the Pooh*, ABC (Burbank, CA: September 8, 1990).

Chapter Seventeen

From Icon to Disneyfication

A Mermaid's Aesthetic Journey

Finn Hauberg Mortensen

As an icon in mass culture, the Little Mermaid has become the official image of Denmark in general, and in particular of its capital, Copenhagen. Its iconicity is intimately tied to two sources: Edvard Eriksen's famous bronze statue erected on the Copenhagen waterfront in 1913 and Hans Christian Andersen's fairy tale from 1837. The complexity of Andersen's fairy tale, however, which lends symbolic value to Eriksen's statue, has been largely ignored because the statue has taken on a life of its own. Historically, it belongs to the final phase of Danish classical sculpture; it has also become the raw material for modernistic artistic expressions. Over the last forty years, the statue has moved toward two distinct representations: the completed statue by Eriksen viewed and revered by the millions of tourists who visit and photograph it, and the fragmented and unfinished work, which has derived from the destruction of the former. This latter "work of art" in turn points to the modernity of which it and Denmark has become a part.

The fragmentation began in 1961, when the statue had its hair painted red and was dressed up in a bra and panties. Two years later she was painted red again. In 1964, these prankish attacks were followed by an act of artistic vandalism when an unknown assailant sawed the head off the body. Later, Jorgen Nash, a Situationist visual artist, claimed responsibility, making a deliberate assault on the Danish national symbol. In 1990, this national symbol lost half of her head; in 1998, the entire head was again severed from her body. The final attack to date took place in 2003, when the mermaid was blown off her stone by expolsives, thrown into the water with injured knees and lips. After reconstructive surgery, she was placed back at "home" on her stone. Since 2008, the daily newspaper *Politiken* has offered a "Genetically

Modified Mermaid" to its readers. It is a small porcelain copy of a large sculpture made by the Danish sculptor Bjorn Norgaard: a monstrosity, clearly intended to function as a commentary on Eriksen's original. Norgaard's mermaid, with deep cuts into her hips, has been "genetically modified" in a biotech laboratory. The point: so-called deconstructed and wounded nature has become a part of culture, not because it has been brought into the living rooms as a knick-knack but as it (re)presents a continual modification of previous cultural representations.

FOLK CULTURE AND MASS CULTURE

Andersen's "Den lille Havfrue" was written in 1836–1837 and first published on April 7, 1837. While the author always maintained that his work had no model, the tale nonetheless draws on traditions of an older feudal oral folk culture. Folk ballads had earlier supplied Danish authors such as Johannes Evald with aspects of the mermaid theme, and Andersen himself had already utilized the topic, as, for example, in "Agnete og Havmanden" ("Agnete and the Merman") from 1833, in which the Agnete can only obtain an immortal soul through love. "Den lille Havfrue" was inspired by works of Andersen's contemporaries. Part of the plot is borrowed from B. S. Ingemann's "Der Underjordiske" ("The Creatures from the Underworld"), while the mermaid longing for an immortal soul and transformation of her body into sea foam derives from a short narrative, *Undine* (1811), by German author Friedrich de ala Motte Fouque. Andersen's text then contributes to the comprehensive reconstitution and remediation of the traditional culture of the romantic period.

A complicated network unfolds in connection with the mermaid. Andersen, for example, draws on several different sources but also many other contemporary works on mermaids from his age that may have served as a basis for the reconstitution and remediation of this figure by mass culture in more recent times. This fairy tale in particular exhibits qualities that changed the course of tradition and supplied modern, industrial, popular, and mass culture with material. More recently, Walt Disney has famously drawn on Andersen's fairy tale and delivered it to movie theatres and VCRs in even the remotest parts of the globe. Although its meaning and understanding presuppose the original title, it appears only in the form of reconstructions and repetitions—remediations that give it meaning while, ironically, taking meaning away.

The Disney film presents not only the text, but also the sculpture purchased in 1913 by the founder of Carlsberg Brewery, Carl Jacobsen, and placed at Langelinje in Copenhagen. The artist Eriksen innocently depicted the dancer Ellen Price on a maritime base and placed the figure on a flat stone near the pier. Eriksen was inspired by the French sculptor Henry Chapu's Jeanne d'Arc (1870), its replica displayed in Copenhagen. Yet Eriksen's is not simply a sculpture. At a diminutive height of 1.25 meters, it serves as a national icon, undoubtedly associated with Andersen, but at the same time it has become disassociated from the author and independently stands today both as a national symbol and a as the springboard for remediations only remotely linked to Andersen, although they play a significant role in today's folk culture (i.e., the tourist and culture industry). While Eriksen's mermaid longs wistfully or tragically for a love that cannot be realized, a steady stream of postcards and merchandise generally manages to portray her as little more than a reference to the first country to lift the criminal ban on pornographic pictures in 1969 or to the world-famous blondes in "Wonderful Copenhagen."

One frequently sees examples of advertisements, pictures in the press, and newspaper articles that ascribe a sexual motive or activity to the mermaid that are altogether foreign to the works of both Andersen and Eriksen. A large billboard advertisement was displayed throughout Rome a few years ago depicting a mermaid whose genital region was merged with half a banana, peel slit slightly upward at the bottom. Evidently, this combination of one male and one female sexual attribute was intended to sell more banana yogurt. Two stories in Danish newspapers reporting on this advertising campaign come to mind.[1] The first reports on the gay pride parade known as the "Danish Mermaid Pride," which was criticized on the street for its march through Copenhagen by a lesbian group arguing that homosexuality should not be portrayed as something unique. The second is from Weeki Wachee, Florida, a water park that has fallen on hard times despite the fact that generations of young girls once fought to appear there dressed in mermaid costume, submerged in a gigantic glass tank before half a million visitors each year. The job is tough, since the girls are not only supposed to swim convincingly and with a smile as they flit about in the cold water with their Lycra tails, but also take in oxygen from time to time from underwater breathing hoses. They must also contend with the stray sea animals that occasionally find their way into the tank from the local river. Given a choice, the girls like the peaceful sea cows the best because they love to be scrubbed on the back while the tank is being cleaned.

In 1964, another, more "sophisticated" meaning was attributed to the statue, its status paradoxically underscored after vandals sawed off the head. Pictures of the defaced statue were seen the world over; the event marked the beginning of a new wave of remediation centering on events arranged by Nash, who kept the migrating tale in motion when he declared himself guilty of "mermaid murder" in 1998. While the extensive media attention that this case received was central to the way events subsequently unfolded, it is debatable whether Nash is correct in claiming that these events rekindled interest in Andersen's fairy tale. A quick glance at the many tourist shots taken daily of the mermaid on Langelinje, the related tourist merchandise available, and the "mermaid murder" suggests rather that the phenomena represent different forms of dilution—the breakdown of tradition—from the perspective of Andersen's text and as an expression of the fact that the mermaid is now living in a modern, industrialized folk culture.

From the perspective of historical consciousness, the long chain of references that have defined the mermaid as a locus of cultural meaning can be divided into three layers: (1) the feudal-popular-pagan traditional culture, with superstitious sailors and their folk ballads about sea creatures; (2) the bourgeois-Christian culture to which both Andersen's fairy tale and Eriksen's statue at Copenhagen's harbor belong; and (3) mass culture, with its multimedia exploitation of Andersen's fairy tale, the most characteristic example of which is Disney's postmodern musical animated film. The issues then are (1) to what does each of the three layers refer, (2) which *tertium comparationis* makes each individual reference possible, and (3) do these three different layers refer to each other to form an interwoven complex of meanings? Answering such problematic questions becomes difficult if not impossible because we cannot escape the necessity of using ourselves as a standard when we assume possession of other cultural traditions. This procession necessarily involves transformation.

ANDERSEN'S MERMAID

Space and Setting

The space of this fairy tale is highly economic in its construction. Vertically, it is organized through an opposition between up and down, sky and seabed. Between these two, there lies a third level, organized horizontally through an opposition between sea surface and dry land. The story takes place here. Customarily, literary/legendary mermaids lure sailors downward from the land to the sea. The Little Mermaid, in contrast, strives with her good deeds to achieve immortality.

The story functions as a frame narrative, as is clear in the introduction, in which listeners are transported from the moment of storytelling in the sitting room far out to sea, where the events take place; and, from there, down to the bottom of the ocean. The embedded nature of the central story in the frame is also thematized when the narrator describes plants and creatures from the deep as phenomena from contemporary daily life. In so doing, features of contemporary life are imparted to the merpeople. These attributions are discrete, well known from other fairy tales by Andersen. This move differs from most of the others since here the scene is placed within the frame. In the final paragraph, the characters are the *Luftens Dotre* (daughters of the air), whom the Little Mermaid has joined and whose good deeds and hopes for an eternal life are projections from the ground. What is up and is down are, therefore, determined from there.

The daughters of the air keep watch from above and turn those children listening to the story into participants in the emancipation process the daughters must undergo. When the children behave well toward their parents, the daughters' trial period is shortened. But misbehavior extends it. This kind of involvement of the audience is reminiscent of a modern computer game, in which the player is able to choose his or her own way through the plot. This resemblance is only superficial, however, since the key is ethical behavior in the bosom of one's family rather than cost-free choices in a fictional universe.

Many regard the finale as an after-the-fact moral appendage; however, both the gradual revelation of the tale's frame and the genesis of the tale dispute this view. Prior to its completion, a friend referred to the text as "Luftens Dottre" ("The Daughters of the Air") in a letter to Andersen, suggesting that this part of the text served as a point of departure. Another argument in favor of interpreting the final paragraph as organic to the text is that the surprise ending of the main story—the mermaid's ascent to the ethereal sphere and, with this, the possibility of obtaining an immortal soul—is overshadowed by the fact that those listening to the narrative are the true agents in this sphere of Christian morality. What child would not want to be on his best behavior if it would put an end to the heroine's sufferings in the bedtime story papa just read and laid on the table next to the bed?

With its focus on the children's behavior, this interactive fairy tale is then similar to surveillance texts typical of children's literature before the breakthrough of which Andersen was a part.[2] The novelty of this focus lies, as it does in the mermaid story, within the tale's regulation of behavior through internal control. Presumptuous children are not corporally punished by a distant, severe father (deity) but learn instead to feel sorrow and shame, as well as a sense of responsibility, for ensuring that innocent representative of goodness are not punished.

Many have argued that the prince is in fact the main character.[3] Certainly, he is at the center of human longing for incorporation into the strange, fertile sea that presents the background of much of the tale about this most human figure, at once a mermaid, a girl, and a child. The longing she feels, however, is more deeply justified as it results in personality development the moment the knife strikes the surface of the water. The prince is left longing but self-reflective. He is neither able to act nor develop a character, and therefore cannot accomplish the task assigned to the children in the frame story: give others an "eternal soul" through love. This is conveyed concretely in terms of the children's responsibility to love and obey their parents, represented by the daughters of the air. Parents in turn are actively involved in reading the tale aloud to their children.

The child's solicitous love for the parents replaces the mermaid's awakening consciousness for her sexual drives as the key to the divine. The main story presents a broken nuclear family at the sea's bottom. But children are given a divine power for controlling the demons of that sea. Instead of transporting its listeners to the realm of superstition, this fairy tale transforms them into participants in the fiction, reinterprets demonic nature, then returns them to their real lives for the choice between good and evil—smiles and tears.

Soul and Gender

This fairy tale follows the structure of the *Bildungsroman*, in terms of both its framing and irs narration: it moves from (a) childhood in the family via (b) the quandaries of youth—the discovery of humans, "the other nature"—to (c) a mature actualization of self among the *Luftens Dotre*. It begins and ends happily, but, as usual, the story focuses on an intervening schism. In this case, the shifts between sky and sea are duplicated in the relationship between dry land and the sea's bottom, as well as the ruptures between good and evil that produce the moments of mistaken identity and gory scenes found in late romantic opera.

Hans Andersen's contemporary Danish author Carsten Hauch wondered at the little creature's ability to follow her own instincts toward the good so purposefully without already possessing the eternal soul for which she so yearned.[4] Had she lacked this drive, however, the story would have been about the demonic. As is, it deals with the relationship between the temporal and the eternal in a process of development necessary for taking possession of oneself. Luther and the children's literature that dominated the period up until preromanticism did not attribute an innately divine soul to the child. Instead, the child acquired one and became human once its wild nature had been disciplined. Both Kierkegaard and Andersen moved beyond this point. The mermaid is not human, but both she and children in general are assumed to possess the instinct to do good from the beginning. Indeed, an upbringing based on internal control would not be possible otherwise.

The Little Mermaid derives from a family sphere that excludes sexuality. Her father is a widower. His mother fills in for the absent mother in the role of "the good mother," but she knows more about the life of humans than she reveals to her grandchildren. This is rendered particularly clear in their encounter with the unfamiliar as they also discover their own sexual identity. She is especially adept at both repressing and driving out what she finds undesirable. She brings the girls face-to-face with the opposition between the surface of the sea and the dry land—the site of the action—so that they will choose, as she did, to remain true to their own fundamental nature. They inherit a comfortable and happy life of three hundred years but no immortal soul. The youngest of the girls is the exception. From the beginning, her longing makes her different. So she attempts to obtain an eternal soul through the realization of her love for a human being. A Faust in reverse, she must sell half of her body as well as her voice to the sea witch, whose appearance, stronghold, and underwater servants identify her as the character into whom the sum of underwater sexuality has been driven—in particular, masculine sexuality, if we are to give credence to the phallic nature of the symbols surrounding her. The description of the sea witch ought to please every Freudian, who can accordingly and reasonably ponder the extent to which she is the embodiment of the masculine force in the story and the demonic helper who exceeds the demonic, a feat neither the sea king nor the land prince is capable of.

The process is irreversible, and the terms harsh: to obtain her eternal soul, the prince must be so in love with her that he forgets both father and mother, marrying the Little Mermaid. This degree of commitment is not only substantial but, beyond that, the narrative's overarching theme. As everyone knows, the project fails. Despite his intuitive love for the one who saved him, the prince sees her as his "little foundling" and does not understand the very limited language left to her.

She strives for both the red and the white. Here, use of color symbolism is but one of the effective narrative devices. After the sisters, in a gesture of self-castration, offer the sea witch their glorious hair in exchange for a knife with which their little sister can reenter the fold, she turns the water red—not by plunging the knife into the heart of the newly wed prince, but by directing the weapon at herself so that drops of blood trickle back into the sea. Liberation lies in self-sacrifice. Her reaction is like that of a man in using the phallic knife, an instinctive act in which the body (again) is offered on behalf of the spirit. Like a reverse Aphrodite, her being dissolves into white foam. She is united with those "hundrede gjennemsigtige, deilige Skabnniner" (hundreds of transparent, beautiful beings) floating in the air who are invisible to humans: "deres Stemme var Melodie, men saa aandig, at intret menneskeligt Ore Kunde hore children" (their voice was melodious, but so ethereal that no human ear was able to hear it).

As is often the case in Andersen, the Little Mermaid as an embodiment of righteousness receives yet another chance: the group of sisters living in the sea for three hundred years of familial comfort is replaced with another group for whom a trial period of three hundred years awaits. This reduplication is an example of deferred gratification—with a vengeance or as an exemplification of the Protestant work ethic as outlined by Max Weber. The children of the air and those in the living room are only able to communicate through good deeds, so one presumes the trial period is not yet over. Andersen's text functions as a *Bildungsroman* concerning the mermaid embedded in a story about conduct addressed to children of the author's day.

To this specific aim, the demons are put into words, so that they can be countered with actions that simultaneously reduce religion to ethics, even as sexuality is removed from love. Consequently, virtue and love for one's parents are able to stand guard together over home life as abstract instantiations of actual parental supervision. In the process, Andersen reveals exceptional daring and bravery in his fascinating account of sexual longing that finds expression during the child's meeting with itself as an adult. Readers have seen enough within and between the lines to grasp how much remains implicit and why. By land, by sea, and by air.

DISNEY'S MERMAID

Children's culture has long been a part of mass culture, both when it was predominantly religious and later under the influence of market forces. It's therefore not surprising that Disney—the most powerful influence on the international market for children's literature—adapted *The Little Mermaid* for a global audience. It is an arresting example of an act of remediation with explicit reference to Andersen's text, which is just as ill protected against reinterpretation and distortion as the folk tradition was when Andersen seized upon it.

Awaited with great expectations, Disney's film arrived in Denmark in the fall of 1990 and was launched with every means available to the modern media industry. It was to be Disney's great comeback to the animated musical film. Andersen's work had already been the subject of an earlier Disney short, "The Ugly Duckling" (1939), and the American version of *The Little Mermaid* more than fulfilled artistic expectations in receiving Oscars for best music and best song. The Danish version of the film was dubbed using the voices and singing talents of eminent domestic artists.

The publicity campaign was set in motion before the film appeared on the screen so children would persuade their parents to purchase posters, records, erases, pencils, action figures, and burgers at McDonald's—all in the name of the Mermaid. This hard-driving commercialism could be one of the reasons serious cultural critics and parents in Denmark turned away; they were not accustomed to seeing a film as the center of an all-encompassing commercial campaign. However, precisely this concept has characterized Walt and the Disney group since the mid-1930s. The strategy was the reason that he, inspired by Tivoli among other things and ignoring opposition among top Disney management, proceeded in 1955 to create Disneyland. Here children would be able to participate in every dimension of Disney's world.

The Danish newspapers dutifully participated in the promotion. Since reviewers paid little attention to the project's financial aspects, they offered two pieces of advice to readers: (1) forget Andersen, and (2) enjoy the film with your children as an impressive artistic experience in its own right. Although the fairy tale is radically reinterpreted, Disney nonetheless expresses something of Andersen. Although the film is an arresting work of art in many respects, it has nonetheless been misunderstood as addressing both parents and their children.[5]

In the film, the mermaid is transformed into a terrestrial figure; that is, Ariel is from the beginning associated clearly with the land more than the sea. In part, this shift in focus results from her human experience, which appears quite lively on the bottom of the ocean, but the transcendental and religious dimension of the fairy tale are notably absent. Also, the worldview and the devices used in the film are clearly grounded in the contemporary American cultural industry. The message of the fairy tale is conveyed in terms suitable for a modern public but is integrated into a product that cheats its intended public of small children by making the daughter's emancipation from puberty into the turning point of the story and offering parents the advice to allow their children *more* freedom.

Similar to other Disney films, this invokes a series of stories alongside the fairy tale. These are not joined in a single well-balanced narrative but instead intrude like loose fragments, not taken seriously on their own but free-floating, manipulatable quotations. If they collectively point toward anything, it must be the filmmaker's—or our own—expectations about postmodernity. It is open to discussion, then, whether the film represents a new tradition that fulfills in a real sense the romantic period's expectations regarding the free work of art, or whether it merely further feeds our confusion. If the film is meant to help resolve the indeterminate position of children in the media age, it could have taken these children as its starting point instead of merely handing them sporadic, momentary experiences. As is customary in the media industry, Disney films gift wrap their product in sexuality and watered-down Freudian clichés. Yet even this is not done consistently, since the sexual instinct is toned down in the film version.

THE MERMAID AS ICON

In Denmark, the film was not on the billboards for long, whereas it became a genuine success in the United States precisely because it gave American girls an opportunity to continue playing the mermaid in a line of costumes launched after the film's release. What does a mermaid "mean," in its history as well as in the Disney Version? An icon is a picture, a statue, or more specifically an image of a saint; Andersen's mermaid does indeed share many features with a female saint of Catholic ideology in that she is a siren in reverse. Instead of seducing human beings, she wishes to live as one herself—is seduced by them, in fact. At the same time, life as a human being is first and foremost a means to eternal life. She wishes, through love, to surpass finitude and temporality and to achieve eternity. Human life is a mode of existence that makes it possible to connect the animal and the divine. From the divine perspective, love amounts to both self-sacrifice and good deeds. Seen in this context, the mermaid with her seductive powers is neither frightening to people nor seduced by them into becoming foreign to her nature. She is already human, and in her bifurcated body—half human, half animal—she exhibits the human split between the supernal divine and the all too human.

The separation between the divine and the human is often perceived as the division between the divine and the animal within human beings. Since ancient times, creatures have been imagined with bodies composed of various natural parts that have been recombined supernaturally; the sphinx is often attributed with wings, a human head, and a lion's body. In Greek folklore, sirens belong to this category. If our need to create meaning leads to the construction of divine creatures at once human and superhuman, then it is plausible to imagine that we also have a need to explore human nature, particularly our own drives, and we do so when we see such drives reflected in the qualities found in animals. The animal in humans is understood as the human in animals, not least in modern society, in which projections of specific human characteristics have been rerouted from paganism's divine relatives and Catholicism's saints to those animals that we associate with ourselves and worship as modern idols.

Mermaids are not holy creatures that parallel cows in India or dogs in the West. Originally derived from actual sea cows, these creatures were the subsequent imaginative constructions of ancient sailors' encounters. They remain today constructions whose beginnings can be found in the human need to understand sexuality and love: their similarities and differences; their interconnectedness, and also oppositional aspects; their complimentary joys and sorrows. In the service of this end, *The Little Mermaid*, via its various incarnations from the folk tradition through Andersen and Eriksen to Disney, has long since passed from fairy tale princess into the realm of legend—that is, to the status of icon.

NOTES

1. See *Fyens Stiftstidende* and *Politiken*, August 17, 2003.
2. See Simonsen, *Den danske Bernebog*, 42ff. On surveillance literature, see Aries, *L'Enfant et la vie familiale*.
3. For further discussion on this topic, see Finn Barlby, *Det dobbelite liv*, 69ff.

4. See Hauch's letter to Ludvig Bodtcher, dated May 22, 1837, cited in Andersen, *Eventyr*, 6:134–35.

5. It is only possible to summarize in context the more general conclusions drawn from an analysis of the film.

WORKS CITED

Andersen, Hans Christian. *Evfentyr.* 7 vols. Edited by Erik Dal. Cophenagen: C.A. Reitzel, 1990.

Aries, Philippe. *L'Enfant et la vie familiale sous L'Ancien Regime.* Paris: Plon 1960.

Barlby, Finn. *Det Dobbelte liv: Om H.C. Andersen.* Copenhagen: Draben, 1994.

Simonsen, Inger. *Den danske Bernebog I des 19: Anrhundrede.* Copenhagen: Nyt Nordsisk Forlag, 1942.

Chapter Eighteen

Disney's *Pocahontas*

History, Legend, and Movie Mythology

Gary Edgerton and Kathy Merlock Jackson

"It is a story that is fundamentally about racism and intolerance and we hope that people will gain a greater understanding of themselves and of the world around them. It's also about having respect for each other's cultures."—Thomas Schumacher, senior vice president of Disney Feature Animation

"The challenge was how to do a movie with such themes and make it interesting, romantic, fun."—Peter Schneider, president of Disney Feature Animation[1]

THE HOLLYWOOD INDIAN

The "Hollywood Indian" is a well-established image that has appeared on movie screens for nearly a century. The parameters of this stereotype are outlined in a handful of useful studies.[2] These focus on representative types and traits, furnishing us with a deeply conflicted and contradictory composite, as in the case of most racial, ethnic, and gender stereotypes. In the essay "The Indians in the Movies," Michael T. Marsden and Jack Nachbar described the cultural context of captivity narratives, dime novels, stage melodramas, and Wild West shows, all of which contributed to the film industry's rendition of the Native American. They also offer a three-part model of American Indian film characterizations in which men compose the first two stereotypes, as "noble anachronisms" or "savage reactionaries," and women are presented as "Indian princesses" in the third, if they are presented onscreen at all.[3]

In this respect, Disney's *Pocahontas* (directed by Mike Gabriel and Eric Goldberg) promised to offer an intriguing departure from the usual male-centered story line, as well as the general portrayal of American Indians. As the epigraphs suggest, the company's executives stressed a seriousness of purpose not usually connected with one of their animated pictures. For Roy Disney, Walt's nephew and the board member who supervised the Feature Animation Division, "Pocahontas is a story that appealed to us because it was basically a story about people getting along together . . . which is particularly applicable to lots of places in the world today."[4] Schneider confirmed, "It is an important message to a generation to stop fighting, stop killing each other because of the color of your skin."[5]

Disney publicists asserted that "in every aspect of the storytelling, the filmmakers tried to treat Pocahontas with the respect she deserved and present a balanced and informed view of the Native American culture."[6] Producer James Pentecost added, "We also tried to tap into [Pocahontas's] spirituality and the spirituality of the Native Americans, especially in the way they relate to nature."[7] Native American activist Russell Means conferred a much-welcomed imprimatur: "When I first read the script, I was impressed with the beginning of the film. In fact, I was overwhelmed by it. It tells the truth about the motives for Europeans initially coming to the so-called New World. I find it astounding that Americans and the Disney Studios are willing to tell the truth."[8] Despite these laudable intentions, Disney's *Pocahontas* raises cultural and historical questions, marking it as a site of controversy.

THE DISNEY VERSION

"You have to approach it carefully. The Disney version becomes the definitive version."—Glen Keane[9]

"Three things are inevitable in 1995: death, taxes, and Disney's Pocahontas."—Pat H. Broeske[10]

Walt Disney Company (WDC) launched its campaign to sell *Pocahontas* on February 3, 1995, with a twenty-four-city mall display, complete with an animation kiosk. Shoppers could electronically paint a cel from the film and view a twenty-six-foot model of John Smith's ship. The promotional juggernaut continued that spring with dozens of tie-ins; Burger King distributed fifty-five million toy replicas of the film's characters with kids' meals, Payless Shoes featured a line of moccasins, while Mattel peddled a Barbie-like *Pocahontas* doll.[11] No doubt the most effective technique was attaching a *Pocahontas* trailer to the March release of *The Lion King* on home video. Disney's marketing of *Pocahontas* peaked with a highly publicized June 10 premiere in New York's Central Park on four eight-story-high screens, before 110,000 spectators. This extravaganza was not only covered by the print and electronic news media but telecast live on the newly launched United Paramount Network. *Pocahontas* eventually earned $91 million in its first four weeks of domestic release and became a certifiable blockbuster by reaping more than $300 million at theaters worldwide during the remainder of 1995.[12]

Fashioned within the no-holds-barred commercial milieu of WDC, this animated feature erupted into the public sphere as the focal point of a massively successful advertising and marketing offensive. The film's story line and characters were soon adapted into other media and provided the basis for an assortment of widely retailed products, generating additional sales and promotions. Pocahontas, the four-hundred-year-old legend, was expertly redesigned to Disney's usual specifications: a full-length animated feature with a host of commodity tie-ins, automatically emerging as the version that most people recognize today.

DON'T KNOW MUCH ABOUT HISTORY

"Moviemakers shouldn't be handcuffed when using real stories as jumping-off places for works of entertainment."—James Pentecost[13]

"We never wanted to do a docu-drama, but something that was inspired by legend."—Peter Schneider[14]

Representatives of WDC inadvertently alienated their chief Native American consultant, Shirley "Little Dove" Custalow McGowan, by sending her mixed signals about the kind of guidance they were seeking. Co-director Eric Goldberg remembers how "we met with surviving members of the Algonquin nation in Virginia and realized that it would be fascinating to show their culture in our film. We wanted to be as faithful as possible."[15] In response, Custalow McGowan recalls, "I was honored to be asked by them . . . but I wasn't at the studio two hours before I began to make clear my objections to what they were doing . . . they had said that the film would be historically accurate. I soon found that it wasn't to be. . . . I wish my name wasn't on it. I wish Pocahontas' name wasn't on it."[16] The filmmakers at Disney never really intended *Pocahontas* to be historically accurate, despite all their rhetoric. After all, they were producing another animated feature. Native American advisors were hired to secure a more positive, even hagiographic, portrayal of Native American characters within an earnestly sympathetic narrative. Studio executives were banking on the likelihood that a postmodern restyling of Pocahontas's legend would prove an immensely popular and profitable version for audiences in the mid-1990s.

Artists and authors have been reshaping Pocahontas for nearly four centuries. In *Pocahontas: Her Life and Legend,* William M. S. Rasmussen and Robert S. Tilton surveyed dozens of depictions, beginning during Pocahontas's lifetime when she was "living proof that American natives could be Christianized and civilized."[17] Fact and fiction were blended from the outset with this legendary personality, symbolizing friendly, advantageous relations between American Indians and English settlers from a distinctly Anglo-American point of view. Disney's animators furthered that tradition, the latest in a series of storytellers, painters, poets, sculptors, and commercial artists who have taken liberties with Pocahontas's historical record for their own purposes.

Disney's *Pocahontas* emerges then as a parable of assimilation, although this time the filmmakers hinted at a change in outlook. Producer James Pentecost reported that "'Colors of the Wind' perhaps best sums up the entire spirit and essence of the film . . . this song was written before anything else. It set the tone of the movie and defined the character of Pocahontas. Once Alan [Menken] and Stephen [Schwartz] wrote that song, we knew what the film was about."[18] Schwartz agreed with Pentecost, adding that his lyrics were inspired by Chief Seattle's famous speech to the United States Congress that challenged white ascendancy in America and the appropriation of American Indian lands.[19] "Colors of the Wind" functions as a rousing anthem, extolling the virtues of tolerance, cross-cultural sensitivity, and respect for others and the natural environment: "You think you own whatever land you land on / The earth is just a dead thing you can claim / But I know ev'ry rock and tree and creature / Has a life, has a spirit, has a name. / You think the only people who are people / Are the people who think and look like you / But if you walk the footsteps of a stranger / You'll learn things you never knew, you never knew."

These lofty sentiments, however, are downplayed by the film's overriding commitment to romantic adventure. Pocahontas sings "Colors of the Wind" in response to John Smith's remark that her people are "savages," but the rest of the technically stirring sequence plays more like an adolescent seduction than a lesson teaching Smith those "things [he] never knew [he] never knew." Pocahontas's search for her "dream," a classic Disney device, particularly in their princess movies, is a case in point. A great deal of dramatic energy is spent on Pocahontas's finding her "true path." She is sprightly though troubled in her conversations with Grandmother Willow. She struggles with her own youthful uncertainties as well as her father's very definite plans for her: "Should I choose the smoothest course / Steady as a beating drum / Should I marry Kocoum / Is all my dreaming at an end? / Or do you still wait for me, dreamgiver / Just around the river bend?" Unsure of Kocoum, but regarding love and marriage as her only options, Pocahontas finally finds her answer in John Smith.

What this development discloses is the conventional viewpoint of the filmmakers: Pocahontas essentially falls in love with the first white man she sees. The scriptwriters chose certain episodes from her life, invented others, and in the process shaped a narrative that highlights some events, ideas, and values while suppressing others. The historical Pocahontas and John Smith were never lovers; she was twelve and he was twenty-seven when they met in 1607. In relying so completely on their romantic coupling, however, Disney's animators minimize the many challenging issues that they raise—racism, colonialism, environmentalism, and spiritual alienation. Clearly, the filmmakers were genuinely trying to offend no one, particularly the Native American community and their consultants. *Pocahontas*'s climactic sequence further emphasizes the film's dominant love-story narrative, albeit with some variations of the classic Disney formula. After English settler Thomas shoots and kills Kocoum, tensions between the American Indians and the British mount. John Smith is captured by Kocoum's companions, blamed for his death, and slated for execution. In a replay of the legendary rescue scene, Pocahontas risks her life to save John Smith, catalyzing peace between the English and American Indians. In the process, the film's animators and scriptwriters complete their upgrade of the Indian princess characterization by making Pocahontas more assertive, determined to realize her "dream" and, according to her father, "wis[e] beyond her years."

Moreover, the film concludes with Pocahontas standing alone on a rocky summit, watching the ship carrying a wounded John Smith sail for England. She presumably resolved to remain in Virginia and take her rightful place alongside her father as a peacemaker, though her actions during the previous eighty minutes suggest that her "path" lies elsewhere. *Pocahontas* therefore reinforces another resilient stereotype: the main purpose of a Disney heroine is to further the interests of love, notwithstanding the bittersweet coda. Pocahontas's newfound ambition to become a mediator, then, is a workable if somewhat disingenuous solution, especially considering the latent historical realities percolating beneath this romantic plotline. The questions then arise: Can a Disney animated feature be substantive as well as entertaining? Can race, gender, and the rest of *Pocahontas*'s postmodernist agenda be presented in a thought-provoking way that still works for the animation feature audience, especially children?

We believe the answer is yes, but also that the studio has an obligation to create a more forward-looking alternative to existing stereotypes and to deal more fully and maturely with the serious issues and charged imagery that it addresses. Consider the title character's redesigning. Supervising animator Glen Keane recalled how former studio chairman Jeffrey Katzenberg charged him with reshaping Pocahontas as "the finest creature the human race has to offer."[20] He also admitted, "I don't want to say a rut, but we've been doing mainly Caucasian faces."[21] Keane, in turn, drew on four successive women for inspiration, beginning with paintings of Pocahontas herself, then Native American consultant Shirley "Little Dove" Custalow McGowan, then twenty-one-year-old Filipino model Dyna Taylor, and finally, white supermodel Christy Turlington. After studio animators spent months sketching, their Pocahontas emerged as a multicultural pastiche. They started with Native American faces, eventually gravitating to more familiar Anglicized looks. Not surprisingly, all key decision makers and supervising artists on *Pocahontas* were white males. Disney and Keane's "finest creature" clearly is the result of a conventional viewpoint.

Accordingly, what of avoiding old stereotypes? Native American actors were cast in all native roles; still, Pocahontas's screen image is less American Indian than fashionably exotic. Many critics, for example *Newsweek*'s Laura Shapiro, refer to the makeover as "Native American Barbie"[22] —in other words, Indian features, such as Pocahontas's eyes, skin color, and wardrobe, only provide a kind of Native American styling to an old stereotype. The British colonists replace Indians as stock villains, with Governor Ratcliffe in particular singing about gold, riches, and power in the appropriately titled song "Mine, Mine, Mine." The film's final impression, therefore, is that, with Ratcliffe bound, gagged, and headed back to England, American Indians and Europeans are now free to coexist peacefully.

Race becomes a dramatic or stylistic device, but the more profound consequences of institutional racism are never allowed even momentarily to invade the audience's comfort zone. Perhaps the Disney studio should trust its patrons more. Fairy tales and fantasies have traditionally challenged children (and adults) with the unpleasant realities lurking just beneath their placid exteriors. Audiences are likely to enjoy added depth and suggestiveness enough to buy plenty of tickets and merchandise. Disney's *Pocahontas* raises important issues but does not fully address them; it succeeds as a king-sized commercial vehicle but fails as a halfhearted revision.

CONTESTED MEANINGS

"The meaning of a text is always the site of a struggle."—Lawrence Grossberg[23]

"History is always interpreted. I'm not saying this film is accurate, but it is a start. I grew up being called Pocahontas as a derogatory term. They hissed that name at me, as if it was something dirty. Now, with this film, Pocahontas can reach a larger culture as a heroine. No, it doesn't make up for 500 years of genocide, but it is a reminder that we will have to start telling our own stories."—Irene Bedard[24]

The comments of Irene Bedard, the Native American actress who plays the voice of Pocahontas, augment many critical responses that surfaced after the film's release. She offers audiences valuable insights into the Native American perspective, especially with her painful recollection of being ridiculed with the surprising taunt, "Pocahontas." As she says, this film signals a welcomed counterbalance to such insults. Significantly, she calls for the emergence and development of a truly American Indian cinema that is the next needed step for fundamentally improving depictions of Native Americans on film.

Until that time, however, we can extend our understanding of *Pocahontas* in particular, and established and alternative views toward Indian people in general, by examining the spectrum of critical reactions that the animated film engendered. The most striking aspect of *Pocahontas*'s critical reception is the contradictory nature of the responses: the film is alternately described as progressive or escapist, enlightened or racist, feminist or retrograde—depending on the critic. Inherently fraught with contradictions, *Pocahontas* sends an abundance of mixed messages, probably underscoring the limits of reconstructing the Native American image at Disney or, perhaps, any major Hollywood studio that operates first and foremost as a marketer of conventional dreams and a seller of related consumer products.

The Native Americans who worked on the film—such as Russell Means, the voice of Powhatan, and Irene Bedard—generally commended it. Means specifically called it "the single finest work ever done on American Indians by Hollywood."[25] His comments especially drew fire from the Native American press, where a number of both columnists and readers who sent letters to the editor wondered if the former head of the American Indian Movement had "sold out to the white man and his money."[26] Means's pronouncements evidently became a source of controversy in a debate that highlights the competing conceptions of American "Indian-ness" that coexist in contemporary America.

A valuable place to start discussion on *Pocahontas* is Robert Berkhofer Jr.'s seminal work *The White Man's Indian: Images of the American Indian from Columbus to the Present*, which underscores that the dominant view of Native Americans has always originated with Euro-American culture, reflecting Anglicized attitudes and preferences and ultimately pushing native perspectives to the margins of society, if not entirely out of view. Disney's *Pocahontas* emerges, then, as another example of the "white man's Indian," mostly because the studio was only willing to partially incorporate its consultants' advice. Berkhofer's book can also be supplemented with Daniel Francis's *The Imaginary Indian: The Image of the Indian in Canadian Culture*, which again emphasizes how most popular representations of Native Americans are the products of white needs, intentions, and purposes.

Moreover, *Pocahontas* is a text in which the issues of race and gender intersect. Bedard found herself at odds with several Native American women writers when she remarked, "When I was growing up, I wanted so much to be Barbie. Now, some little girl might want to be Pocahontas. That's a step in the right direction."[27] Martina Whelshula and Faith Spotted Eagle countered Bedard's sentiment in their review of the film in the *Spokane Review-Perspective*, reprinted in *Indian Country Today*. They stated that Disney's *Pocahontas* is "part of Barbie culture. A culture that relies on sexism, capitalism and lookism . . . where a woman is elevated only on her appearance . . . where a heroine lives only for approval from men."[28]

This flashpoint supplies a productive basis on which to encourage discussion on the social construction of beauty standards and race. From it can be garnered a sense of the profound distress still elicited in the native community by the longstanding traditions of the "Hollywood Indian." Even Disney's relatively benign portrayal prompted consultant Shirley "Little Dove" Custalow McGowan to say her "heart sorrowed" upon seeing the film.[29] Two letters to the editor of *Indian Country Today* likewise expressed dismay and anger, especially over Disney's use of the song "Savages," which the authors found highly offensive.[30] University of Texas anthropologist Pauline Turner Strong aptly explains the reasons behind such a reaction when she writes that

> for many Native Americans "savage" is the "S" word, as potent and degrading as the word "nigger." I cannot imagine the latter epithet repeated so often, and set to music in a G-rated film and its soundtrack. It is even more shocking to write it in a review. Is "savage" more acceptable because it is used reciprocally? But then does this not downplay the role the colonial ideology of savagism played in the extermination and dispossession of indigenous people?[31]

The portrayal of the English in *Pocahontas* similarly triggered outrage in the British press. The July 30, 1995, *Times*, for instance, referred to Pocahontas as

> history's most famous squaw. . . . The English are thugs, all greed, gold, and guns, and they treat natives like savages. The Indians, by contrast, are civilized, peace-loving and eco-conscious. The animators have significantly made the Redskins look pretty much like modern paleface Americans, and speak like them, too. . . . Disney's fable of an arcadian American history wrecked by incursions from the Old World is obviously a means of allaying a bad conscience, while voicing xenophobic resentments about corrupt Europeans.[32]

Evidently, Disney's symbolic inversion can lead to a fruitful exchange about multiculturalism and the function of stock villainy in popular film. As Betsy Sharkey wrote in the *New York Times*, "British males seem to be one of the few safe villains in these politically correct times."[33] Paying attention to such cues can produce striking illustrations of intercultural differences in perspective, allowing us all to "learn [some] things [we] never knew [we] never knew."

The majority of America's mainstream press coverage also concentrated on *Pocahontas*'s racial and gender depictions. On the one hand, Caryn James of the *New York Times* called *Pocahontas* "a sharp revision of the classic Disney fairy tale formula . . . [and] a model of how smartly those elements can be reinvigorated." Moreover, she viewed *Pocahontas* as "the most subversive heroine in the Disney canon."[34] In contrast, Owen Gleiberman of *Entertainment Weekly* provided a scathingly glib description:

> Pocahontas herself has been conceived as a strapping, high-cheek-boned update of the usual Disney Princess—she's an aerobicized Native American superbabe, with long, muscular brown legs, regal shoulder blades, and silky black hair flowing down to her waist. With her vacuous Asian doll eyes, she looks ready to host Pocahontas' House of Style.[35]

Mal Vincent of the *Virginian-Pilot and Ledger-Star* concurred with James that "'Pocahontas' is a signal that Disney animators are willing to take new, and daring, risks";[36] David Sterritt of the *Christian Science Monitor* disagreed, saying that Disney is

> Clinging to formulas that refuse to grow in any but superficial ways. True enough, "Pocahontas" tips its hat to such trendy (and worthy) causes as conservation and environmentalism, and even delivers a hearty endorsement of interracial dating. Yet the studio can hardly be congratulated for "taking a stand" on socially relevant issues, since it's careful to wrap its ideas in an aura of nostalgic fantasy that neutralizes their ability to challenge or stimulate us.[37]

Whether regarded as "subversive" or "sexist," "daring" or "reactionary," *Pocahontas* is a deeply conflicted text. Also undeniable is the film's effect: *Pocahontas*'s widespread popularity has produced a corresponding upsurge in interest in the historical Pocahontas and in Native Americans. After its release, admissions to the Jamestown Settlement rose 60 percent over those of July 1994,[38] eventually reaching 38 percent more than the average for the previous five summers.[39] Although other factors contributed to Jamestown's increased tourism, such as various marketing strategies and the four hundredth anniversary celebration of the birth of Pocahontas, the Disney film contributed greatly to the upturn.

In the words of one Jamestown historical interpreter, tourists are "coming here to learn. I've been pleasantly surprised at how much parental concern there is for children getting more than was shown in the movie."[40] In conclusion, *Pocahontas* can be used as a springboard to encourage our students and children to look beyond the movie and the merchandise. Jean Fritz's young adult history, *The Double Life of Pocahontas*, is a wonderful place to start, along with informative books such as Philip Barbour's *Pocahontas and Her World*, William Rasmussen and Robert Tilton's *Pocahontas: Her Life and Legend*, and Robert Tilton's *Pocahontas: The Evolution of an American Narrative*, other rewarding alternatives to the ubiquitous Disney Version.

NOTES

This chapter was previously published as "Redesigning *Pocahontas*" in "Disney, the 'White Man's Indian,' and the Marketing of Dreams," published by and copyright of *Journal of Popular Film & Television*, vol. 24, no. 2 (1995), 90–98. *Journal of Popular Film & Television* is the property of Taylor & Francis Ltd., and its content may not be copied or emailed to multiple sites or posted to a listserv without the copyright holder's express written permission. Individuals may, however, print, download, or email articles for individual use.

1. Both epigraphs come from *Pocahontas: Press Kit*, 35 and 37.
2. See Bataille and Silet, *Pretend Indians*.
3. Marsden and Nachbar, "Indians in the Movies." In the first category, a "noble anachronism" embodies Rousseau's notion of "natural man and his inherent goodness," who is ultimately doomed by the onslaught of Euro-American culture. Second, a "savage reactionary" confronts white manifest destiny with violent defiance but is also annihilated for the overall good of advancing civilization. Lastly, an "Indian princess" is rooted in the legend of Pocahontas. She is typically maidenly, demure, and deeply committed to some white man—for example, John Smith in the case of Pocahontas.
4. *Pocahontas: Press Kit*, 33.
5. Ibid., 37.
6. Ibid., 34.
7. Ibid., 33.
8. Ibid., 34.
9. Gleiberman, "Disney's Indian Corn," 42.
10. Broeske, "Pocamotion," 8.
11. Ibid.
12. Kilday and Thompson, "To Infinity and Beyond," 27–32.
13. Kim, "Whole New World?," 24.
14. *Pocahontas: Press Kit*, 37.
15. Ibid., 34.
16. Vincent, "Disney vs. History," E5.
17. Rasmussen and Tilton, *Pocahontas*, 7.
18. *Pocahontas: Press Kit*, 51–52.
19. Ibid., 52.
20. Kim, "Whole New World?," 24.
21. Cochran, "What Becomes a Legend Most?," 42.
22. Shapiro and Chang, "Girls of Summer," 57.
23. Grossberg, "Reply to the Critics," 86.
24. Quoted in Vincent, "Disney vs. History," E5.
25. *Pocahontas: Press Kit*, 34.
26. Rattler, "Letters to the Entertainment Editor," D1.
27. Quoted in Vincent, "Disney vs. History," E5.
28. Whelshula and Spotted Eagle, "Pocahontas Rates an 'F,'" D1.
29. Silver, "Pocahontas for Real," 61.
30. Rattler, "Letters to the Entertainment Editor," D2.
31. Strong, "Review of *Pocahontas*."
32. Adair, "Animating History," 10.

33. Sharkey, "Beyond Teepees," 2:1.
34. James, "Belle and Ariel," F1.
35. Gleiberman, "Disney's Indian Corn," 42.
36. Vincent, "Pocahontas," E2.
37. Sterritt, "'Pocahontas' Doesn't Stray," 13.
38. Holland, interview, October 2, 1995.
39. "Renewed National Interest," 3.
40. Holland, interview, October 2, 1995.

WORKS CITED

Adair, Gilbert. "Animating History." *(London) Sunday Times*, July 30, 1995, 10.

Barbour, Phillip. *Pocahontas and Her World*. Boston: Houghton Mifflin, 1970.

Bataille, G., and C. Silet, eds. *The Pretend Indians: Images of Native Americans in the Movies*. Ames: Iowa State University Press, 1980.

Berkhofer, Robert, Jr. *The White Man's Indian: Images of the American Indian from Columbus to the Present*. New York: Vintage, 1979.

Biskind, Peter. "Win, Lose—But Draw." *Premiere*, July 1995, 81.

Broeske, Pat H. "The Pocamotion: Promotion of Walt Disney's 'Pocahontas.'" *Entertainment Weekly*, February 5, 1995, 8.

Cochran, Jason. "What Becomes a Legend Most?" *Entertainment Weekly*, June 16, 1995, 42.

Francis, Daniel. *The Imaginary Indian: The Image of the Indian in Canadian Culture*. Vancouver: Arsenal Pulp, 1992.

Friar, R., and N. Friar. *The Only Good Indian . . . : The Hollywood Gospel*. New York: Drama Book Specialists, 1972.

Fritz, Jean. *The Double Life of Pocahontas*. New York: Puffin, 1983.

Gleiberman, Owen. "Disney's Indian Corn." *Entertainment Weekly*, June 16, 1995, 42.

Grossberg, Lawrence. "Reply to the Critics." *Critical Studies in Mass Communication* 3 (1983): 86–95.

Holland, Erik. Interview by authors. October 2, 1995. Jamestown Settlement. Powhatan Village.

James, Caryn. "Belle and Ariel Never Chose Duty over Love." *New York Times*, June 18, 1995, F1.

Kilday, Gregg, and Anne Thompson. "To Infinity and Beyond." *Entertainment Weekly*, February 2, 1996, 27–32.

Kim, Albert. "Whole New World?" *Entertainment Weekly*, June 23, 1995, 22–25.

"Letters to the Entertainment Editor." *Indian Country Today*, July 6, 1995, D2.

Mallory, Michael. "American History Makes Animation History." *Disney Magazine*, Spring 1995, 22–24.

Marsden, Michael, and Jack Nachbar. "The Indians in the Movies." In *Handbook of North American Indians*, vol. 4, *History of Indian–White Relations*, ed. Wilcomb E. Washburn, 607–16. Washington, DC: Smithsonian Institution, 1988.

Mossiker, Frances. *Pocahontas*. New York: Alfred A. Knopf, 1976.

O'Connor, J. *The Hollywood Indian: Stereotypes of Native Americans in Films*. Trenton: New Jersey State Museum, 1980.

Pocahontas: Press Kit. Burbank, CA: Walt Disney Pictures, 1995.

Rasmussen, William M. S., and Robert S. Tilton. *Pocahontas: Her Life and Legend*. Richmond: Virginia Historical Society, 1994.

Rattler, Terri. "Letters to the Entertainment Editor: Do We Teach History or Fiction to Our Children?" *Indian Country Today*, July 6, 1995, D1.

"Renewed National Interest in Pocahontas Has Impact at Jamestown Settlement." *Jamestown-Yorktown Foundation Dispatch*, Fall 1995, 3.

Shapiro, Laura, and Yahlin Chang. "The Girls of Summer." *Newsweek*, May 22, 1995, 56–57.

Sharkey, Betsy. "Beyond Teepees and Totem Poles." *New York Times*, June 11, 1995, 2:1, 22.

Silver, Marc. "Pocahontas for Real." *U.S. News and World Report*, June 19, 1995, 61.

Sterritt, David. "'Pocahontas' Doesn't Stray Far from Disney Game Plan." *Christian Science Monitor*, June 23, 1995, 13.

Strong, Pauline Turner. "Review of *Pocahontas*." H-Net Discussion List, Popular Culture and American Culture Associations. June 30, 1995. https://networks.h-net.org/node/24029/reviews/30033/strong-pocahontas.

Tilton, Robert S. *Pocahontas: The Evolution of an American Narrative*. Cambridge: Cambridge University Press, 1994.

Vincent, Mal. "Disney vs. History . . . Again." *Virginian-Pilot and Ledger-Star*, June 20, 1995, E1, E5.

———. "'Pocahontas': Discarding the History, It's Still a Terrific Show." *Virginian-Pilot and Ledger-Star*, June 24, 1995, E1–E2.

Whelshula, Martina, and Faith Spotted Eagle. "Pocahontas Rates an 'F' in Indian Country." *Indian Country Today*, July 6, 1995, D1–D2.

Woodward, Grace Steele. *Pocahontas*. Norman: University of Oklahoma Press, 1969.

Chapter Nineteen

"Driven to Sin"

Victor Hugo's Complex Vision of Humanity in Disney's
The Hunchback of Notre Dame

Michael Smith

At first pass, Victor Hugo's dark, gothic tragedy *Notre-Dame de Paris* (1837) (popularly retitled *The Hunchback of Notre Dame*) would seem the *least* promising literary ground for Disney animators hoping to unearth literary nuggets for a potential children's feature. This is, after all, a novel that ends with the wholly innocent female lead hung in the public square, a hangman clinging to her like a monkey as her body swings from the gallows.[1] What's more, poor Esmeralda is executed only *after* a joyful reunion with her long-lost mother, a pathetic wretch who has spent the past fifteen *years* weeping in a walled-up cell. The novel's acute, increasingly grotesque levels of devastation do not offer obvious fare for the family audience. Of course, in adapting the book for just such a project, WDC made enormous changes and modulations.

Most obviously, hideously deformed Quasimodo is transformed into a bucktoothed, lumpish, but still adorably sweet-faced boy-hero. He swings/ sings of his longing for acceptance "out there"—that is, beyond the cathedral's confines.[2] This exists in sharp contrast to Hugo's Quasimodo, an outcast, victim of his own appearance, someone who inspires fear and disgust. He is also almost willfully misanthropic. At the beginning of the novel, Quasimodo seems to be a monster at peace with *being* a monster. It is a tribute to Hugo's genius that often it's difficult to tell whether Quasimodo longs for human contact or actually *prefers* the company of the cathedral and its bells to humans.[3] Who could blame Quasimodo if he *did* prefer such straightforward company, since the majority of characters we meet are hypocrites, bored, or cruel?[4] Worst is the crowd, which cheers with equal fervor for someone's public humiliation as for their rescue. In the end, the entertainment, the spectacle, is all that matters.[5]

Here is the simplest way to express the difference between the two works: When he is out in public, Hugo's hunchback whirls on the children who trail after him (some trying to puncture his hump with pins), snarling contemptuously at them. Disney's cuddly "Quasi," meanwhile, wants only a hug.[6] This necessarily radical revisioning doesn't stop there. The novel's internally grotesque but outwardly handsome Captain Phoebus becomes a generous, noble prince-rescuer archetype. Kevin Kline allows him a gentle, self-deprecating sense of humor, dispelling audience outrage that it's the good-looking blond dude in golden armor who captures Esmeralda's heart over lovable Quasi.[7] Indeed, the filmmakers go to considerable lengths in trying to preemptively address the question of just why it is that Quasi and Esmeralda *can't* end up together. It is a Disney film, after all, and Quasi's the underdog hero, so why doesn't he get the girl? One decision they make is to give Phoebus more to do, positioning him in the presumptive role of romantic lead. In the novel, Phoebus is almost a stereotypical frat boy. When not drinking and picking up women, he cracks jokes about doing so. The only action he takes to "earn" Esmeralda's love is to foil Frollo's kidnapping attempt. Even this appears more a matter of accident than bravery: he happens to comes across Quasimodo struggling with Esmeralda in the night while comfortably backed by his fellows.[8]

In the film, Phoebus is more active, standing up for the persecuted gypsies. The first time we meet him, Phoebus helps Esmeralda escape from two fellow officers when they try to shake her down for money. Later, he intervenes when the villain traps a gypsy family in their house. Finally, he goes to warn hiding gypsies that their secret lair has been discovered and they face an imminent attack. He does this at considerable professional and personal risk—he's captain of the guard, after all, and stands to lose not just his position but his life for defying orders.

Also, the filmmakers adjust the characters' ages in significant ways. Disney's Phoebus is roughly the same age as in the book—early to midtwenties. Esmeralda's age, however, is given a significant boost. In the novel, she's a naïve, credulous sixteen year old; in the film, an independent young woman, apparently in her midtwenties.[9] The film's Quasimodo is a teenager, and a *young* one at that (that is, a tween). More than once, he's seen playing with action figures—actually, wooden figurines of Parisians he has carved. We could ascribe some of that playing to loneliness, for, unlike in the book, this Quasimodo has been forbidden from *ever* stepping foot outside the cathedral. As voiced by Tom Hulce, Quasimodo even *sounds* young; consistently, Disney films feature protagonists only a few years older than the target audience's age so that child viewers can relate but also emulate. By making

Quasimodo younger and Esmeralda older, it's less plausible—less accept-able, really—that they could or should be together. Her affection for him can only be sisterly or it turns gross, possibly even criminal. His romantic interest in her becomes something like a shy schoolboy's first crush, cute but harm-less, something she can indulge up to a point. [10] As a result, it's "safe" for her to choose Phoebus.

Still, many children and adults will feel some measure of disappointment that, in the end, Esmeralda "disses" Quasimodo. [11] This situation illustrates a fundamental contradiction—an impossibility, really—confronted by WDC in taking on this particular adaptation. One presumed message of almost any children's movie featuring an ugly or deformed protagonist is that you shouldn't judge people by how they look; it's what's on the *inside* that matters since true beauty comes from within. The film's ending must bear this out. But what Disney's *Hunchback* does is try to communicate that message—finesse it, really—while *still* making sure the ugly guy doesn't get the hot girl.

Why *can't* Esmeralda be with Quasimodo? Why couldn't Disney make it work? Because one idea that remains absolutely central to the source—to Hugo's tragic vision, to the book's essential idea—is that for the vast major-ity of people, what matters is *outer* beauty. The book hammers at this, again and again. It appears in Esmeralda's infuriating, all-consuming devotion to Phoebus. He is a pure cad, but she assumes that because he's gorgeous he must be good on the inside. Nothing he does can disabuse her of this belief. He shows up for their romantic evening stinking drunk and, with no prelimi-naries, takes her directly to what is for all intents and purposes a rent-by-the-hour room, stating as he begins to undress her, "You must abandon this strange outfit when you are with me." [12] We are told that she becomes "ab-sorbed in her own charming thoughts, was drinking in the intoxicating tones of his voice without listening to the meaning of his words." [13] A moment later, "Phoebus snatched away her shawl," leaving her shoulders and chest exposed. This is momentarily enough to rouse her; Esmeralda begs for her shawl. Yet Phoebus only has to say, "I see plainly you do not love me," to send her into a panic at the possibility of losing him—or an idealized version of him existing in her mind. "Not love you, my Phoebus!" she cries. "Cruel man to say so! Do you want to break my heart? Take me! Take every-thing!" [14] She throws herself at him, then submits: "The young girl, eyes turned toward the ceiling, fell back, trembling and palpitating under his kiss." [15]

Esmeralda is so committed to the idea of a rapturous encounter that she remains blind to what today might be described as Phoebus's "rapey-ness," as well as the hideousness of his interior vacuity. Later, when Phoebus takes up with another woman, doing nothing to aid Esmeralda in her witchcraft trial, Hugo comments on Esmeralda's continued dedication, her love for the way he *appears*: "the blinder the passion the more tenacious it is. Never is it stronger than when it is most unreasonable."[16]

Superficial attractiveness trumps inner beauty in Quasimodo's relationship to Esmeralda. When he rescues her from her public shaming and imminent execution, invoking sanctuary, he risks everything for her—not just his relationship with Frollo, his adopted father and the only person to show him anything like love, but his very life.[17] Still, she can't bring herself to look at him.[18] He must take continual care to remain out of her sight, to "station himself . . . to spare the girl the disagreeable spectacle of his ungainly person."[19] Quasimodo comes to understand some unpleasant, all-too-human truths when he sees her turn wildly rapturous at the sight of Phoebus riding in the street. Tearing out his hair, he cries, "Damnation! That is how one should look, then! One only has to be handsome on the outside!"[20]

Later, Esemeralda overhears Quasimodo singing to himself, darkly ruminating on this reality: "Do not look at the face, / Young girl, look at the heart . . . That which is not beautiful is wrong to be at all / Beauty loves only beauty."[21] Yet this Esmeralda is too obtuse even to contemplate such ideas and instead "passed her days in petting Djali [her goat] . . . talking to herself of Phoebus."[22] While the filmmakers could radically depart from certain literary aspects, departing *too* radically would be fundamentally inauthentic, at odds with the tragic reality of human nature according to Hugo—this unpleasant truth about who we are that we prefer not to face. The nature of that truth? As Quasimodo says, "One only has to be handsome on the outside."[23] So putting Quasimodo and Esmeralda together would be just too . . . *icky*.[24] You don't want your audience leaving the theater disgusted and ashamed. The movie's ending proves that the audience doesn't always *really* want what it thinks it wants. Quasi joins Esmeralda's and Phoebus's hands together, giving them his blessing. This may be dissatisfying, but it is, truthfully if sadly, the best the filmmakers can do while maintaining integrity to the thematic premise upon which this story is built.

It might be argued that the film's happy ending stays strangely true to Hugo's vision. While it is surely Disneyfied, it's also grounded in our unspoken understanding of how the world actually works, which Hugo articulated: say what you want about how the only thing that matters is what's on the inside, when you get right down to it, appearance is what counts.[25] The film effectively articulates more of Hugo's vision by incorporating the book's eroticism.[26] This includes, to an unnerving extent, the sexual torment and hypocrisies of archdeacon Claude Frollo. But Disney's Frollo is not an archdeacon or holy man but rather a *judge*. All powerful in Paris, at film's end he orders the guard to violate the tradition of holy sanctuary by laying siege to Notre-Dame, only Phoebus daring to question his orders.

The reasons for this change are relatively straightforward. In the novel, Frollo is a tragic, complex figure. He is a serious, disciplined man. Though he is severe and coldly distant from people he serves, there's little question that he is a *good* man. After the death of his parents, the young Frollo became responsible for the upbringing of his infant brother, Jehan, a "poor, frail, fair, delicate creature," who "moved him to the bottom of soul."[27] Frollo "bestowed on him all possible care. . . . He was more than a brother . . . he became a mother."[28] As a result of his feelings of "infinite compassion," Frollo spoiled the child. Here again appears another instance of Hugo's essential argument. Jehan grew up handsome, charming, and funny. He is also a letch, a lazy drunkard, and a liar. Owing to the depth of his love, Frollo continually blinds himself to his brother's ugly inner reality.

Frollo is outwardly cold—his congregation fears him—but possesses a tremendous reservoir of tenderness. When the infant Quasimodo was abandoned, Frollo adopted him; before that, the insensitive crowd's rising sentiment held that the demonic-looking creature should be burned at the stake.[29] He vowed "to bring up this [hideous] boy for the love of his [spoiled] brother, that, whatever the faults little Jehan might possess, he could have the benefit of this act of charity performed on his behalf."[30] Frollo sees the adoption as a "small stock of good work that he determined to store up for his brother [to eventually be] accepted at the gates of Paradise,"[31] committing to raising a deformed child in hopes this might save his brother's soul. Here is a selfless, *responsible* act. Hugo's Frollo is essentially good on the inside if outwardly unpleasant. He is also an intellectual, a seeker—with a deep interest in learning, in alchemy, in finding answers to physical mysteries.[32] This makes his eventual fall into sexual obsession, self-betrayal, and degradation sympathetic, even tragic. However, the film's Frollo is *almost* a straight-up snarling old-time movie villain: a harsh, arrogant, and corrupt judge, drunk on his own power and self-righteousness. Considering WDC's ambitions for the piece and their loyal intended audience, how could a children's movie depict a Catholic priest as an increasingly sex-obsessed madman? How could the Disney Version of Frollo in any way remain sympathetic?

In truth, the filmmakers were right in line with the spirit of Hugo's novel by settling on his profession. Some of Hugo's most scathing portraits of hypocrisy involve judges and their indifference to human suffering amid their smug desire to exercise power arbitrarily. The most humorous and awful example is the deaf judge who cannot hear any testimony but pretends he can. His "infirmity . . . passed [with many] for profundity, and with some few for stupidity."[33] We are told he maintains this fiction because "the honor of the magistracy remained unimpeached . . . it is better to be thought a stupid judge than a deaf one."[34] The ability to properly decide on matters of right and wrong, then, is beside the point. In a court of law, only the judge's hold on his position counts.[35]

One widespread assumption about the book—especially among people who have not read it—is that Quasimodo is the hero. Actually, Frollo is the novel's protagonist, a good man tragically brought down by his flaws. By denying and disciplining himself so severely, and taking pride in that denial and discipline, he has left himself open to being overwhelmed by the flood of erotic feeling he experiences at first sight of Esmeralda. He is simply unprepared—he has not allowed himself the life experience—to know how to handle it.[36] In the film, he's the antagonist, the bad guy. In becoming a judge who seeks to "purge the world of vice and sin," rounding up all the gypsy "vermin," the character is stripped of almost all complexity. That "almost," though, is a necessary qualifier. There are some curious moments that render Frollo slightly ambiguous, casting him in a light less shaded by pure malice. This renders him almost human, bringing him closer to Hugo's tormented figure. One involves Quasi's adoption, the other the film's depiction of Esmeralda and the nature of Frollo's fixation.

The matter of why Disney's Frollo adopts Quasi is nowhere near as nuanced or multilayered as in Hugo's book. Still, Frollo can be read in multiple ways that humanize him. In the opening, the judge and his men spring a trap on gypsies. A woman clutching a bundle—"Stolen goods, no doubt," Frollo mutters—flees. He viciously tears a bundle from her and she dies after falling, cracking her skull on Notre-Dame's steps. Frollo then sees the now orphaned infant Quasimodo. Horrified, he moves to toss "this unholy demon" in a well. Then, this Frollo pauses, gazing up at the cathedral. All the statues appear to glare down at him in judgment. His eyes go wide, he blanches, gulps, sees the statue of the Virgin Mary holding the infant Jesus. Clopin, the street minstrel and prologue narrator, sings, "And for one time in his life / Of power and control / . . . Frollo felt a twinge of fear / For his immortal soul." Here there is a sense of entrapment, fear, panic—that is, human emotions. To save face and some semblance of authority, he insists the poor thing must live out all of its days in the cathedral, reflecting, "Even this foul creature may yet prove one day to be of use to me."

None of this renders Frollo a warm, cuddly character. It does elevate him above the status of a mustache-twirling Snidely Whiplash type. He is not a simplistic cartoon villain who enjoys enacting evil for its own sake. On some level, this judge *is* doing what he thinks is right. While he may only be selfishly concerned about the disposition of his soul, *at least he is concerned about his soul!* Purely evil characters are not. As a human, however unpleasant, he knows he must bend to the will of God or burn eternally. But then: All right, he says, you win. This likely is God's special plan for me, a tool that might be useful someday. This final bit of self-deception renders the Disney Frollo especially complex, especially human. The logic of it goes like this: I am a good man who didn't do anything wrong. But if I did do something wrong, it was all part of God's plan anyway. Because I am a Godly man, I'll accept the consequences—except not fully.

The backing up, the rationalization, the distortions humans engage in to avoid an unpleasant truth is a consistent idea in Hugo. In *Les Miserables* (1862), the bishop lies when he tells the gendarmes that the parolee Jean Valjean did not steal the church's silver; the bishop gave it to him so Jean could go free. The bishop does this to provoke a change in Valjean, to encourage him to become a good man. Once free, the next thing Valjean does is steal a coin from the street urchin Gervais. Hugo's point: change takes time. Initially, the idea of a good life "fills him with tremors and anxiety." He believes the bishop has "assaulted him," has "humiliated" him. This is, according to Hugo, what humans do, how we deal, or fail to deal adequately, with what occurs in the world. [37]

More of this complexity is evidenced in the Disney Frollo's first sight and fixation upon Esmeralda, who, in the film, as a young woman appears in direct control of her sexuality. In the book, Esmeralda is a victim, innocent of the spellbinding effect she has on men. Her innocence is in fact *part* of the appeal. She is described not as a human being but as a "fairy, an angel" or "a vision."[38] When she sings, her voice, "like her dancing and her beauty, was indefinable, something pure, sonorous, aerial, winged."[39] She seems totally unaware of the erotic impulses her presence engenders. This is evident when Hugo's Frollo, trying to deny what he feels at the sight of Esmeralda dancing before a campfire, yells, "Sacrilege! Profanation!" She "pouts," yes, but it is in the manner of a put-upon child told to stop playing, not for conscious seductive effect.[40] In the novel, it is the very innocence of her pout, beyond any allure of her body movements, that exerts the most powerful erotic effect.

Contrast Hugo's moment to how Disney's Esmeralda appears when she dances in front of Frollo in the "Feast of Fools" sequence. Esmeralda is voiced by Demi Moore, who possesses an especially husky, smoky voice, essential to Moore's sex appeal. We might also note that within weeks of *The Hunchback of Notre-Dame*'s release, Moore also appeared in *Striptease*, playing a reluctant stripper; the actress's dancing, which captives a powerful politician in that movie, creates a relationship between that R-rated film and this family item. While Disney's mature Esmeralda remains (lightly) clothed, some parents might still find themselves taken aback by the way Esmeralda swirls around, her ample bosom barely contained in a flimsy pink top. Her bare midriff undulates; she winks and cavorts across the stage. She slithers into the judge's lap and wraps a filmy scarf around his neck, pecks him on the nose, mincing away in the manner of a stripper who knows that the more she alternates seduction with dismissal, the bigger the tip.

This is meant to signal Esmeralda's power over the all-powerful judge. The gypsy plays with him, mocks his authority, reveals him as yet another open-mouthed rube. She uses her sex appeal for political effect. But whether this is exactly a *feminist* take on the character is open for discussion. One might suggest Esmeralda only establishes power in a familiar, approved way—through her looks, her ability to be what men want. The film might be accused of placing her in a helpless, objectified position, needing to be rescued by *other* men. While the scene is surely a radical departure from Hugo—and for Disney!—it triggers a powerfully contradictory reaction in Disney's Frollo. The complexity of that reaction again aligns with Hugo's complex vision of humanity.

The increasing depth of Frollo's self-deception, denial, and rationalization become apparent during the "Hellfire" sequence, as a flaming likeness of Esmeralda appears inside Frollo's furnace. The faceless image has a plunging neckline and, as it dances, strokes its own neck and chest, beckoning to him provocatively. (Indeed, the MPA ratings board almost assigned a PG to the film.) Horrified, entranced, ashamed, Frollo compares that fire—his own desire, his lust—to the fires of Hell, complaining that he is being "driven to sin." Before he snaps back to himself, he insists, "It's not my fault / I'm not to blame / It is the gypsy girl / Who sent this flame / It's not my fault / If in God's plan / He made the devil so much stronger than a man."

The dissembling—Frollo's seeming admission of guilt followed by an immediate backing away from it, all along insisting he's a good man and none of this is his fault—mirrors the film's opening. Frollo takes such pride in being "so much purer than the common, vulgar, weak, licentious crowd" that he casts all the blame on God. Then he has the gall to beg God for help.

What could be more human than this?

The Disney film, despite its necessary simplifications of the original's narrative, is absolutely fully in keeping with Hugo's vision of what it is like to be human—never uniformly good or evil in the abstract. Instead of some Manichean divide between good and evil, we witness the psychology of flawed, believable humans. We in the audience, like characters in Hugo's novel *or* Disney's film, exist in how we choose to exercise—or fail to exercise—control over our own minds and bodies.

NOTES

1. Victor Hugo, *Notre-Dame de Paris*, trans. Catherine Liu (New York: Modern Library, 2002), 507.

2. *The Hunchback of Notre Dame*, directed by Gary Trousdale and Kirk Wise (1996; Burbank, CA: Walt Disney Studios/Buena Vista Home Entertainment, 2013), DVD.

3. Hugo, *Notre-Dame de Paris*, 149: "After all, he had turned toward humankind with reluctance; his cathedral was enough for him."

4. Ibid., 303–11. At the conclusion of Esmeralda's trial, a judge complains about the nerve of that "bothersome girl" for bringing torture on herself "when we ought to be at supper!"

5. Ibid., 353–54.

6. My wife's youngest cousin spent the night in our house. She had a stuffed Quasi that she slept with and treated like a teddy bear. She would sooner die than be parted with it, for even one second.

7. The Captain Phoebus of the novel shares the vacuity of Kline's character Otto in *A Fish Called Wanda* (1988).

8. Hugo, *Notre-Dame de Paris*, 69-70. While Phoebus sees three figures initially, Frollo slips away and Phoebus is untroubled by the disappearance. This gives us some indication of his relative abilities and commitment.

9. She stands up to Frollo and the increasingly out-of-control crowd when she frees Quasimodo.

10. When he sneaks her out of the cathedral, she does stimulatingly kiss him.

11. See the moment where she kisses the wounded Phoebus in front of Quasimodo when she knows very well that the hunchback has a crush on her. Also see the Fanpop.com poll on whether Esmeralda should have ended up with Phoebus or Quasimodo (Fanpop.com, "Did You Like That Esmeralda").

12. Hugo, *Notre-Dame de Paris*, 298.

13. Ibid.

14. Ibid., 299.

15. Ibid.

16. Ibid., 373.

17. Ibid., 370. After rescuing her and invoking sanctuary, Quasimodo tells Esmeralda, "But do not leave the church either by night or by day, or they will catch you and kill you, and it will be the death of me."

18. Ibid., 493. There is a way of viewing Esmeralda in much the same way as superficial Phoebus. She is stunningly beautiful, a terrific dancer, and has a charming goat. But she cannot help herself from crying out, "Oh, my Phoebus!" at the most inopportune times. Near the book's end, when she is desperately hiding from the watch, she hears a snatch of Phoebus's voice and jumps up and gives herself away: "Phoebus! My Phoebus! Come here!" She is just sixteen, yes, and caught up in romantic delusions, but she is also just plain dumb.

19. Ibid., 378.

20. Ibid.

21. Ibid., 384.

22. Ibid.

23. We continue to assume, almost as a matter of course, that the most beautiful people in our culture are also the most intelligent and virtuous. See any issue of *People* magazine.

24. Consider the public reaction when Lyle Lovett married Julia Roberts, or when Billy Bob Thornton married Angelina Jolie.

25. To be clear, I'm not suggesting that this is right, or that Hugo is arguing that this is right. Rather, he is arguing that this is the way it is for most people, and the film ultimately must uphold this idea.

26. Much of this was cut or mollified in earlier translations. The Liu translation does the best job of restoring the erotic and borderline fetishistic elements.

27. Hugo, *Notre-Dame de Paris*, 143.

28. Ibid.

29. Ibid., 137–39.

30. Ibid., 145.

31. Ibid.

32. Ibid., 163–72.

33. Ibid., 194

34. Ibid.

35. Ibid., 194–98. Hugo milks this idea of the law's indifference for all it is worth when he brings the deaf Quasimodo before this deaf judge.

36. Ibid., 59. When he first sees Esmeralda dancing, Frollo's deep-set eyes hold an "expression of extraordinary youth, ardent life, and deep passion," but he quickly grows "pained" and "gloomy" as he struggles to contain his excitement.

37. Note that the popular musical is missing this sense, as the bishop's action provokes an immediate and total change in Valjean. He instantly becomes a good man, out of keeping with the spirit of the novel. See chapters 12 and 13 in book 2 of Victor Hugo, *Les Miserables*, trans.

Isabel F. Hapgood, (New York: Thomas Y. Crowell & Co., 1887), http://www.gutenberg.org/files/135/135-h/135-h.htm#link2HCH0026.

38. Hugo, *Notre-Dame de Paris*, 58.
39. Ibid., 62.
40. Ibid., 61.

BIBLIOGRAPHY

Fanpop.com. "Did You Like That Esmerelda Ended Up with Phoebus or Do You Think She Should Have Ended Up with Quasimodo?" http://www.fanpop.com/clubs/the-hunchback-of-notre-dame/picks/results/43734/did-like-esmerelda-ended-up-with-phoebus-think-should-ended-up-with-quasimodo.

Hugo, Victor. *Les Miserables*. Translated by Isabel F. Hapgood. New York: Thomas Y. Crowell & Co., 1887. http://www.gutenberg.org/files/135/135-h/135-h.htm#link2HCH0026.

———. *Notre-Dame de Paris*. Translated by Catherine Liu. New York: Modern Library, 2002.

The Hunchback of Notre Dame. Directed by Gary Trousdale and Kirk Wise. 1996. Burbank, CA: Disney/Buena Vista Home Entertainment, 2013. DVD.

Moore, Demi. Interview by Barbara Walters. *The Barbara Walters Oscar Night Special*. ABC, March 25, 1996. Available at https://www.youtube.com/watch?v=-dhLGk4aFpg.

Striptease. Directed by Andrew Bergman. 1996. Atlanta, GA: Turner Home Entertainment, 2010. DVD.

Chapter Twenty

The Integrity of an Ape-Man

Comparing Disney's Tarzan *with Burroughs's*
Tarzan of the Apes

Stanley A. Galloway

When WDC chose to adapt Edgar Rice Burroughs's novel *Tarzan of the Apes*[1] into a feature animation film, they entered an already-crowded media milieu. Two different television series had run earlier in the decade.[2] One year prior, Warner Brothers released *Tarzan and the Lost City*;[3] Sony, anticipating Disney's movie, offered audiences an unauthorized animated adaptation in March,[4] preceding Disney's June 1999 release.[5] Disney producer Bonnie Arnold reflected in the DVD commentary, "The good news was Tarzan was a character and a title that was so easily recognizable, but the tough part was everybody thinks they've already seen that movie."[6] Feature animation president Thomas Schumacher admitted that was the project's "biggest deficit."[7] "What could Disney do with Tarzan that hadn't been done before?" asks Howard E. Green, then vice president of studio communications.[8]

Most Tarzan adaptations focus on his adulthood. After the initial silent version (1918), only *Greystoke: The Legend of Tarzan* (1984) spent any significant time on Tarzan's maturation process.[9] "The most remarkable part of that movie is its opening—long sequences without language, depicting Tarzan raised by apes, entering into intimate, loving relations with them," writes cultural critic Marianna Torgovnick.[10]

The response of the Disney development team was to return to Burroughs's original and refocus on the family aspects of Tarzan's growth. Coproducer Chris Buck wrote in his journal on August 12, 1996, "The character relationships need to be at the core of our film."[11] Green affirmed the directors' awareness that this "would ultimately succeed or fail based on the strength of its characters and their relationships to one another."[12] Scott Tracy Griffin, a Burroughs film historian, affirms, "Tarzan's relationship with his adoptive primate family . . . wasn't extensively explored in previous big-screen incarnations."[13] That is the direction Disney chose to take.

Ken Cerniglia admits, in his essay exploring Disney's adaptations for film and Broadway, "this narrative reframing took the traditional Tarzan story in a decidedly new direction."[14] Just as *Greystoke* had begun with a close rendition of what Burroughs wrote, then veered into a significantly different plot, so too with Disney. "During the story development process, a debate emerged over the third act. [Tab] Murphy [screenwriter] suggested following Burroughs and having Tarzan go to England [Tarzan does *not* go to England in *Tarzan of the Apes*, but to Paris and America] but directors [Kevin] Lima and Buck felt strongly that after acts establishing a family in the jungle, abandoning it for the human world would not gel"; following the directors' inclinations, "the story took a turn into uncharted territory,"[15] ending with Jane and her father remaining in Africa.

While differences in plot can be enumerated, the mix of fidelity and departure in characterization is telling. This is unquestionably Tarzan's story. A child orphaned as an infant, adopted and raised to adulthood by Kala, confronted with his difference and his humanity, Tarzan has to choose how to proceed; Burroughs and Disney agree on this much. The difference has to do with choice: for Burroughs, it is to leave the jungle and follow his human desires (at least until well into the second novel), for Disney, to make a paradise of the jungle where Jane's family can live in harmony with nature.

Burroughs describes Tarzan's "straight and perfect figure, muscled as the best of the ancient Roman gladiators must have been muscled, and yet with the soft and sinuous curves of a Greek god, [a] wondrous combination of enormous strength with suppleness and speed"; and, further, "With the noble poise of his handsome head upon those broad shoulders, and the fire of life and intelligence in those fine, clear eyes, he might readily have typified some demigod of a wild and warlike bygone people."[16] Here is the prototype of a modern superhero or the legacy of legend. Also, Tarzan is the champion of genetic gentility.

When Disney recasts the character, though, Tarzan is "far from epitomizing the modernist notion of an all powerful male in total control," writes Pieter Swanepoel.[17] Animator Glen Keane explains: "We didn't want him to have a big chin like a superhero, so the jaw is rather narrow with a point on the chin. But at the same time I wanted it to be strong, so I gave him a lot of muscles at the back of his jaw, as if he'd been chewing bamboo all his life."[18] Still, Tarzan is no average human. In the summer of 1996 Keane noted, "[Tarzan] has to think instinctively. Eyes that see, ears that hear. A mind that comprehends. Tuned in to everything around him. As a blind man is in touch with hypersensitivity, so Tarzan has developed these senses," making Tarzan a "stunning contradiction of animal skill, courage, cunning, and human intelligence, spirit, and soul."[19]

In addition to his "extreme-sports kind of active life," Tony Goldwyn, voice of Disney's Tarzan, understands "he's also sensitive and introspective."[20] Lee Artz describes a similar dichotomy between his "angular, muscular, Aryan" features empowering "athletic and coordinated" action contrasted with "dialogue [that] is innocent and naïve."[21] Tarzan's character might be considered contradictory, featuring bold confidence while "stand[ing] in the sign of uncertainty."[22] Keane emphasized that the animation had to keep Tarzan from becoming "a really dark character"; to do that, he intended to "play up the side of him that was a daredevil, the side that loves life."[23] This becomes, in the words of Richard Corliss, "a safari into the interior of Tarzan's conflicted soul."[24]

Disney's refocus on family transforms Tarzan's central purpose into that of an individual seeking acceptance. "Like the Little Mermaid and the Beast," Edward Rothstein points out in his *New York Times* review, "Tarzan is an outsider who yearns to be accepted in a society he seems ill suited for . . . an immigrant determined to earn his credentials."[25] In the decade of the 1990s, he claims, this recurring theme of Disney movies turns on itself to provide less the assimilation of the main character than respect for the character's difference.

Lima points out that Phil Collins's song "Son of Man" "show[s] Tarzan actually gaining agility and control of his world, which is for us all about the journey from adolescence into adulthood."[26] The lyrics point to a central question Tarzan must answer, whether man or ape; the song answers that he will be a man, given time. That answer is grasped from Tarzan's point of view in Collins's later song, "Strangers Like Me," where he finds uncanny familiarity with humans. The search for identity was so crucial in Disney's vision that the direct-to-DVD sequel, *Tarzan II*,[27] focuses solely on this. A new theme song by Collins is titled "Who Am I?" Burroughs made that question central as well.

In the novel, the mud-covering scene is enacted with grislier results. The narrator reveals Tarzan "was nearly ten before he commenced to realize that a great difference existed between himself and his fellows."[28] In an attempt to be more like his companions, "he attempted to obviate this [difference] by plastering himself from head to foot with mud."[29] While comparing his reflection in the lake with that of a companion, Tarzan pities himself, realizing the extent of his physical differences. Sabor (the name Burroughs gives to every lioness) attacks and kills Tarzan's companion. Tarzan is saved by his plunge into the lake, something apes won't do. In Disney, Tarzan does this alone; instead of a deadly attack, he is met with motherly assurance that heartbeats and hands are more to be trusted than feelings of inferiority.

Lima believes "ultimately Tarzan is his own villain" rather than Sabor or, later, Clayton. He continues, "Tarzan's conflict is internal and we searched throughout the film to find ways to take his internal journey and make it external."[30] This internal quest prepares Tarzan for the arrival of Jane. In the first half, Tarzan learns to balance "fitting in" and "being unique." Keane writes in his journal for July 16, 1997, "When he meets Jane, the dormant drive of his search for identity is reborn—he finds himself in her."[31] This is emphasized in Collins's song "Strangers Like Me," Collins singing from Tarzan's point of view, "Every gesture, every move that she makes, makes me feel like never before. / Why do I have this growing need to be beside her?"[32] This meeting marks a turning point: Tarzan discovers in himself "a long-suppressed feeling of belonging."[33] This fascination and attraction captures the same impulse as in Burroughs, especially Tarzan's internal conflict, though the circumstances have changed.

In both novel and movie, Kala is the maternal figure who protects Tarzan while he grows. Erling B. Holtsmark suggests the Greek feminine adjective *kala* as Burroughs's linguistic source, a word that "speaks to those qualities of Greek culture which entail the concepts of the beautiful, the moral, the right, the fine."[34] She is the most beloved of all apes. As such, Kala may be the least changed of all characters in the adaptation. The only substantial difference is her death, which Swanepoel calls the "most prominent loss within the context of the Tarzan story and the Tarzan identity."[35] Disney removes that by keeping her alive. Artz points out, "Indicative of Disney's naturalistic style, animal stars are always thoroughly anthropomorphized to instantiate the fiction of some human characteristic in animal behavior: motherly owl, devious hyena, playful bear."[36]

In *Tarzan*, Kala represents especially the love of an adoptive mother. The bond that is established in the treehouse when Kala finds Tarzan is an "emotional tent pole" in Disney's adaptation, according to Arnold, "the piece of the Tarzan that we'd never really seen in any of the [previous] movies."[37] The focus on family that Disney has chosen (and which thematically connects this film from Burroughs's book to the entire Disney canon) succeeds because of Kala, who teaches the central theme: "Family is made up more by those who love and support you rather than blood ties."[38] Glenn Close, who voiced the character, explained, "What's lovely about Kala is that she teaches Tarzan that your worth is what's inside."[39] She has to believe Tarzan learns that sufficiently to make a mature choice, even if that means leaving her when the humans arrive. Buck says that Kala "has this incredible fear of losing his love,"[40] though that fear is never verbalized—the analog of every parent who fears the day the child will leave home.

In Disney, the parental death transfers from Kala to Kerchak. Buck points out, "in the original novel Kala is the one who actually gets killed, and we . . . [chose] to put it upon Kerchak."[41] By doing so, Kala remains to anchor

Tarzan's sense of family, central in the Disney Version. Tarzan loses that sense in Burroughs's book when Kala is killed and shortly he kills Kerchak, claiming leadership. But Tarzan does not retain a sense of belonging once Kala is taken from him. Though Kala dies by the middle of the first novel, she is mentioned in three-quarters of the Tarzan novels Burroughs wrote (twenty-four total). Even in her death and absence, she represents family, though the apes themselves become secondary in Tarzan's later adventures as his interests shift from animal to human.

Jane, as Burroughs created her, is the nineteen-year-old daughter of an eccentric academic from Baltimore who is treasure hunting as a means of discharging his debts. Her education and interests are never revealed. She has a tendency to faint and require rescuing. It is only in later novels that she develops skills of jungle self-sufficiency.[42] In Disney, she and her father become naturalists from England, an improvement in terms of gender equality.[43] Noni White, one of WDC's screenwriters, calls Jane "feisty, intelligent, and feminine."[44] Ken Duncan, lead animator for Jane, identified her as "an innocent character with a lot of energy and a great sense of curiosity."[45] Minnie Driver, who voiced Jane, said, "Jane is not the sort of 'damsel in distress' that we've seen in the other *Tarzan* films [or the original novel]. She's very adventurous, funny, and clever."[46] Arnold clarified that she was redesigned to "feel more contemporary"[47] than the Victorian setting dictated. It is, after all, Jane who initiates the kiss at the end; she has control of herself and, to an extent, of Tarzan, since his education in romance is dependent on her.

One scene transformed by Disney but true in intent is Tarzan's rescue of Jane from, in Burroughs's case, abduction and rape by Terkoz and, in Disney, threat of bodily harm by baboons. Jane's mixed response is clear in each. In the novel, while Jane is borne away, Tarzan's arrival is "as wine to sick nerves" and "she saw in him only a protector and friend."[48] During the battle, "the veil of centuries of civilization and culture was swept from the blurred vision of the Baltimore girl."[49] After Tarzan has killed Terkoz, "it was a primeval woman who sprang forward with outstretched arms toward the primeval man who had fought for her and won her."[50] But during their kiss, "as suddenly as the veil had been withdrawn it dropped again, and an outraged conscience suffused her face with its scarlet mantle, and a mortified woman thrust Tarzan of the Apes from her and buried her face in her hands."[51] When the confused Tarzan continues to press close, "she turned upon him like a tigress, striking his great breast with her tiny hands."[52]

The violence and sexual tension in Burroughs is subdued but not absent in Disney. Jane is pursued by baboons, "with a ferocity that would appear to place her in mortal danger," according to David Whitley.[53] After he rescues her, Tarzan, in Whitley's analysis in *The Idea of Nature in Disney Animation*,

approaches her cautiously on all fours till he achieves an intimate bodily
proximity that alarms the bemused Jane. He then proceeds to sniff her from
different angles, even progressing tentatively towards lifting the edge of her
dress so he can extend his exploration to that most fascinating region for
olfactory encounters—between her legs. Jane finally regains her self-control at
this point and firmly slaps him down.[54]

Jane has nowhere to go, her back against a tree. She resists, saying, "Now
you stay away from me, like a very good wild man. You stay! I'm warning
you. My father won't take kindly to you—No, that's, now that's close
enough! How dare y—," at which point he catches her striking hand. Comparing palms and fingers, finding similarity that he did not have in the parallel scene with Kala, he puts the side of his face between her breasts, while
Jane grimaces and closes her eyes. This "comedy of manners,"[55] as Whitley
calls it, keeps alive the sexual tension Jane is feeling but on a level, presumably, still comfortable for young viewers. The core of the scene, though,
comes straight from Burroughs; this is one of the clearest examples of Disney's change to the exterior without damaging the interior.

Another alteration involves Kerchak. The novel's Kerchak is leader of the
tribe of apes that raised Tarzan, but not the mate of Kala. That role belongs to
Tublat. Tarzan's relationship with Tublat is adversarial, Oedipal in many
ways, leading to Tarzan killing him to protect Kala.[56] Disney has merged
Kerchak with Tublat. In the novel, Kerchak is first named in chapter 4, where
he kills two fellow apes in rage, then pursues Kala through the trees, causing
the death of her baby. This event is transferred from Kerchak to Sabor in
Disney's version. Burroughs's Kerchak is fearsome and unsympathetic; he
"ruled with an iron hand and bared fangs."[57] The same day as the death of
Kala's baby, Kerchak kills Tarzan's father (another event Disney shifts to
Sabor) and Kala rescues Tarzan from Kerchak.

White said, "For me, the heart of this movie is the dignity of the apes and
the family structure they have."[58] This "dignity" is something different than
what Burroughs intended. Tarzan tries to teach the apes to look after one
another (particularly in *Jungle Tales of Tarzan*)[59] with limited success. Burroughs's apes rarely think beyond the moment. Disney's Kerchak is more
contemplative. Margareta Ronnberg analyzes that change: "Kerchak is not an
'evil father figure' as much as a reluctant and remote role model."[60] He sets
the tone for that distance with two sentences when Kala insists she keep the
infant: "I said he could stay," followed by, "That doesn't make him my son."
It is only at the moment of death that Kerchak relents, having seen Tarzan's
attempt to undo the damage he set in motion, revealing Tarzan's strength and
humility. Disney's Kerchak represents a small departure from Burroughs in
this regard.

The character of Clayton, by contrast, takes a wide departure. Clayton is the family name of Tarzan's ancestors. His father is "a certain young English nobleman, whom we shall call John Clayton, Lord Greystoke."[61] By this token, it is Tarzan's name as well. Later, Tarzan's cousin, William Cecil Clayton, appears, a bit of a dandy, accompanying Jane and her father in the search for treasure. He also is consistently called Clayton. Disney's re-creation draws from film history rather than Burroughs. Hunters became Tarzan's nemesis, beginning with Holt, in *Tarzan the Ape Man* (1932),[62] searching for the elephant graveyard. Ronnburg suggests he is a visual composite of "Clark Gable, Gaston in *Beauty and the Beast* and Walt Disney himself";[63] John Newsinger calls him "a reincarnation of Captain Hook."[64] Brian Blessed, voice of Clayton, says he "has enjoyed a lifelong romance with himself. . . . The character is a total egomaniac."[65] During character development, Randy Haycock, animation supervisor for Clayton, said, "He went from being a very big, bombastic character to being actually subtle for a villain."[66] The directors wrestled with Clayton's character, Arnold says, trying not to make him "too big and over the top as far as his villainy" is concerned because to do so detracts from Tarzan's own internal conflict.[67]

Few people find Clayton subtle. Cerniglia calls him a "narcissistic and self-serving blowhard."[68] Rothstein adds, "there is little doubt about the evil tendencies of a big-chinned character named Clayton: he wants to cage friendly apes, has little respect for women and likes to shoot first and ask questions later. He embodies egotistical maleness, . . . the epitome of contemporary villainy."[69] Artz points out his relative size in predictable characterization: "Like other Disney villains, Clayton is the largest human character in the film—graphically representing dangerous power."[70] But while Clayton's villainy seems obvious, there are some subtleties. "When we first meet Clayton," art director Dan St. Pierre writes, "he is cutting down the bamboo forest and letting more light break in"; "light" he explains, "equals danger, and darkness or subdued light is safety."[71] The preparation of light as danger begins in the opening, with the lightning over the endangered ship.

In a final comparison, Lima points out that Clayton wears the "same colors as Sabor and he even looks kind of spotted . . . and his ascot is the same color as Sabor's tongue,"[72] including a medial cleft. Arnold says later, "Clayton really becomes an animal himself."[73] In Clayton's final scene, many elements parallel the earlier sequence in which Tarzan defeated Sabor. Clayton pushes into the trees, slicing at the vines even as Sabor clawed through foliage to get at Tarzan. Both Sabor and Clayton meet their death in a descending motion. Tarzan's character is developed in contrast to Clayton. Both represent forms of masculinity (as does Kerchak), but the variations embodied are oppositional. Clayton is offensively violent; Tarzan, competently defensive. When Clayton taunts Tarzan in their final scene, "Be a man," Tarzan's response is clear: "Not a man like you." Embodied in that exchange is the moral lesson that power protects rather than takes.

Lewis Beale identifies another radical change, leading his review of the film with, "what moviegoers won't see—even though the story is set in the jungles of Africa—are any black characters."[74] In Burroughs's original, Tarzan is orphaned in an apparently uninhabited area on the African coast. Only after Tarzan reaches an age around eighteen does the tribe of Mbonga relocate nearby. They become a significant catalyst for Tarzan's maturation by killing Kala, an act that, regardless of any cultural/racial qualities, pits Tarzan against them. He associates all blacks with the pain of the loss of his mother. Later, Tarzan consequently prepares to kill several black workers. The Frenchman who takes him to civilization, Paul D'Arnot, stops this and corrects his misperception that all black men are evil: "Do not assume that men are your enemies until they prove it."[75] Thereafter, Tarzan understands that character rather than race determines how humans get along.[76]

That Disney chose to eliminate the narrative portion including the African village is not surprising, for Burroughs characterized it by cruelty and violence on both sides. This village is cannibalistic; Tarzan's relationship with D'Arnot comes through rescuing him from Mbonga's cooking pots. D'Arnot's forces attack the village in a "battle [that] turned to a wild rout, and then to a grim massacre," stopping only "because there lived to oppose them no single warrior of all the savage village of Mbonga."[77] Newsinger decries Disney's decision to remove Mbonga's village, claiming "the film does not escape its imperial origins. . . . The stories had relations between black and white," but Disney ducks "these issues by not having any black characters."[78] Beale speculates the reason stems from "criticism the studio received for allegedly biased minority depictions in *The Lion King* and *Pocahontas*."[79] Schumacher writes in the press release for the latter, "It is a story that is fundamentally about racism and intolerance and we hope that people will gain a greater understanding of themselves and of the world around them. It's also about having respect for each other's cultures."[80] Gary Edgerton and Kathy Merlock Jackson, challenging Schumaker's intent, write, "the more profound consequences of institutional racism are never allowed even momentarily to invade the audience's comfort zone."[81]

Schumacher's goal did not change in the four years between *Pocahontas* and *Tarzan* though. Disney wanted to nip any chance of potential offense. Likely the sting still throbbed from 1993 when the company made two costly changes to films after they had been released.[82] The absence of blacks in *Tarzan* has been seen by Peter Rainer as "the neutron-bomb version of political correctness" in avoiding "the ooga-booga stereotype"[83] that may have been inescapable given Burroughs's original context. Disney's awareness of the potential racial contention is compressed into a single reference—Tantor's exclamation upon first seeing the human camp: "The horror!" The phrase echoes the dying words of Mr. Kurtz in Joseph Conrad's novella *Heart of Darkness*. What appears to be a throwaway line becomes, in the eyes of David Whitley, "a ludicrous reconfiguring of the nihilistic despair expressed by the character of Kurtz."[84] Marlow, the narrator in Conrad's story, tries to determine what the words mean: "this was the expression of some sort of belief; it had candor, it had conviction, it had a vibrating note of revolt in its whisper, it had the appalling face of a glimpsed truth—the strange commingling of desire and hate . . . and a careless contempt for the evanescence of all things."[85]

Few children who watch Disney's film will be familiar with Conrad's work. Whitley suggests the line is "designed to entertain Disney's adult audience" and that "it does show the scriptwriters' awareness of more complex issues underlying the film's major themes."[86] Later, Whitley calls that line "a deliberate echoing and pastiche,"[87] trivializing the travesty of colonialism. Picking up on Conrad's language, Alex Vernon concludes, "The blacks have been erased; the brutes have been exterminated"; thus "Disney's Africa is an animal-only community."[88]

Condemnation is not the universal response, by any means. Marie Woolf, writing for the *Observer*, credits Disney's treatment for removing the "sexist and racist trappings" of the original.[89] Rothstein suggests a reading that allows *Tarzan* to address racial issues in a constructive way, where species are seen to represent races. He explains that Tarzan "is like the child of a biracial or bicultural marriage. The ethnic issue is by no means clear; allegiance can be declared, but it can't be made absolute. The xenophobic ape and the xenophobic human, with their opposing versions of ethnic supremacy, are both to be scorned. Ethnic pride must be tempered."[90] Corliss as well, in his article for *Time*, raised some eyebrows when he suggested one of the themes of the movie was "the pain and triumph of racial . . . assimilation."[91] Such a reading cannot be coerced from Burroughs. It only works within the framework of the new ending provided by Disney.

Ronnberg provides a simple conclusion to the issue of difference: "the answer to the question of what actually differentiates humans from animals is finally, 'nothing, really': both eat, sleep, play, love, and defend those whom they love."[92] This is true not only with species dissimilarities but, importantly, racial and cultural differences. Shakespeare's Shylock says much the same thing: "Hath not a Jew eyes? Hath not a Jew hands, organs, dimensions, senses, affections, passions? Fed with the same food, hurt with the same weapons, subject to the same diseases. . . . If you prick us do we not bleed? If you tickle us, do we not laugh? If you poison us, do we not die?"[93] Compared to what has been done with the Tarzan character in the history of film, Disney's ape-man remains surprisingly close to Burroughs's. Buck and Lima, unlike some viewers, are not concerned with fidelity to the original plot but characterization. Phil Burger, in his addendum to Richard Lupoff's book *Master of Adventure*, believes "the mighty ape-man with [then] an eighty-five-year history is now associated in the public's mind with Disney rather than Burroughs."[94] As with any adaptation, there are always differences. Some credit Disney; their grandparents credit Johnny Weissmuller. For more than a hundred years, some have known the original story Burroughs wrote.

Vernon, in his self-professed "idiosyncratic consideration," says insightfully that Disney's "isn't Burroughs's Tarzan; he only started there."[95] The story Burroughs wrote is but partly told in Disney's film. Its focus has changed; because of that, many characters and their motivations have been adjusted or eliminated. Yet Danton Burroughs, grandson of Edgar Rice, wrote to Keane after the initial screening, "You have without a doubt mastered the portrayal of Tarzan. If my Grandfather were alive he would embrace you for your keen awareness of his creation."[96] Schumacher said, "We were honest and faithful to the intention of the material. In a sense our version was closer [to the novel] than many" other movies.[97] In terms of physical and conceptual artifacts—Burroughs's novel(s) and Disney's film(s)—to borrow from the song that opens Disney's film, we have two story worlds, but in each of them, Tarzan has a single heart.

NOTES

1. Edgar Rice Burroughs, *Tarzan of the Apes* (Chicago: McClurg, 1914).
2. *Tarzan* (Balenciaga Productions, 1991–1994) and *Tarzan: The Epic Adventures* (Keller Siegel Entertainment, 1996).
3. *Tarzan and the Lost City*, directed by Carl Schenkel (Burbank, CA: Warner Bros., 1998).
4. *Tarzan of the Apes*, produced by Diane Eskenazi and Darcy Wright (New York: Sony Wonder, 1999).
5. *Tarzan*, directed by Chris Buck and Kevin Lima (Burbank, CA: Disney, 1999).
6. Bonnie Arnold, Chris Buck, and Kevin Lima, "Directors' Commentary," *Disney's Tarzan: Special Edition* (Burbank, CA: Disney, 2005).
7. Quoted in Howard E. Green, *The Tarzan Chronicles* (New York: Hyperion, 1999), 19.
8. Ibid., 12.
9. *Tarzan of the Apes*, directed by Scott Sidney (National Film Corporation of America, 1918), and *Greystoke: The Legend of Tarzan*, directed by Hugh Hudson (Burbank, CA: Warner Bros., 1984).
10. Marianna Torgovnick, *Gone Primitive: Savage Intellects, Modern Lives* (Chicago: University of Chicago Press, 1990), 71.
11. Quoted in Green, *Tarzan Chronicles*, 21.
12. Ibid.
13. Scott Tracy Griffin, *Tarzan: The Centennial Celebration* (London: Titan, 2012), 264.
14. Ken Cerniglia, "Tarzan Swings onto Disney's Broadway," in *Global Perspectives on Tarzan: From King of the Jungle to International Icon*, ed. Annette Wannamaker and Michelle Ann Abate (New York: Routledge, 2012), 42.
15. Ibid., 43.
16. Burroughs, *Tarzan of the Apes*, 159, 160.

The Integrity of an Ape-Man

221

17. Pieter Swanepoel, "Tarzan: The Man We Love to Hate," in *Taking a Hard Look: Gender and Visual Culture*, ed. Amanda Du Preez (Cambridge: Cambridge Scholars, 2009), 223.

18. Quoted in Russell Schroeder and Victoria Saxon, *Disney's Tarzan: Special Collector's Edition* (New York: Disney, 1999), 49.

19. Quoted in Green, *Tarzan Chronicles*, 54.

20. Quoted in Liz Smith, "Tony Goldwyn, Voice of Tarzan," *Disney Magazine*, Summer 1999, 36.

21. Lee Artz, "Animating Hierarchy: Disney and the Globalization of Capitalism," *Global Media Journal* 1, no. 1 (2002), http://www.globalmediajournal.com/open-access/animating-hierarchy-disney-and-the-globalization-of-capitalism.php?aid=35055.

22. Swanepoel, "Tarzan," 223.

23. Quoted in Green, *Tarzan Chronicles*, 62.

24. Richard Corliss, "Him Tarzan, Him Great," *Time*, June 14, 1999, 221.

25. Edward Rothstein, "From Darwinian to Disneyesque," *New York Times*, July 15, 1999, http://www.nytimes.com/1999/07/15/movies/critic-s-notebook-darwinian-disneyesque-tarzan-s-evolution-new-theory-survival.html. Note: the print version on E1 and E8 contains only the first of four sections of this article.

26. Quoted in Green, *Tarzan Chronicles*, 174.

27. *Tarzan II*, directed by Brian Smith (Burbank, CA: Disney, 2005).

28. Burroughs, *Tarzan of the Apes*, 57.

29. Ibid., 58.

30. Quoted in Green, *Tarzan Chronicles*, 26.

31. Quoted in ibid., 68.

32. Phil Collins, *Disney's Tarzan* (Walt Disney Music Company [Dist. Milwaukee: Hal Leonard], 1999), 38–39.

33. Green, *Tarzan Chronicles*, 182.

34. Erling B. Holtsmark, *Tarzan and Tradition: Classical Myth in Popular Culture* (Westport, CT: Greenwood, 1981), 89.

35. Swanepoel, "Tarzan," 228.

36. Artz, "Animating Hierarchy."

37. Arnold, Buck, and Lima, "Directors' Commentary."

38. Schroeder and Saxon, *Disney's Tarzan* , 26.

39. Quoted in ibid., 31.

40. Arnold, Buck, and Lima, "Directors' Commentary."

41. Ibid.

42. Jane's most notable roles occur in *Tarzan the Terrible* (Chicago: McClurg, 1921) and *Tarzan's Quest* (Tarzana, CA: ERB, 1936).

43. Disney is not the first to give her a scientific bent. In the television series *Tarzan* (distributed by Keller Entertainment), which ran 1991 through 1994, the years immediately before Disney starts writing, Jane is an environmental scientist focused on wildlife ecology.

44. Quoted in Green, *Tarzan Chronicles*, 37.

45. Quoted in ibid., 83.

46. Quoted in ibid., 84.

47. Arnold, Buck, and Lima, "Directors' Commentary."

48. Burroughs, *Tarzan of the Apes*, 256.

49. Ibid., 256–57.

50. Ibid., 257.

51. Ibid.

52. Ibid.

53. David Whitley, *The Idea of Nature in Disney Animation* (Burlington, VT: Ashgate, 2008), 125.

54. Ibid., 121–22.

55. Ibid., 122.

56. Disney used Tublat's name in its follow-up television series, *The Legend of Tarzan* (directed by Steve Loter and Lisa Schaffer [Burbank, CA: Disney Television Animation, 2001–2003]), for a rival ape trying to wrest control of Kerchak's tribe.

57. Burroughs, *Tarzan of the Apes*, 46.

58. Quoted in Green, *Tarzan Chronicles*, 41.

59. Edgar Rice Burroughs, *Jungle Tales of Tarzan* (Chicago: McClurg, 1919).

60. Margareta Ronnberg, *Why Is Disney So Popular?* (Uppsala: Filmforlaget, 2002), 186.

61. Burroughs, *Tarzan of the Apes*, 2.

62. *Tarzan the Ape Man*, directed by W. S. Van Dyke (Beverly Hills, CA: MGM, 1932).

63. Ronnberg, *Why Is Disney So Popular?* 185.

64. John Newsinger, "Me Disney, You Tarzan," *Race and Class* 42, no. 1 (2000): 81.

65. Quoted in Green, *Tarzan Chronicles*, 93.

66. Quoted in ibid., 91.

67. Arnold, Buck, and Lima, "Directors' Commentary."

68. Cerniglia, "Tarzan Swings onto Disney's Broadway," 43.

69. Rothstein, "From Darwinian to Disneyesque"

70. Artz, "Animating Hierarchy."

71. Quoted in Green, *Tarzan Chronicles*, 136.

72. Arnold, Buck, and Lima, "Directors' Commentary."

73. Ibid.

74. Lewis Beale, "Walt Disney's 'Tarzan' Target of Many Minority Complaints," *Spokane Spokesman-Review*, June 30, 1999, D9.

75. Burroughs, *Tarzan of the Apes*, 349.

76. For more about racism in Burroughs's original text, see my fuller development in *The Teenage Tarzan* (Jefferson, NC: McFarland, 2010), as well as Phillip Burger, "Forty More Years of Adventure," in *Master of Adventure: The Worlds of Edgar Rice Burroughs*, by Richard A. Lupoff (Lincoln: University of Nebraska Press, 2005), 224–61.

77. Burroughs, *Tarzan of the Apes*, 303–4.

78. Newsinger, "Me Disney, You Tarzan," 80.

79. Beale, "Walt Disney's 'Tarzan,'" D9.

80. *Pocahontas: Press Kit* (Burbank, CA: Disney, 1995), 35.

81. Gary Edgerton and Kathy Merlock Jackson, "Redesigning *Pocahontas*," *Journal of Popular Film and Television* 24, no. 2 (1996): 90–98.

82. Those changes were revising lyrics in *Aladdin* (directed by Ron Clements and John Musker [Burbank, CA: Disney, 1992]) and taking, in *The Program* (directed by David S. Ward [Burbank, CA: Touchstone, 1993]), "the virtually unprecedented action of removing a scene from a movie while it is still playing in theaters" (David J. Fox, " Disney to Cut Film's Scene Tied to Fatality," *Los Angeles Times*, October 20, 1993).

83. Peter Rainer, "*Tarzan*: In *Tarzan*, the Animation Really Swings," *New York Magazine*, June 28, 1999.

84. Whitley, *Idea of Nature in Disney Animation*, 124.

85. Joseph Conrad, *Heart of Darkness* (New York: Penguin, 2007), 88.

86. Whitley, *Idea of Nature in Disney Animation*, 124.

87. David J. Whitley, "The Wild and the Cute: Disney Animation and Environmental Awareness," in *Kidding Around: The Child in Film and Media*, ed. Alexander N. Howe and Wynn Yarbrough (New York: Bloomsbury, 2014), 215.

88. Alex Vernon, *On Tarzan* (Athens: University of Georgia Press, 2008), 165.

89. Marie Woolf, "Me Tarzan, You Jane, We PC: Disney Sanitises Lord of the Jungle's Dark Continent Adventures," *Observer*, November 12, 1995.

90. Rothstein, "From Darwinian to Disneyesque."

91. Corliss, "Him Tarzan, Him Great," 221.

92. Ronnberg, *Why Is Disney So Popular?* 185.

93. William Shakespeare, *The Merchant of Venice*, in *William Shakespeare: Complete Works*, ed. Jonathan Bate and Eric Rasmussen (New York: Modern Library, 2007), act 3, scene 1, lines 40–45.

94. Burger, "Forty More Years of Adventure," 232–33.

95. Vernon, *On Tarzan*, 5.

96. Quoted in Green, *Tarzan Chronicles*, 74.

97. Quoted in Cerniglia, "Tarzan Swings onto Disney's Broadway," 55 (brackets Cerniglia's).

Index

The Absent Minded Professor (1961), 67
Aladdin (1992), 24, 109, 129
Alice (in Cartoonland) series, 57
Alice in Wonderland (1951), 51, 52, 53, 54, 55, 56, 81
Alice in Wonderland (2010), 55, 56, 57, 58
Allende, Isabel, 41
Anderson, Hans Christian, 2, 178, 179, 180, 184, 185
Annakin, Ken, 72
Avery, Tex, 53

Baby Weems (1941), 25
Bambi (1942), 27, 46, 47, 48, 49, 50, 53
Barrie, James, 79, 81
The Beatles, 124
Beauty and the Beast (1991), 24, 129
Benchley, Robert, 25, 26, 27, 31
Blackbeard's Ghost (1968), 67
Brave (2012), 82
Burroughs, Edgar Rice, 211, 212, 213, 214, 215, 216, 217, 218, 219, 220
Burton, Tim, 51, 55, 56, 57, 58

Capote, Truman, 121
Carroll, Lewis, 51, 55, 56, 57, 81
Cinderella (1950), 8
Collodi, 2, 13, 14, 15, 16, 17, 18, 19, 21

Dali, Salvador, 53

Darby O'Gill and the Little People (1959), 67
Davy Crockett, King of the Wild Frontier (1955), 72, 74, 76, 96
Dickens, Charles, 151, 152
Disney, Lillian, xi
Disney, Roy, xi, 46
Disney's A Christmas Carol (2009), 152, 158, 159, 160, 172
Douglas, Kirk, 94, 102
Dumbo (1940), 25, 45, 118, 122, 123, 136

Ebert, Roger, xv
Education for Death: The Making of a Nazi (1943), 130
Eisenstein, Sergei, xvi

Fantasia (1940), 24, 135, 136
Finch, Peter, 74
Fleischer, Max and Dave, xii, 1, 4, 7, 8, 9, 10, 96
Flynn, Errol, 72
Ford, Henry, xi

Galsworthy, John, 45
Graham, Kenneth, 26, 28
The Great Gatsby (novel), xi
Grimm, Jacob and Wilhelm, xii, 2, 3, 6, 10
Gulliver Mickey (1934), 4, 5
Gulliver's Travels (1939), 1, 7, 8, 9, 10

Harris, Joel Chandler, 33, 34, 35, 36, 37, 38, 39, 40, 41
Haskin, Byron, 62, 64
House of Mouse (TV), 8
"How to Ride a Horse" (1950), 25
Hugo, Victor, 201, 202, 203, 204, 205, 206, 207, 208
The Hunchback of Notre Dame, 24, 201, 202, 203, 204, 205, 206, 207, 208

Iwerks, Ub, xi, xii

James, Henry, 64
Johnson, Ollie, 119
Jung, Carl, 105
The Jungle Book (1967), 117, 118, 119, 120, 121, 122, 123, 124, 125, 129, 136

Keane, Glen, 212
Kidnapped (1960), 64, 65, 66, 67, 68, 69
Kipling, Rudyard, 117, 118, 119, 120, 121, 122, 123, 124

Lady and the Tramp (1955), 109
"Laugh-O'Grams," xi, 4
Lilo & Stitch (2002), 24
The Lion King (1994), 24, 75
The Little Mermaid (1989), 74, 84, 87, 88, 109, 178, 179, 184, 185
"Little Red Riding Hood" (1922), 4

Maleficent (2014), 110
Mary Poppins (1964), 67, 141, 142, 144, 145, 146
Mason, James, 94
McCay, Winsor, xiv
McDaniel, Hattie, 36
Méliès, Georges, xiv, 51, 101
Melville, Herman, 96
The Mickey Mouse Club (TV, 1955–1959), 132, 133
"Mickey's Christmas Carol" (1983), 152, 153, 154, 155, 160
Milne, A. A., 165, 166, 173
Mulan (1998), 8, 24, 129
multiplane camera, xii

The New Adventures of Winnie the Pooh (TV), 167, 168, 169, 170, 171, 172, 173

Newton, Robert, 63

The Old Mill (1937), xii, 5
Old Yeller (1957), 67
Oliver & Company (1988), 152, 155, 156, 157, 158

Parker, Fess, 74
Perrault, Charles, xii, 2, 105
Perri (1957), 45
Peter Pan (1953), 55, 79, 80, 81, 82, 83, 84, 85, 86, 87, 88, 136
Pinocchio (1940), 13, 17, 18, 19, 20, 21, 22, 24, 49, 72, 119, 120, 132, 136
Pocahontas (1995), 8, 189, 190, 191, 192, 193, 194, 195

The Reluctant Dragon (1941), 23, 25, 26, 27, 28, 29, 30, 31
Richter, Hans, xv
Robin Hood (1973), 24, 72, 74, 75, 76, 77

Salten, Felix, 45, 46, 47, 48
Seal Island (1948), 132
The Shaggy Dog (1959), 45
Shakespeare, William, xi
Sherman Brothers, Robert and Richard, 146
Silly Symphonies (series), 5, 53
The Skeleton Dance (1929), 5
Sleeping Beauty (1959), 105, 106, 107, 108, 109, 110, 111, 112, 130, 132, 136
Snow White and the Seven Dwarfs (1937), xii, 1, 2, 3, 4, 5, 6, 7, 8, 9, 10, 17, 49, 107, 132
Song of the South (1946), 33, 34, 35, 36, 37, 38, 39, 40, 41, 118, 131
Son of Flubber (1963), 67
The Sorcerer's Apprentice (2010), 136
Stevenson, Robert, 67
Stevenson, Robert Louis, 61, 62, 63, 64, 65, 66, 67, 68, 69, 70
The Story of Robin Hood and His Merrie Men (1952), 72, 73, 74, 76, 93, 97
Swift, Jonathan, 4
The Sword and the Rose (1953), 109
The Sword in the Stone (1963), 119, 129

Tarzan (1999), 211, 212, 213, 214, 215, 216, 217, 218, 219, 220

Tchaikovsky, Peter, 105

Temple, Shirley, 36

The Three Little Pigs (1937), 6, 8

Thomas, Frank, 119

Travers, P. L., 141, 142, 144, 145, 146, 147, 148

Treasure Island (1950), 62, 63, 64, 65, 93

True-Life Adventures (series), 132, 133

Twain, Mark, 36

20,000 Leagues under the Sea (1954), 93, 94, 95, 96, 97, 98, 99, 100, 101, 102

The Ugly Duckling (1939), 184

Van Dyke, Dick, 147

Verne, Jules, xiv, 93, 94, 95, 96, 97, 98, 99, 100, 101, 102

Wells, H. G., xiv, 102

White, T. H., 130, 132, 133

Winnie the Pooh (franchise), 165

Winnie the Pooh and the Blustery Day (1968), 166

Winnie the Pooh and the Honey Tree (1966), 166

Winnie the Pooh and Tigger, Too (1974), 166

The Wizard of Oz (1939), 6

Wordsworth, William, 45

Zemeckis, Robert, 160

About the Editors

Douglas Brode is a screenwriter, playwright, novelist, graphic novelist, film historian, and award-winning journalist. He developed and offered diverse courses in cinema studies and popular culture for several decades at Syracuse University's Newhouse School of Public Communications in the TV/Film/Radio and Digital Media Department. Several of his more than forty books on movies have dealt with the ongoing phenomenon of Disney, including *From Walt to Woodstock: How Disney Created the Counterculture* and *Multiculturalism and the Mouse: Sex and Race in Disney Entertainment*. He was one of the Disney scholars chosen to comment on camera for the PBS TV miniseries *Walt Disney: The American Experience*. Brode's latest books include *Sex, Drugs, and Rock 'n' Roll: The Evolution of an American Youth Culture* (2014) and *Fantastic Planets, Forbidden Zones, and Lost Continents: The 100 Greatest Science Fiction Films* (2015).

Shea T. Brode graduated from Buffalo State College, part of the State University of New York, in 2007 with a BA in humanities. While a student, he contributed numerous articles on theater, film, and other cultural events, both classical and popular, to various campus publications. He then relocated to Madrid from 2009 to 2012 as a member of the Saint Louis University students abroad program. In spring 2012 he received an MA in literature and cultural studies from the University of Autonoma in Madrid. He is the coeditor of *Gene Rodenberry's Star Trek: The Original Cast Adventures* and *The Star Trek Universe: Franchising the Final Frontier* (Rowman & Littlefield, 2015).

About the Contributors

Jean-Marie Apostolidès is professor of literature and drama at Stanford University. Author of more than twenty-five volumes, he is also a playwright and a stage director. His book *The Metamorphosis of Tintin* was published in 2010.

Susan Aronstein is professor of English and director of honors at the University of Wyoming. She is the author of *Hollywood Knights: Arthurian Cinema and the Politics of Nostalgia* (2005) and *British Arthurian Narrative* (2012), as well as coeditor (with Tison Pugh) of *Disney's Middle Ages: A Fairy-Tale and Fantasy Past* (2012). Her articles have appeared in *Exemplaria, Prose Studies, Assays, Cinema Journal, Theatre Survey, Women's Studies*, and *Studies in Medievalism*.

Elizabeth Bell received her PhD in communication in 1983 from the University of Texas, Austin. She is professor of communications, former chair of the Department of Women's and Gender Studies, and currently associate dean of faculty affairs in the College of Arts and Sciences at the University of South Florida. Bell has published dozens of journal articles and is the coeditor of *From Mouse to Mermaid: The Politics of Film, Gender, and Culture* (1995). Her textbook, *Theories of Performance* (2008), is the first performance theory textbook aimed at the undergraduate communications classroom.

Sarah Boslaugh holds a PhD from City University of New York and an MPhil from Saint Louis University. She has worked as a biostatistician for approximately twenty-five years while also engaging in critical conversations about cultural topics, including gender and sexuality and film and television. Her bestselling book is *Statistics in a Nutshell* (2nd ed., 2012), and she has also served as the general editor for the Sage *Encyclopedia of Epidemiology* (2008) and the Sage *Encyclopedia of Pharmacology and Society* (2015).

Gary Edgerton is professor and dean of the College of Communication at Butler University. He has published twelve books and more than eighty-five essays on a variety of television, film, and culture topics in a wide assortment of books, scholarly journals, and encyclopedias. He also coedits the *Journal of Popular Film and Television*.

Alexis Finnerty graduated from Syracuse University with an MA in media studies in 2014. Previously published essays include "The Dangers of Innocence: An Analysis of Film Representations of Female Vampire Children," in *Dracula's Daughters: The Female Vampire on Film* (2014), and "Authorial Primacy and Literary Adaptation: TOS and William Shatner's 'Captain's Trilogy,'" in *The Star Trek Universe: Readings on the Films and Franchise* (2014). She is currently teaching English in Japan with the JET Program.

Stan A. Galloway teaches English at Bridgewater College in Virginia's Shenandoah Valley. His book *The Teenage Tarzan: A Literary Analysis of Edgar Rice Burroughs' Jungle Tales of Tarzan* (2010) addresses Tarzan's early years as well as Burroughs's writing in general. He also writes poetry, such as *Just Married* (2013).

Shari Hodges Holt is an instructional assistant professor of English at the University of Mississippi, where she teaches courses in British literature and film studies. She has authored articles on Charles Dickens, Gothic fiction, and film adaptations of literature and is the coauthor of *Ouida the Phenomenon* (2008). Her present research examines cinematic adaptations of Dickens's novels as critical interpretations of their literary originals that demonstrate how Dickens is "read" under varying cultural and historical circumstances.

Kathy Merlock Jackson is professor of communication at Virginia Wesleyan College, where she teaches courses in media studies and children's culture. She has written or edited eight books and published numerous articles, reviews, encyclopedia entries, and chapters in various popular culture and film journals and books. A former president of the American Culture Association, she edits the *Journal of American Culture*.

David McGowan is a professor of animation history at the Savannah College of Art and Design (SCAD) in Savannah, Georgia. His PhD thesis focused on reading American theatrical short animation through the prism of star studies. He is an alumnus of the University of Warwick and Loughborough University. His research interests include animation, video games, home video, stardom, screen comedy, and silent cinema.

Greg Metcalf teaches film in relation to other arts at the Universities of Maryland, Maryland Institute College of Arts, and New York University. His book *The DVD Novel: How the Way We Watch Television Changed the Television We Watch* (2012) remains the only comprehensive consideration of the development of longform TV. Other publications include the essay "Them like US, Then like Now: The Modernized Historical and the Americanized Foreign in Disney's Animated Films," which appears in *The Americanization of History: Conflation of Time and Culture in Film and Television*, edited by Kathleen A. McDonald (2010).

Cynthia J. Miller is a cultural anthropologist specializing in popular culture and visual media. She is the editor or coeditor of eight scholarly volumes, including the award-winning *Steaming into a Victorian Future: A Steampunk Anthology*, *International Westerns: Re-locating the Frontier*, and *Horrors of War: The Undead on the Battlefield*. She serves as the series editor for Rowman & Littlefield's Film and History book series and is director of communication for the Center for the Study of Film and History, governing board member for the PCA/ACA, and editorial board member for the *Journal of Popular Television* and Bloomsbury's Guide to Contemporary Directors series.

Finn Hauberg Mortensen (1946–2013) was universally considered the greatest Danish scholar to analyze his homeland's history, legends, and myths for their treatment in contemporary popular culture. His most wide-read and critically acclaimed books include *Danskfagets Didatik* (1979) and *Kierkergaard Made in Japan* (1996). He taught at Odense Universitet. The editors wish to express our appreciation to his wife and grown children for allowing us to include a particularly apt article from his writings.

Scott Allen Nollen was educated in history and film at the University of Iowa, later serving as an archivist for the National Archives and Records Administration. He has written and edited more than forty books on film, literature, music, and African American studies and has been widely recognized for his work on Robert Louis Stevenson, among many others. He still lectures extensively and contributes to scholarly panels and the Hawaii Public Radio program *Sinatra: The Man and the Music*.

David Payne is associate professor of communication at the University of South Florida. His work embodies the perspective of media ecology and has focused on psychologistic themes in film and the rhetoric of identity in contemporary culture. He is the author of *Coping With Failure: The Therapeutic Uses of Rhetoric* (1989) and a previous essay on Disney adaptations included in *From Mouse to Mermaid: The Politics of Film, Gender, and Culture* (1995).

Tison Pugh is professor of English at the University of Central Florida. His recent books include *Precious Perversions: Humor, Homosexuality, and the Southern Literary Canon* and *Chaucer's (Anti-)Eroticisms and the Queer Middle Ages*. With Susan Aronstein, he edited *The Disney Middle Ages: A Fairy-Tale and Fantasy Past*.

Peggy A. Russo is a retired assistant professor of English at the Pennsylvania State University, Mont Alto. She is coeditor (with Paul Finkelman) of *Terrible Swift Sword: The Legacy of John Brown* (2005) and has published articles in such journals as *Shakespeare Bulletin, Southern Literary Journal, Journal of American Culture, Shakespeare and the Classroom,* and *Selected Papers of the Ohio Valley Shakespeare Conference*. She is currently editing a second collection of essays on John Brown.

David S. Silverman is the Animation Division chair of the Popular Culture Association and is an associate professor of communication studies and theater arts at Kansas Wesleyan University. His first book, *"You Can't Air That": Four Cases of Censorship and Controversy in American Television Programming*, was an editor's pick in *Choice* magazine. He currently resides in Salina, Kansas, with his wife, Olga, and their daughter, Stephanie.

Olga Silverman is a secondary English teacher at Solomon High School in Solomon, Kansas, and is a Kansas Horizon Award winner. Born and raised in Riga, Latvia, she completed a master's degree in industrial engineering at the University of Latvia, later receiving her BA in English and secondary education from Kansas Wesleyan University. She currently resides in Salina, Kansas, with her husband, David, and their daughter, Stephanie.

Anne Collins Smith is professor of philosophy and classical studies in the Division of Multidisciplinary Programs at Stephen F. Austin State University in Nacogdoches, Texas. Her current research involves exploring philosophical issues in Harry Potter and other science fiction and fantasy texts.

Michael Smith is an associate professor of writing, rhetoric, and technical communication at James Madison University, where he has created courses